Introduction to

Google™
Apps

Introduction to

Google™ Apps

Michael Miller

Prentice Hall

Upper Saddle River, NJ–Columbus, OH

Library of Congress Cataloging-in-Publication Data

Miller, Michael, 1958-
  Introduction to Google apps / Michael Miller.
      p. cm.
  ISBN 0-13-245747-4
  1. Google. 2. Web search engines. 3. Application software. I. Title.
  TK5105.885.G66M57 2009
  005.75'8--dc22

                        2008050024

VP/Editorial Director: Natalie E. Anderson
Editor-in-Chief: Michael Payne
Director, Product Development: Pamela Hersperger
Product Development Manager: Eileen Bien Calabro
Editorial Project Manager: Meghan Bisi
Development Editor: Jennifer Campbell
Editorial Assistant: Marilyn Matos
AVP/Director of Online Programs, Media: Richard Keaveny
AVP/Director of Product Development: Lisa Strite
Editorial Media Project Manager: Alana Coles
Production Media Project Manager: John Cassar
Marketing Manager: Tori Olson Alves
Marketing Coordinator: Susan Osterlitz
Marketing Assistant: Angela Frey
Senior Managing Editor: Cynthia Zonneveld
Associate Managing Editor: Camille Trentacoste
Production Project Manager: Rhonda Aversa
Manager of Rights & Permissions: Charles Morris
Senior Operations Specialist: Nick Sklitsis
Operations Specialist: Natacha Moore
Senior Art Director: Jonathan Boylan
Art Director: Anthony Gemmellaro
Interior Design: Anthony Gemmellaro
Cover Design: Anthony Gemmellaro
Cover Illustration/Photo: Shutterstock Images
Manager, Cover Visual Research & Permissions: Karen Sanatar
Composition: Black Dot Group
Full-Service Project Management: Black Dot Group
Printer/Binder: Webcrafters Inc.
Typeface: 11/12 Garamond 3

Google™ products referenced herein are either trademarks or registered trademarks of Google™ in the U.S.A. and other countries. Screen shots and icons reprinted with permission from Google™. This book is not sponsored or endorsed by or affiliated with Google™.

Pearson Education Ltd., London
Pearson Education Singapore, Pte. Ltd
Pearson Education, Canada, Inc.
Pearson Education–Japan
Pearson Education Australia PTY, Limited

Pearson Education North Asia Ltd., Hong Kong
Pearson Educación de Mexico, S.A. de C.V.
Pearson Education Malaysia, Pte. Ltd.
Pearson Education, Upper Saddle River, New Jersey

Prentice Hall
is an imprint of

www.pearsonhighered.com

10 9 8 7 6 5 4 3 2 1
ISBN-13: 978-0-13-245747-7
ISBN-10: 0-13-245747-4

About the Author

Michael Miller has written more than 80 non-fiction how-to books over the last two decades, including *Googlepedia: The Ultimate Google Resource, Photopedia: The Ultimate Digital Photography Resource, Absolute Beginner's Guide to Computer Basics,* and *The Complete Idiot's Guide to Music Theory.* His books have collectively sold more than 1 million copies worldwide. Miller has established a reputation for his conversational writing style and for clearly explaining complex topics to casual readers. More information can be found at the author's website, located at www.molehillgroup.com.

To Sherry, as always.

Contents

Contributors

We'd like to thank the following people for their work on *Introduction to Google Apps:*

Instructor Resource Authors:

Barbara Stover, *Marion Technical College*
Julie Boyles, *Portland Community College*

Technical Editors:

Elizabeth Lockley
Janet Pickard
Julie Boyles
Tom McKenzie

Google Apps Survey Participants:

Ashish Soni, *University of Southern California*
Charles Esparza, *Glendale Community College and University of Phoenix*
Gary L. Whitten, *Trident Technical College*
Gary Marrer, *Glendale Community College*
Jim Patridge, *SUNY at Oswego*
Kamaljeet Sanghera, *George Mason University*
Karen Allen, *Community College of Rhode Island*
Kim Cannon, *Greenville Technical College*
Kuan Chen, *Purdue University Calumet*
M. Carl Drott, *Drexel University*
Marilyn Hibbert, *Salt Lake Community College*
Marlene Roden, *Asheville-Buncombe Technical Community College*
Michele Budnovitch, *Pennsylvania College of Technology*
Pamela Silvers, *Asheville-Buncombe Technical Community College*
Pindaro Demertzoglou, *Rensselaer Polytechnic Institute*
Rocky Belcher, *Sinclair Community College*
Subodha Kumar, *University of Washington*

Visual Walk-Through

Many of today's introductory computing courses are moving beyond coverage of just the traditional Microsoft® Office applications. Instructors are looking to incorporate newer technologies and software applications into their courses, and on some college campuses new alternative courses based on emerging technologies are being offered.

We developed *The NEXT Series* to provide innovative instructors with a high-quality, academic teaching solution that focuses on the next great technologies. There is more to computing than Microsoft® Office, and the books in *The NEXT Series* enable students to learn about some of the newer technologies that are available and becoming part of our everyday lives.

The NEXT Series...making it easy to teach what's *NEXT!*

▶ Whether you are interested in creating a new course or you want to enhance an existing class by incorporating new technology, *The NEXT Series* is your solution.

Included in this series are books on alternative productivity software application products, Google Apps and Open Office, as well as new technologies encompassed in Web 2.0 such as social networking, information sharing, and collaboration tools.

▶ *Introduction to Google Apps* is a teaching and learning tool that was designed for use in a classroom setting, encouraging students to learn by using this new technology hands-on.

The text includes in-chapter activities, end of chapter exercises, and instructor supplements.

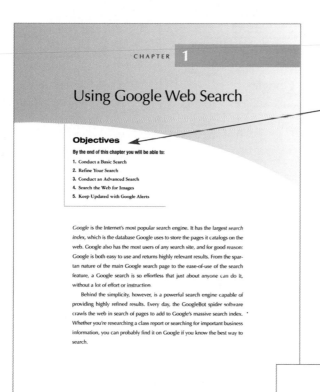

Each chapter opens with a list of **Objectives**, clearly outlining what students will be able to accomplish after completing the chapter.

Learn-by-doing approach

Students learn how to use Google Apps by completing a series of **Activities**.

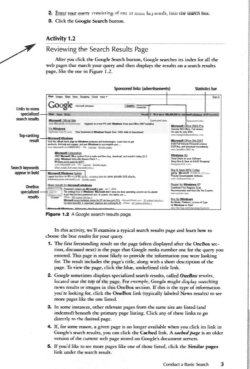

Notes are used to call attention to important items in the text

Key terms are defined in the margins

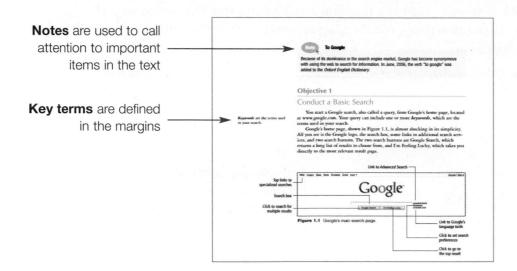

Alert boxes call attention to items that might cause students to get hung up.

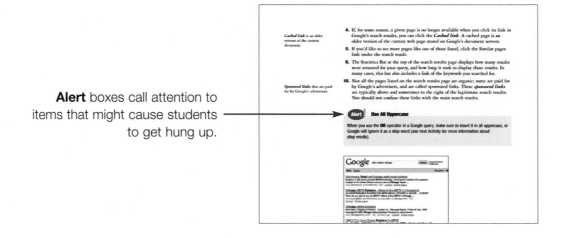

Tip boxes provide students with useful tips and tricks

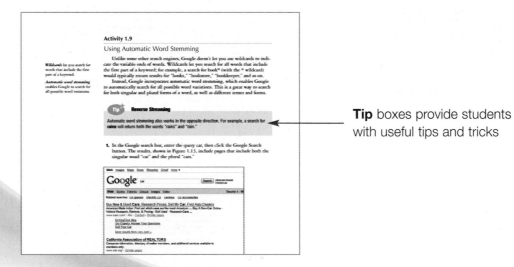

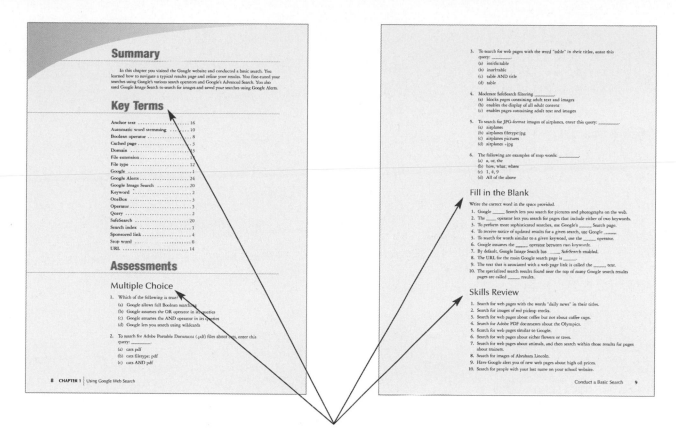

End-of-chapter material

Includes a **Summary** of Key Terms as
well as Multiple Choice, Fill in the Blank,
and Skills Review **Assessments**

CHAPTER 1

Using Google Web Search

Objectives

By the end of this chapter you will be able to:

1. Conduct a Basic Search

2. Refine Your Search

3. Conduct an Advanced Search

4. Search the Web for Images

5. Keep Updated with Google Alerts

Google is the Internet's most popular search engine. It has the largest **search index**, which is the database Google uses to store the pages it catalogs on the web. Google also has the most users of any search site, and for good reason: Google is both easy to use and returns highly relevant results. From the spartan nature of the main Google search page to the ease-of-use of the search feature, a Google search is so effortless that just about anyone can do it, without a lot of effort or instruction.

Behind the simplicity, however, is a powerful search engine capable of providing highly refined results. Every day, the GoogleBot spider software crawls the web in search of pages to add to Google's massive search index. Whether you're researching a class report or searching for important business information, you can probably find it on Google if you know the best way to search.

Google The Internet's most popular search engine.

Search index The organization of data to allow for fast and accurate searching.

To Google

Because of its dominance in the search engine market, Google has become synonymous with using the web to search for information. In June, 2006, the verb "to google" was added to the *Oxford English Dictionary*.

Objective 1

Conduct a Basic Search

Query A search for information.

Keyword A term used in a search query.

You start a Google search, also called a *query*, from Google's homepage, located at **www.google.com**. Your query can include one or more *keywords*, which are the terms used in your search.

Google's homepage, shown in Figure 1.1, is almost shocking in its simplicity. All you see is the Google logo, the search box, some links to additional search services, and two search buttons. The two search buttons are **Google Search**, which returns a long list of results to choose from, and **I'm Feeling Lucky**, which takes you directly to the most relevant result page.

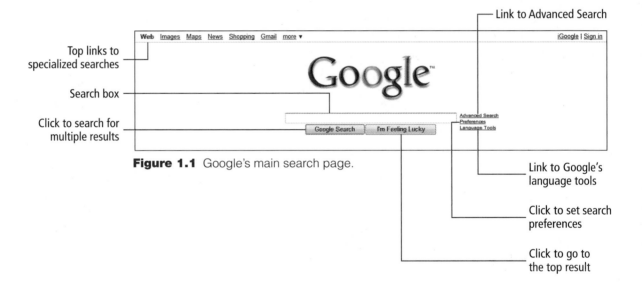

Figure 1.1 Google's main search page.

 Comparing Your Screen with the Figures in This Book

Because Google is constantly updating its feature set, the pages you see on your own computer might not always match those displayed in this book. In addition, because Google's search results are updated daily (if not hourly!), the search results displayed here may be different from the search results you obtain when you work through these exercises.

Activity 1.1

Entering a Query

In this activity, we'll initiate a basic search from Google's main search page. It's as easy as entering one or more keywords and clicking a button.

1. From your web browser, go to Google's main page, located at **www.google.com**.

2. Enter your query, consisting of one or more keywords, into the search box.

3. Click the **Google Search** button.

Activity 1.2

Reviewing the Search Results Page

After you click the Google Search button, Google searches its index for all the web pages that match your query and then displays the results on a search results page, like the one in Figure 1.2.

Figure 1.2 A Google search results page.

In this activity, we'll examine a typical search results page and learn how to choose the best results for your query.

1. The first freestanding result on the page (often displayed after the OneBox section, discussed next) is the page that Google ranks number one for the query you entered. This page is most likely to provide the information you were looking for. The result includes the page's title, along with a short description of the page. To view the page, click the blue, underlined title link.

OneBox Specialized search results.

2. Google sometimes displays specialized search results, called *OneBox* results, located near the top of the page. For example, Google might display matching news results or images in this OneBox section. If this is the type of information you're looking for, click the **OneBox** link (typically labeled News results) to see more pages like the one listed.

3. In some instances, other relevant pages from the same site are listed (and indented) beneath the primary page listing. Click any of these links to go directly to the desired page.

Cached page A page that is stored on Google's document servers, and may be slightly older than the current version of the page, or outdated.

4. If, for some reason, a given page is no longer available when you click its link in Google's search results, you can click the **Cached** link. A *cached page* is an older version of the current web page stored on Google's document servers.

5. If you'd like to see more pages like one of those listed, click the **Similar pages** link under the search result.

6. The Statistics Bar at the top of the search results page displays how many results were returned for your query and how long it took to display those results. In many cases, this bar also includes a link to definitions of the keywords you searched for.

7. Not all the pages listed on the search results page are the result of your specific search; some are paid for by Google's advertisers and are called *sponsored links*. These sponsored links are typically above and sometimes to the right of the legitimate search results. You should not confuse these links with the main search results; they may have only indirect relevance to your query.

Sponsored link Links on a search results page that are paid for by Google's advertisers.

Note **Universal Search Results**

Before mid-2007, Google presented the results of all its various types of searches separately; you had to click separate links to view matching images, news stories, and the like. Google now presents Universal Search results, which displays relevant results from all of Google's search indexes on the same search results page. You can, if you like, display only certain types of results by clicking the links on the left side of the Statistics Bar. For example, if a search returned a mix of web, image, and news results, you'll see links for Web, Images, and News; to view only the image results, click the **Images** link.

Activity 1.3

Extending Your Search Results

For many searches, you can find what you want simply by clicking a few page titles on the first search results page. But don't assume that the only relevant results will appear on the first page. Some queries return literally thousands (if not *millions*) of matching pages, and even though the most relevant results are supposed to be listed first, it's possible to find much useful information buried deeper in the results.

1. To display the next page of search results, scroll to the bottom of the first page and click the **Next** link.

2. To go directly to a specific page in the search results, scroll to the bottom of the first page and click a page number, as shown in Figure 1.3.

Click to go to the next page of results

Click to go to a specific page of results

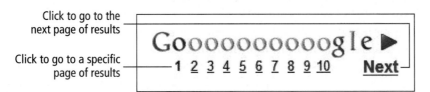

Figure 1.3 The bottom of a typical search results page; click a page number to jump to that page of results.

3. To view a page beyond the first ten listed, click on the **Page 10** link; this displays page numbers 1–19. Keep clicking to the right to view more and more pages of results.

Activity 1.4

Searching Within Your Results

There's another useful feature to be found at the bottom of the search results page. The **Search within results** link lets you narrow your results by refining your query and applying the new search solely to the original results. In this activity, we'll learn how to use this feature.

1. From any search results page, scroll to the bottom and click the **Search within results** link.

2. When the Search within results page appears, as shown in Figure 1.4, enter a new query into the search box.

Enter new query here

Click to initiate the refined search

Figure 1.4 Refine your query on the Search within results page.

3. Click the **Search within results** button. Google now searches the existing results, using your new query. The new, refined results appear on a subsequent search results page.

Objective 2

Refine Your Search

Most users enter a keyword or two into Google's search box, click the **Search** button, and are satisfied with the results. This is a rather brute force method of searching, however, and typically generates a multitude of (mostly unwanted) results.

There is a better way to search that generates a smaller, more targeted list of results. To generate fewer, better results, you have to refine your query using a defined series of search operators.

 Note **Understanding Operators**

An **operator** is a symbol or word that causes a search engine to do something special with the word directly following the symbol.

Operator A symbol or word that causes a search engine to do something special with the word directly following the symbol.

Activity 1.5

Changing the Word Order

In a Google query, the order of your keywords matters. Google weights the importance of your keywords by order of appearance, so that the first keyword is considered most important, the second keyword the second most important, and so on. In this activity, we'll examine how this word order works.

1. From the main Google search page, enter **hdtv retailers chicago**, then click the **Google Search** button. The search results should look something like the page shown in Figure 1.5.

Figure 1.5 The results of a search for **hdtv retailers chicago**.

2. Return to the Google search page and enter **chicago retailers hdtv**, then click the **Google Search** button. Note that the search results for this query, shown in Figure 1.6, differ slightly from those of the original query.

Figure 1.6 The search results of **chicago retailers hdtv**—the first result is the same as the previous query, but the second result is different and the order varies slightly.

 Similar Results

In many cases, the very top results will be the same no matter what the word order. The difference tends to come as you move deeper into the result listings.

Activity 1.6

Using AND/OR Operators

When constructing a query from multiple keywords, know that Google automatically assumes the word "and" between all the words in your query. That is, if you enter two words, it assumes you're looking for pages that include both those words—word one *and* word two. It doesn't return pages that include only one or the other of the words.

This is different from assuming the word "or" between the words in your query. With an "and" query, the results would include pages that contain both words. With an "or" query, the results include pages that contain either word—potentially a much larger set of results.

In this activity, we look at the differences between "and" and "or" queries.

1. Let's start with an explicit "and" query. In the Google search box, enter **birds AND fish**, then click the **Google Search** button. The results, as shown in Figure 1.7, include pages that contain both words.

Figure 1.7 Using the AND operator in a Google query.

2. Now let's see how Google assumes the "and" query. In the Google box at the top of the results page, enter **birds fish**, then click the **Search** button. The results should be nearly identical to those in step 1.

3. Finally, let's compare "and" and "or" queries. Perform the query **birds OR fish**. The results, shown in Figure 1.8, now include pages that contain either word, not necessarily both.

Figure 1.8 Using the OR operator in a Google query.

Use All Uppercase

When you use the **OR** operator in a Google query, make sure to insert it in all uppercase, or Google will ignore it as a stop word (see next activity for more information about stop words).

 Boolean Operators

Boolean operator Words that are used to refine a search and that come from Boolean logic and mathematics, such as AND, OR, and NOT. Google supports only the Boolean OR operator.

Boolean operators come from Boolean logic and mathematics and are words used to refine a search. The **OR** operator is the only Boolean operator accepted by the Google search engine. The Boolean **AND** operator is assumed in all Google searches; the Boolean **NOT** operator is replaced by the Google – (minus sign) operator.

Activity 1.7

Working with Stop Words

Stop word A small, common word, such as "and," "the," "where," "how," and "what," that Google ignores when performing a query.

Google automatically ignores small, common words, called *stop words*, in a query. Stop words include "and," "the," "where," "how," "what," "or" (unless uppercase), and other similar words, along with certain single digits and single letters (such as "a").

Including a stop word in a search normally does nothing but slow down the search, which is why Google excises them. As an example, Google takes the query **how a toaster works**, removes the words "how" and "a," and creates the new, shorter query **toaster works**.

You can override the stop word exclusion by telling Google that it *must* include specific words in the query. You do this with the + (plus sign) operator in front of the otherwise excluded word. In this activity, we learn how this works.

1. In the Google search box, enter **where is mars**, then click the **Google Search** button. The results, shown in Figure 1.9, ignore the stop words "where" and "is."

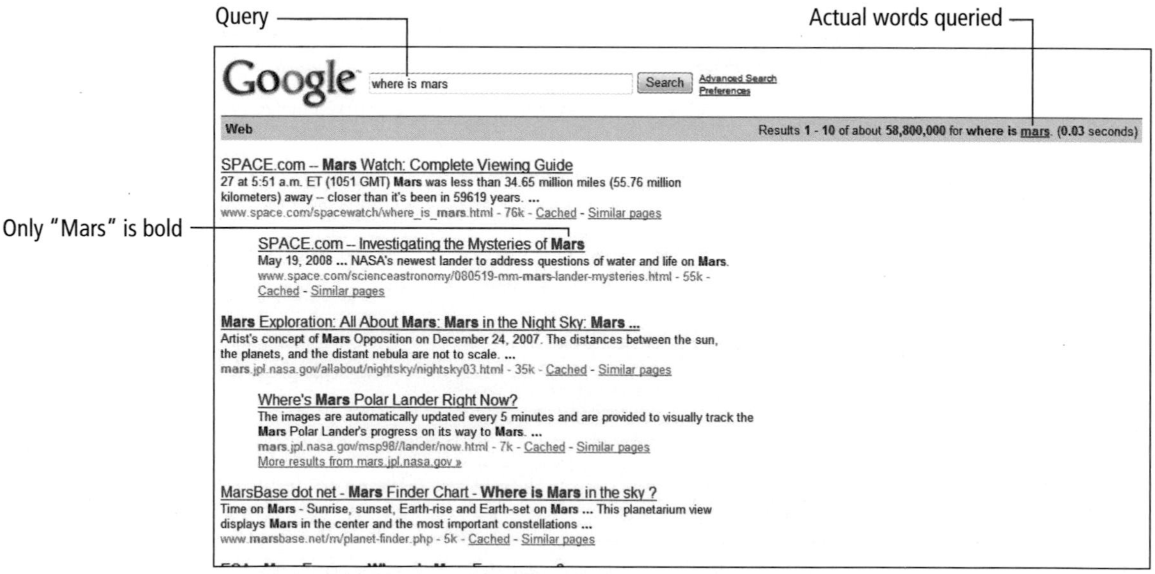

Query ―――――   Actual words queried ―

Google where is mars   Search Advanced Search
                                  Preferences

Web   Results 1 - 10 of about 58,800,000 for where is mars. (0.03 seconds)

SPACE.com -- Mars Watch: Complete Viewing Guide
27 at 5:51 a.m. ET (1051 GMT) Mars was less than 34.65 million miles (55.76 million kilometers) away -- closer than it's been in 59619 years. ...
www.space.com/spacewatch/where_is_mars.html - 76k - Cached - Similar pages

Only "Mars" is bold ― SPACE.com -- Investigating the Mysteries of Mars
May 19, 2008 ... NASA's newest lander to address questions of water and life on Mars.
www.space.com/scienceastronomy/080519-mm-mars-lander-mysteries.html - 55k - Cached - Similar pages

Mars Exploration: All About Mars: Mars in the Night Sky: Mars ...
Artist's concept of Mars Opposition on December 24, 2007. The distances between the sun, the planets, and the distant nebula are not to scale. ...
mars.jpl.nasa.gov/allabout/nightsky/nightsky03.html - 35k - Cached - Similar pages

Where's Mars Polar Lander Right Now?
The images are automatically updated every 5 minutes and are provided to visually track the Mars Polar Lander's progress on its way to Mars. ...
mars.jpl.nasa.gov/msp98/lander/now.html - 7k - Cached - Similar pages
More results from mars.jpl.nasa.gov »

MarsBase dot net - Mars Finder Chart - Where is Mars in the sky ?
Time on Mars - Sunrise, sunset, Earth-rise and Earth-set on Mars ... This planetarium view displays Mars in the center and the most important constellations ...
www.marsbase.net/m/planet-finder.php - 5k - Cached - Similar pages

Figure 1.9 Google automatically excises small stop words, such as "where" and "is."

2. Now perform the query **+where +is mars**. These results, shown in Figure 1.10, include the words "where" and "is."

Query ⎯⎯⎯⎯⎯⎯⎯⎯⎯ Actual words queried ⎯⎯⎯⎯⎯⎯

"Where" and "is" are bold because they were included in the search

Figure 1.10 Use the + operator to force inclusion of stop words.

> **Alert!** **Include a Space**
>
> Be sure to include a space before the + sign, but not after it.

Activity 1.8

Excluding Words from Your Results

Sometimes you want to refine your results by excluding pages that include a specific word. You can exclude words from your search by using the – (minus sign) operator; any word in your query preceded by the – sign is automatically excluded from the search results. Remember to always include a space before the – sign, and none after.

In this activity, we examine word exclusion by looking at a word that has several meanings—"bass," which can be a fish, a male singer, a type of guitar, a type of drum, several other deeply pitched musical instruments, or a brand of beer.

1. In the Google search box, enter **bass**, then click the **Google Search** button. The results, shown in Figure 1.11, include pages about both fish and singers.

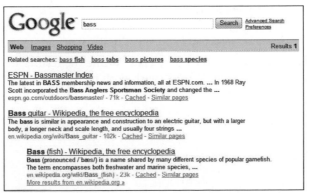

Figure 1.11 Search results that include all meanings of the keyword "bass."

2. To focus your results more closely on the bass that's a male vocalist, you want to exclude pages that include the word "fish," "guitar," "drum," and "beer." Perform the query **bass -fish -guitar -drum -beer**. The results, shown in Figure 1.12, no longer include fish-, guitar-, drum-, and beer-related pages.

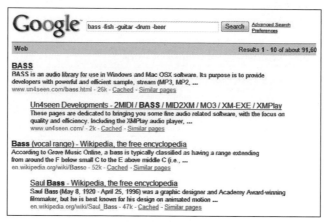

Figure 1.12 Use the – operator to exclude most non-singer meanings of the word "bass" from the search results.

Wildcard Allows you to search for all words that include the first part of a keyword. For example, search for **book*** to return results for "books," "bookstore," and "bookkeeper." Unlike other search engines, Google does not support wildcard searches.

Automatic word stemming A feature that enables Google to automatically search for all possible word variations.

Activity 1.9

Using Automatic Word Stemming

Unlike some other search engines, Google doesn't let you use wildcards to indicate the variable ends of words. *Wildcards* let you search for all words that include the first part of a keyword; for example, a search for **book*** (with the * wildcard) would typically return results for "books," "bookstore," "bookkeeper," and so on.

Instead, Google incorporates *automatic word stemming*, which enables Google to automatically search for all possible word variations. This is a great way to search for both singular and plural forms of a word, as well as different tenses and forms.

 Tip **Reverse Stemming**

Automatic word stemming also works in the opposite direction. For example, a search for **rains** will return both the words "rains" and "rain."

1. In the Google search box, enter the query **car**, then click the **Google Search** button. The results, shown in Figure 1.13, include pages that contain both the singular word "car" and the plural "cars."

2. Now perform the query **cars**. While the results aren't identical to the first query, they also include pages with both the words "car" and "cars."

Figure 1.13 Automatic word stemming in action—results for "car" and "cars."

Activity 1.10

Searching for Similar Words

Not sure you're thinking of the right word for a query? Do you worry that some web pages might use alternative words to describe what you're thinking of?

Fortunately, Google lets you search for similar words by using the ~ (tilde) operator. Just include the ~ character (located to the left of the 1 key on your keyboard) before the word in question, and Google will search for all pages that include that word and all appropriate synonyms.

1. In the Google search box, enter the query **elderly**, then click the **Google Search** button. The results include only pages with the word "elderly."

2. To expand your search, perform the query **~elderly**. As you can see in Figure 1.14, the results now include pages that contain not just the word "elderly," but also the words "senior," "aged," "nursing homes," and so on.

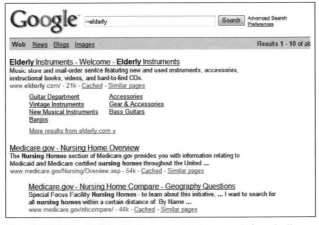

Figure 1.14 Using the ~ operator to search for similar words.

 Listing Synonyms Only

To list *only* synonyms without returning matches for the original word, combine the ~ operator with the – operator, like this: **~keyword –keyword**. This excludes the original word from the synonymous results. Using the previous example, to list only synonyms for the word "elderly," enter **~elderly –elderly**.

Activity 1.11

Searching for an Exact Phrase

When you're searching for an exact phrase, you won't get the best results simply by entering all the words in the phrase as your query. Google *might* return results including the phrase, but it will also return results that include all those words, not necessarily in that exact order.

When you want to search for an exact phrase, you should enclose the entire phrase in quotation marks. This tells Google to search for the precise keywords in the prescribed order, as you'll learn in this activity.

1. In the Google search box, enter the query **monty python** (no quotation marks), then click the **Google Search** button. The results include pages that contain both the words "monty" and "python"—not just pages about the British comedy troupe, but also web pages about snakes named Monty, guys named Monty who have snakes for pets, and any other pages where the words "monty" and "python" occur on the same page.

2. To limit the results just to pages about the Monty Python troupe, you want to search for pages that include the two words in that precise order as a phrase. To do this, perform the query **"monty python"**, making sure to surround the phrase with the quotation marks as shown in Figure 1.15. This way, if the word "monty" occurs at the top of a page and "python" occurs at the bottom, that page won't be listed in the search results.

Figure 1.15 To search for an exact phrase, include it in quotation marks.

Activity 1.12

Filetype A particular way of encoding data in a computer file. Most programs store their data in their own filetypes; filetypes are indicated by specific file extensions.

File extension A 3- or 4-character suffix that indicates the program in which a file was created.

Restricting Your Search to Specific Filetypes

Google can search for information contained in all sorts of documents, not just HTML web pages. Each document format is called a *filetype*, and Google can search by filetype using the file's 3- or 4-digit *file extension*, which indicates the program a file was created in. Google can recognize and search for filetypes, including the following, in addition to normal web pages:

- Adobe Portable Document Format (pdf)
- Adobe PostScript (ps)
- Autodesk (dwf)
- Google Earth (kml, kmz)
- Lotus 1-2-3 (wk1, wk2, wk3, wk4, wk5, wki, wks, wku)
- Lotus WordPro (lwp)

- MacWrite (mw)
- Microsoft Excel (xls, xlsx)
- Microsoft PowerPoint (ppt, pptx)
- Microsoft Word (doc, docx)
- Microsoft Works (wdb, wks, wps)
- Microsoft Write (wri)
- Rich Text Format (rtf)
- Shockwave Flash (swf)
- Text (ans, txt)

If you want to restrict your results to a specific filetype, use the **filetype:** operator followed by the file extension, in this format: **filetype:***filetype*. To eliminate a particular filetype from your search results, use the **filetype:** operator preceded by the – operator and followed by the file extension, like this: **-filetype:***filetype*.

In this activity, we learn how to use the **filetype:** operator to search for files of a particular type.

1. To limit your search to only Adobe PDF documents, enter **filetype:pdf** along with the rest of your query, as shown in Figure 1.16.

2. To eliminate PDF files from your results, enter **-filetype:pdf** followed by the rest of your query.

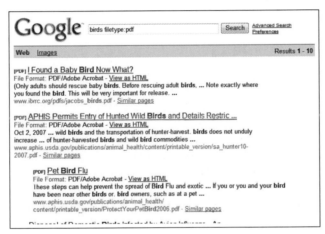

Figure 1.16 Use the **filetype:** operator to limit your search to specific types of documents.

 Viewing Non-HTML Documents

When your search results return a non-HTML document (something other than a web page, such as an Acrobat PDF or Word DOC file), Google displays a **View as HTML** link in the page listing. Clicking this link translates the original document into web page format, which often displays faster in your browser.

Activity 1.13

Restricting Your Search to a Specific Domain or Website

Domain A specific type of site on the web, indicated by the domain name after the final "dot" separator. For example, the .edu domain is used to indicate education sites.

Web sites are organized by top-level ***domain***, which is the two- or three-digit name that defines a type of Internet site. Google lets you search for sites within a specific top-level web domain, such as .com or .org or .edu—or, perhaps, within a specific country's domain, such as .uk (United Kingdom) or .ca (Canada). You do this by using the **site:**

operator. Just enter the operator followed by the domain name, like this: **site:.***domain*.

URL A web address.

The **site:** operator can also be used to restrict your search to a specific website. In this instance, you enter the site's top-level *URL*, or web address, like this: **site:www.***website.domain*.

1. To limit your search to sites in the .edu domain, enter your query followed by **site:.edu**, as shown in Figure 1.17.

2. To limit your search to pages within the Microsoft website (www.microsoft.com), enter your query followed by **site:www.microsoft.com**.

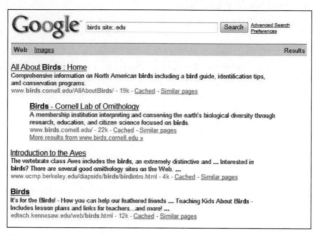

Figure 1.17 Use the **site:** operator to limit your search to a specific top-level domain.

Activity 1.14

Restricting Your Search to the Page's Title

The title of a web page appears in the browser title bar. Sometimes you only want to search the titles of web pages, while ignoring the pages' body text; this helps focus your search to those pages that are primarily, rather than peripherally, focused on the topic at hand. Google offers two ways to do this, depending on how many words you have in your query.

If your query contains a single word, use the **intitle:** operator at the beginning of your query. If your query contains multiple words, use the **allintitle:** operator. The following activity shows how this works.

1. To look for pages with the word "football" in the title, perform the query **intitle:football**, as shown in Figure 1.18. Make sure not to leave a space between the **intitle:** operator and the keyword.

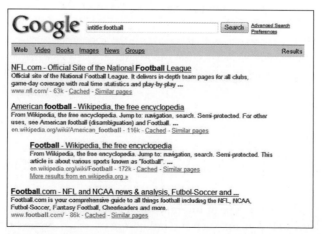

Figure 1.18 Use the **intitle:** operator to restrict your search to web page titles only.

2. To look for pages with the word "football arena" in the title, perform the query **allintitle: football arena**. Notice that when you use the **allintitle:** operator, all the keywords after the operator are searched for; you separate the keywords with spaces.

 Alert **Multiple Keywords with the Intitle: Operator**

If you enter **intitle:football arena**, Google will only search for the word "football" in the page titles; it will conduct a normal full-page search for the word "arena." This is why you want to use the **allintitle:** operator if you have multiple keywords in your query.

Activity 1.15

Restricting Your Search to the Page's URL

Similar to the **intitle:** and **allintitle:** operators are the **inurl:** and **allinurl:** operators. These operators let you restrict your search to words that appear in web page addresses (URLs). You use these operators in the same fashion as **intitle:** and **allintitle:**—**inurl:** to search for single words and **allinurl:** to search for multiple words.

1. To search for sites that have the word "molehill" in their URLs, perform the query **inurl:molehill**, as shown in Figure 1.19. Make sure not to leave a space between the **inurl:** operator and the keyword.

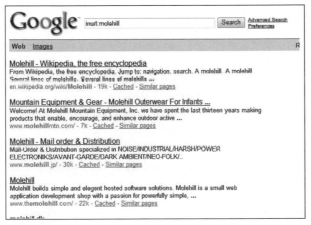

Figure 1.19 Use the **inurl:** operator to restrict your search to web page addresses.

2. To search for sites that have both the words "molehill" and "group" in their URLs, perform the query **allinurl:molehill group**. As with the **allintitle:** operator, all the keywords you enter after the **allinurl:** operator are searched for; you separate the keywords with spaces.

Activity 1.16

Restricting Your Search to the Page's Body Text

While you can limit your searches to page titles and URLs, it's more likely that you'll want to search the body text of web pages. You can restrict your search to body text only (excluding the page title, URL, and link text) by using the **intext:** and **allintext:** operators. The syntax is the same as with the previous operators; use **intext:** to search for single words and **allintext:** to search for multiple words.

1. To search for pages that include the word "birds" in their body text, perform the query **intext:birds**, as shown in Figure 1.20. Make sure not to leave a space between the **intext:** operator and the keyword.

2. To search for pages that include both the words "birds" and "nest" in the body text, perform the query **allintext:birds nest**.

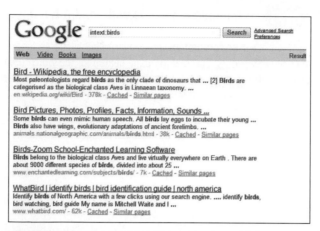

Figure 1.20 Use the **intext:** operator to restrict your search to just the body of web pages.

Activity 1.17

Restricting Your Search to the Page's Anchor Text

The web is built around *hyperlinking*—the ability to click on an underlined piece of text to jump to a related web page. The underlined text that accompanies a link to another web page is called the *anchor text*, and Google lets you search only the anchor text on a web page. You use the **inanchor:** operator to restrict your search to a single word in the anchor text; the **allinanchor:** variation lets you search for multiple words in the anchor text.

1. To search for links that reference the word "cat," enter **inanchor:cat** as your search query, as shown in Figure 1.21. Make sure not to leave a space between the **inanchor:** operator and the keyword.

2. To search for links that reference the words "cat" and "dog," perform the query **allinanchor:cat dog**.

Figure 1.21 Use the **inanchor:** operator to search for links that reference the given keyword.

Activity 1.18

Listing Similar Pages

Have you ever found a web page you like or find helpful and then wondered if there were any more like it? Fortunately, you can use Google's **related:** operator to display pages that are in some way similar to the specified page.

1. If you enter only a page's URL as your query, Google returns various pages on that website. For example, enter **www.cnn.com** in the Google search box; the results are all pages on the CNN website.

2. To find websites that are like the CNN site, enter **related:www.cnn.com** as your query. As you can see in Figure 1.22, the results now include similar news sites.

Figure 1.22 Use the **related:** operator to search for pages that are somehow like a given page.

Objective 3

Conduct an Advanced Search

Don't want to spend the time to learn all of Google's complicated search operators but still want to fine-tune your search beyond the basic keyword query? Use Google's Advanced Search page, which performs most of these same advanced search functions via a series of simple pull-down menus and checkboxes.

Activity 1.19

Accessing Google's Advanced Search Page

You access the Advanced Search page by clicking the **Advanced Search** link on Google's homepage. The Advanced Search page contains a number of options you can use to fine-tune your searches without having to learn all those advanced operators. All you have to do is make the appropriate selections on the page, and Google will do all the fine-tuning for you.

1. Go to Google's main search page, located at **www.google.com**.

2. Click the **Advanced Search** link.

3. Make your selections on the Advanced Search page, shown in Figure 1.23 then click the **Advanced Search** button.

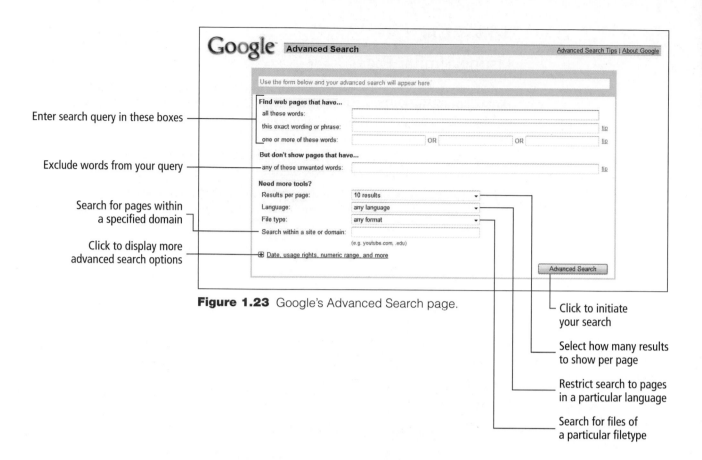

Enter search query in these boxes

Exclude words from your query

Search for pages within a specified domain

Click to display more advanced search options

Figure 1.23 Google's Advanced Search page.

Click to initiate your search

Select how many results to show per page

Restrict search to pages in a particular language

Search for files of a particular filetype

The top of the Advanced Search page is where you enter your query. This section functions much like Google's various search operators; you can choose to search for *all these words* (the default "and" search), *this exact wording or phrase* (the quotation marks operator), or *one or more of these words* (the OR operator). You can also choose to dismiss pages that include selected words by using the *But don't show pages that have any of these unwanted words* option.

More fine-tuning is available farther down on the Advanced Search page, which we'll examine in the following activities.

Activity 1.20

Changing the Search Results Display

In this activity, we'll learn how to use the Advanced Search page to change the way that Google displays its search results for a given query. In particular, you can change the number of results displayed on each page; you're not limited to the normal ten results.

1. From the main Google search page, click the **Advanced Search** link.

2. Click the **Results per page** list arrow and select how many results you want to display per page—10, 20, 30, 50, or 100.

3. Enter your query into the Find web pages that have section of the page.

4. Click the **Advanced Search** button.

Activity 1.21

Searching for Pages in a Specific Language

If you're searching for information written in a particular language, you can use the Advanced Search page to limit your search results to only those pages written in that language. This activity shows you how.

1. From the main Google search page, click the **Advanced Search** link.
2. Click the **Language** list arrow and select which language you want to search for.
3. Enter your query into the Find web pages that have section of the page.
4. Click the **Advanced Search** button.

Activity 1.22

Searching for Recent Web Pages

Often, you will want to search for the most recent information available. Google lets you do this via the Date function on the Advanced Search page.

1. From the main Google search page, click the **Advanced Search** link.
2. Click the + (plus sign) next to the **Date, usage rights, numeric range, and more** link to view additional options, as shown in Figure 1.24.

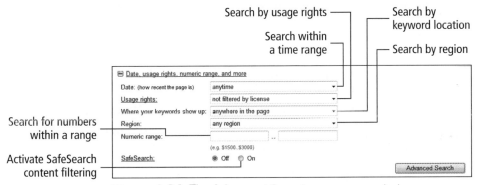

Figure 1.24 The Advanced Search page, expanded.

3. Click the **Date** list arrow and select how recent the pages you want returned in your search results. This restricts your search to web pages updated during the past 24 hours, week, month, 2 months, 3 months, 6 months, year, or anytime.
4. Enter your query into the Find web pages that have section of the page.
5. Click the **Advanced Search** button.

Activity 1.23

Searching Within a Numeric Range

Google also lets you search for values within a specified numeric range. For example, you might want to search for people with salaries between $50,000 and

$100,000; you do this by instructing Google to search for pages that include numbers that fall within that range.

1. From the main Google search page, click the **Advanced Search** link.
2. Click the + (plus sign) next to the **Date, usage rights, numeric range, and more** link to view additional options.
3. Enter the lower number of the range you're searching for into the first Numeric range box.
4. Enter the higher number of the range you're searching for into the second Numeric range box.
5. Enter your query into the Find web pages that have section of the page.
6. Click the **Advanced Search** button.

Activity 1.24

Activating SafeSearch

SafeSearch A filter used to exclude adult websites and images from your Google search results.

The final important option on Google's Advanced Search page is SafeSearch content filtering. You use *SafeSearch* to filter adult websites and images from your Google search results—an effective way to ensure that younger computer users aren't exposed to unwanted content.

There are two levels of SafeSearch filtering. Moderate filtering affects only the images returned on Google's search results pages and is activated from Google's Image Search page; it blocks the display of potentially offensive images. Strict filtering, activated from the Advanced Search page, applies the same standards to all your search results, whether image- or text-based.

In this activity, we learn how to activate Google's SafeSearch content filtering to all of Google's search results.

1. From the main Google search page, click the **Preferences** link.
2. When the Preferences page appears, scroll down to the SafeSearch Filtering section, shown in Figure 1.25.

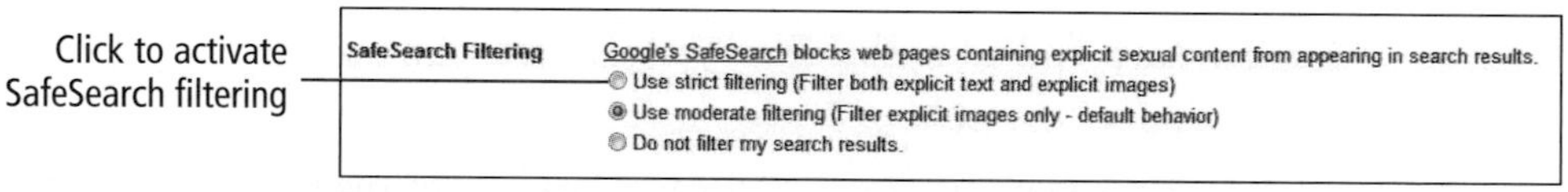

Click to activate SafeSearch filtering

SafeSearch Filtering   Google's SafeSearch blocks web pages containing explicit sexual content from appearing in search results.
○ Use strict filtering (Filter both explicit text and explicit images)
◉ Use moderate filtering (Filter explicit images only - default behavior)
○ Do not filter my search results.

Figure 1.25 Activating Google's SafeSearch filtering.

3. Select the **Use strict filtering** option button.
4. Click the **Save Preferences** button.

Objective 4

Search the Web for Images

Google Image Search A subset of Google's basic web search that lets you search for photos, drawings, logos, and other graphics files on the web.

Google offers many types of specialized searches, from news search to blog search. Among these specialized searches, the most popular is Google Image Search, also known as Google Images. *Google Image Search* is a subset of Google's basic web search that lets you search for photos, drawings, logos, and other graphics files on the web. It's a great way to find pictures online.

There are two ways to access Google Image Search: You can click the **Images** link on any Google search page, or you can go directly to **images.google.com**. And, of course, Google Image Search results appear as part of Google's universal search results when you search from the main search box.

Activity 1.25

Entering a Basic Query

For most users, searching Google Image Search is as easy as entering your query into the search box and clicking the **Search Images** button. Here's how it works.

1. Go to the Google Image Search page, located at **images.google.com**.

2. Enter one or more keywords into the search box at the top of the page, as shown in Figure 1.26.

3. Click the **Search Images** button.

Figure 1.26 The homepage for Google Image Search.

Activity 1.26

Viewing Image Search Results

When you click the **Search Images** button on the Google Image Search page, Google returns the first page of results. As you can see in Figure 1.27, the matching images are displayed in a grid of thumbnail pictures, ranked in terms of relevance. This activity takes you on a tour of the image search results page and the pages that follow.

Select images by size —

Thumbnail image —

Figure 1.27 The results of a Google image search.

1. For each thumbnail image, Google lists an image caption, the dimensions of the image (in pixels), the size of the image file (in kilobytes), the filetype, and the host website. To view the original image, click the thumbnail image.

2. The original page where the image appears is now displayed in a frame at the bottom of the next page, as shown in Figure 1.28. At the top of the page is the Google Images frame, which includes the image thumbnail, information about the image, and a few important links.

Click to view host page without the Google frame

Click to return to image search results

Click to view full-size image —

Google frame —

Host page —

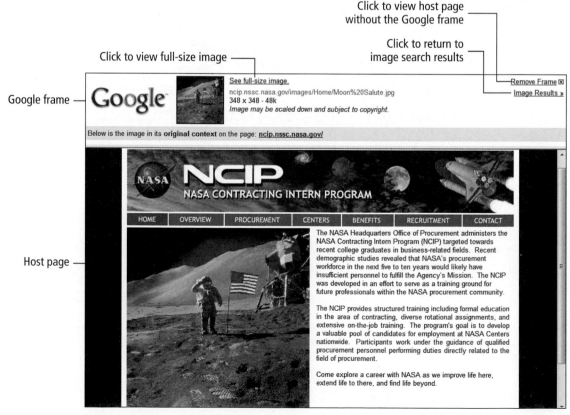

Figure 1.28 Viewing an image found with Google Image Search.

3. To view the host page without the Google frame, click the **Remove Frame** link.

4. To view the picture full-size, outside the host page, click the **See full-size image** link.

5. To return to your search results, click the **Image Results** link.

Activity 1.27

Searching by File Size

If you want to fine-tune your image search, the best way to do it is to use the Advanced Image Search page. One of the most useful options on this page is the ability to search for images of a certain size. This lets you find a larger picture for high-resolution print purposes or a small picture for web use.

1. From the main Google Image Search page, click the **Advanced Image Search** link.

2. When the Advanced Image Search page appears, as shown in Figure 1.29, click the **Size** list arrow and select a sizing option (small, medium, large, extra large, or any size).

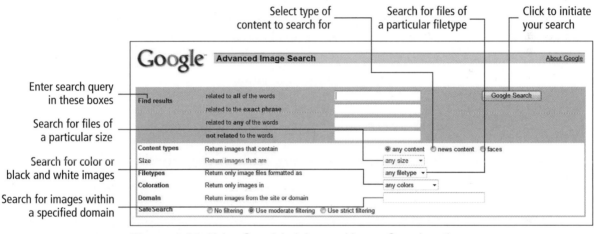

Figure 1.29 Using Google's Advanced Image Search options.

3. Enter your query in the Find results section of the page.

4. Click the **Google Search** button.

Activity 1.28

Searching by Graphic Filetype

Google also lets you search for images of a particular filetype. You can limit your search to JPG, GIF, PNG, or BMP (bitmap) files.

1. From the main Google Image Search page, click the **Advanced Image Search** link.

2. When the Advanced Image Search page appears, click the **Filetypes** list arrow and select a filetype (JPG, GIF, PNG, BMP, or any filetype).

3. Enter your query in the Find results section of the page.

4. Click the **Google Search** button.

 Tip **Search Operators in Image Search**

You can also use any of Google's advanced search operators within an image search query. Of particular use is the **filetype:** operator, which you can use to limit your search to JPG or GIF image files.

Activity 1.29

Searching for Color or Black and White Images

Black and white photography is not only artistic in its own right; it's sometimes exactly what you need for various types of print media such as newspapers. Google makes it easy to find black and white images—or color images, for that matter.

1. From the main Google Image Search page, click the **Advanced Image Search** link.

2. When the Advanced Image Search page appears, click the **Coloration** list arrow and select a color option (black and white, grayscale, full color, or any colors).

3. Enter your query in the Find results section of the page.

4. Click the **Google Search** button.

Objective 5

Keep Updated with Google Alerts

If you're a frequent Google user, you may get tired of entering the same searches over and over, trying to find the latest search results. Wouldn't it be great if Google could email you when new web pages appear that match your search criteria, or if there are recent news articles that match your interests?

That's where Google Alerts come in. A *Google Alert* is an email that Google sends you when it finds new items of interest. All you have to do is sign up for an alert and then wait for your email inbox to fill up with new search results.

Google Alerts An email that Google sends you when it finds new items of interest.

Activity 1.30

Saving a Search as an Alert

Signing up for a Google Alert is as easy as entering a search query and then activating the alert service. If you have a Gmail account, your Google Alerts are automatically sent to your Gmail inbox; if you don't have a Gmail account, you'll need to specify which email address you want your alerts sent to.

You sign up for alerts from the Google Alerts homepage. This activity shows you how.

1. Go to the Google Alerts homepage (**www.google.com/alerts/**), shown in Figure 1.30.

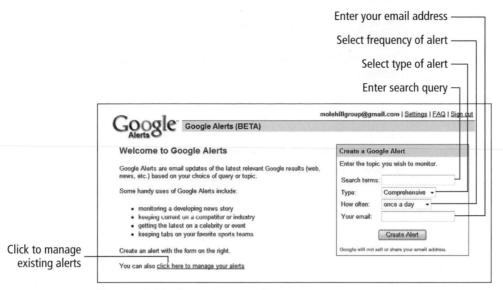

Enter your email address
Select frequency of alert
Select type of alert
Enter search query

Click to manage existing alerts

Figure 1.30 Creating a new Google Alert.

2. Enter your query into the Search terms box.

3. Click the **Type** list arrow and select which type of alert you want to receive (News, Blogs, Web, Comprehensive, Video, or Groups).

4. Click the **How often** list arrow and select how often you want to receive alerts (once a day, as-it-happens, or once a week).

5. Enter your email address.

6. Click the **Create Alert** button.

 Note **Beta Status**

Many Google services (such as Google Alerts) are labeled "beta," meaning they're still in a public testing phase. Google tends to keep the beta designation longer than most companies do; many of Google's supposed "beta" services have actually been in wide public use for several years!

 Tip **Which Type of Alert?**

Use different types of alerts for different types of searches. To receive results from a typical web search, select the Web option. To receive results of all types, select Comprehensive.

Activity 1.31

Changing the Frequency of an Alert

You manage your existing alerts from the Google Alerts page. One of the things you can do from the Google Alerts page is change how often you receive an alert.

1. Go to the Google Alerts homepage.

2. Click the **sign in to manage your alerts** link.

3. When the Manage your Alerts page displays, click the **edit** link next to the alert you wish to edit to open all the fields for editing, as shown in Figure 1.31 for the bird sighting alert.

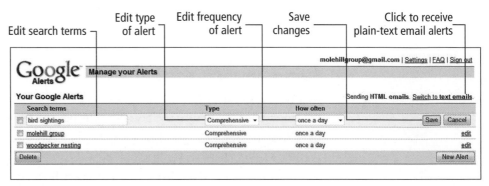

Figure 1.31 Getting ready to edit your Google Alerts.

5. Click the **How often** list arrow and select a new frequency (once a day, once a week, or as-it-happens).

6. When you're done making changes, click the **Save** button next to the alert or click the Cancel button to keep your original settings.

Activity 1.32

Changing the Format of an Alert

By default, your Google Alerts come to you with fancy HTML formatting. If you are using a cell phone, other portable device, or email program that doesn't allow formatted messages, you can configure Google Alerts to receive plain-text email messages instead.

1. Go to the Google Alerts homepage.

2. Click the **click here to manage your alerts** link.

3. When the Manage your Alerts page appears, click the **Switch to text emails** link at the top of the page.

 Tip **Switching Back to HTML Emails**

You can always switch back to HTML format emails by returning to the Manage your Alerts page and clicking the **Switch to HTML emails** link.

Summary

In this chapter, you visited the Google website and conducted a basic search. You learned how to navigate a typical results page and refine your results. You fine-tuned your searches using Google's various search operators and Google's Advanced Search. You also used Google Image Search to search for images and saved your searches using Google Alerts.

Key Terms

Anchor text 16

Automatic word stemming 10

Boolean operator 8

Cached page 3

Domain 13

File extension 12

Filetype 12

Google 1

Google Alerts 24

Google Image Search 20

Hyperlinking .16

Keyword 2

OneBox 3

Operator 5

Query 2

SafeSearch 20

Search index 1

Sponsored link 4

Stop word 8

URL 14

Wildcard 10

Assessments

Multiple Choice

1. Which of the following is true?
   (a) Google allows full Boolean searching.
   (b) Google assumes the OR operator in its queries.
   (c) Google assumes the AND operator in its queries.
   (d) Google lets you search using wildcards.

2. To search for Adobe Portable Document (.pdf) files about cats, enter this query: _____.
   (a) cats pdf
   (b) cats filetype:pdf
   (c) cats
   (d) cats AND pdf

3. To search for web pages with the word "table" in their titles, enter this query: _____.
   (a) intitle:table
   (b) inurl:table
   (c) table AND title
   (d) table

4. Moderate SafeSearch filtering _____.
   (a) blocks pages containing adult text and images
   (b) enables the display of all adult content
   (c) enables pages containing adult text and images
   (d) blocks pages containing adult images

5. To search for JPG format images of airplanes, enter this query: _____.
   (a) airplanes
   (b) airplanes filetype:jpg
   (c) airplanes pictures
   (d) airplanes +jpg

6. The following are examples of stop words: _____.
   (a) a, or, the
   (b) how, what, where
   (c) 1, 4, 9
   (d) All of the above

7. To search for web pages that contain the phrase "these are the times," enter this query: _____.
   (a) these are the times
   (b) these are +the times
   (c) "these are the times"
   (d) these times

8. To search for pages about all birds except woodpeckers, enter this query: _____.
   (a) birds +woodpeckers
   (b) birds −woodpeckers
   (c) birds NOT woodpeckers
   (d) woodpeckers OR birds

9. Thanks to automatic word stemming, a search for the keyword "step" will return pages containing the following words: _____.
   (a) step
   (b) stepped
   (c) steps
   (d) All of the above

10. Which of the following is true?
   (a) A Google Alert is a notification of new pages that match a given search query.
   (b) Google Alerts are sent via instant messaging.
   (c) Sign up for Google Alerts from any search results page.
   (d) Google Alerts are sent hourly.

Fill in the Blank

Write the correct word in the space provided.

1. Google _____ Search lets you search for pictures and photographs on the web.
2. The _____ operator lets you search for pages that include either of two keywords.
3. To perform more sophisticated searches, use Google's _____ Search page.
4. To receive notice of updated results for a given search, use Google _____.
5. To search for words similar to a given keyword, use the _____ operator.
6. Google assumes the _____ operator between two keywords.
7. By default, Google Image Search has _____ SafeSearch enabled.
8. The URL for the main Google search page is _____.
9. The text that is associated with a web page link is called the _____ text.
10. The specialized search results found near the top of many Google search results pages are called _____ results.

Skills Review

1. Search for web pages with the words "daily news" in their titles.
2. Search for images of red pickup trucks.
3. Search for web pages about coffee but not about coffee cups.
4. Search for Adobe PDF documents about the Olympics.
5. Search for web pages similar to Google.
6. Search for web pages about either flowers or trees.
7. Search for web pages about animals, and then search within those results for pages about trainers.
8. Search for images of Abraham Lincoln.
9. Have Google alert you of new web pages about high oil prices.
10. Search for people with your last name on your school website.

CHAPTER 2

Using Other Google Search Tools

Objectives

By the end of this chapter you will be able to:

1. Search the Google Directory

2. Search for People

3. Search for Scholarly Information

4. Search for Books and Publications

5. Search for News Articles

6. Search for YouTube Videos

7. Search for Locations and Directions

8. Search for Words and Definitions

9. Use Google as a Calculator

10. Use Google to Find Constants and Conversions

Google lets you do more than just search the web. You can also use Google to search books and scholarly resources, find current news headlines, display driving directions, perform mathematical calculations, and even view videos online. It's all a matter of knowing where—and how—to search.

Objective 1

Search the Google Directory

Google Directory Google's human-edited directory of websites.

Most Google users search the web via Google's massive search index. But Google also offers a more focused search: the human-edited **Google Directory.**

The difference between a search engine and a directory is in how the listings are compiled. Google's main search engine works by sending automated GoogleBot software out to crawl the web and then using a formula to match the pages to users' search queries. This process guarantees a huge number of results for most queries, but it's all automated. There's no good way to truly judge the content or quality of a page; it's all about numbers.

Directory A collection of websites assembled by human editors.

In contrast, a **directory** is assembled by a team of human editors—not machines. The human editors find and evaluate pages on the web, annotate the page listings, and organize them into relevant categories. Unlike computers, human beings can make qualitative judgments about a page's content and can evaluate the actual meaning of the page. A directory is not about numbers; it's about content.

Because of how it is compiled, the Google Directory is likely to have higher-quality results than Google's search engine. It's also likely to have fewer results because of the need to closely examine each individual page before it's added to the directory. Where the Google search index includes billions of listings, the Google Directory contains approximately 4.6 million listings—less than one tenth of one percent of what's in the search index.

It's the difference between casting a wide net and taking everything that's caught inside (as with Google's search engine), and dropping a single fishing line in the water with the intent of catching a particular type of fish (as with Google Directory). You get lots of fish with the wide net approach, but you get the fish you want by using a rod and reel.

Activity 2.1

Browsing the Google Directory

Browsing Locating a website within a directory by clicking through a hierarchical organization of information.

If you're accustomed to using Google to search for information, browsing might be new to you. **Browsing** uses the concept of hierarchical organization of information into topic categories and subcategories to locate information by being increasingly more specific as you continue to click through the hierarchy.

In this activity, you learn to browse the categories and subcategories of the Google Directory until you find the precise listing you want.

1. From your web browser, go to the Google Directory homepage, located at **directory.google.com.**

2. As shown in Figure 2.1, the Google Directory consists of 16 main categories, each of which contains subcategories. Click the link to the main category that matches your interest.

3. When the main category page appears, like the one shown in Figure 2.2, it lists all the subcategories within the major category, as well as a handful of related categories. Click a subcategory link to proceed.

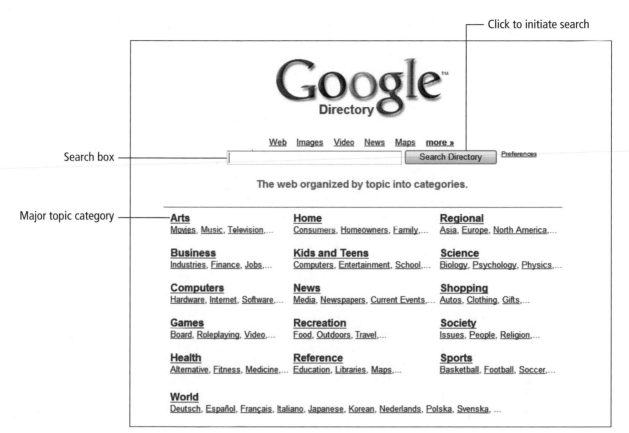

Click to initiate search

Search box

Major topic category

Figure 2.1 The Google Directory homepage.

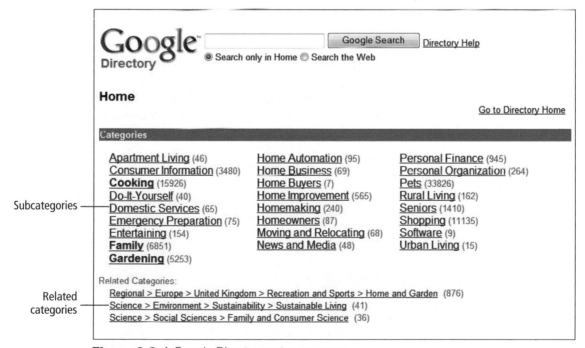

Subcategories

Related categories

Figure 2.2 A Google Directory category page.

4. The subcategory page, like the one shown in Figure 2.3, typically contains more subcategories, along with a list of web pages within the subcategory ranked in order of relevance. The green bar to the left of each page listing visually indicates the relevance; the longer the green bar, the more relevant the result. Each listing also includes the title of the page (click to jump to the page), the page's URL, and the editor's description of the page. Click a link to open a web page of interest.

Figure 2.3 A subcategory page in the Google Directory.

 Listing Alphabetically

If you'd rather view the listings within a category alphabetically instead of by relevance, click the **View in Alphabetical Order** link at the top of the listings.

Activity 2.2

Searching the Google Directory

Most users opt to use the Google Directory much as they do the regular Google search page—that is, by searching within the directory rather than browsing it. In this activity, you learn how to search the Google Directory.

1. From your web browser, go to the Google Directory homepage, located at **directory.google.com**.

2. Enter one or more keywords into the search box at the top of the page.

3. Click the **Search Directory** button.

4. Google now displays a search results page like the one in Figure 2.4. This page looks much like a standard web search results page. Each result listing also features a link to the category in which it is included. You can click a category link to view all the pages listed in that category or click any single result to view that page.

Page name

Directory category

Editor's description

Page URL

Search results

Figure 2.4 A Google Directory search results page.

Objective 2

Search for People

Google Phonebook Google's database of personal names, streets addresses, and phone numbers.

Sometimes you may need—or want—to look up a person's street address or phone number. As part of its massive database of information, *Google Phonebook* includes listings for millions of U.S. households. You search these listings from the main Google search box, using specific query parameters.

Activity 2.3

Searching by Name

You can most often find a person's street address by searching for that person's name with the **phonebook:** operator. To narrow your results, you need to include more information than just the name—such as the person's city, state, or ZIP code. Table 2.1 details the different ways you can search for a person, along with an example of each. In this activity, you'll learn how to conduct a Google Phonebook search.

Table 2.1	Ways to Search for People and Households	
Query	**Example**
First name (or initial), last name, city	**john smith minneapolis**
First name (or initial), last name, state or state abbreviation	**john smith mn**
First name (or initial), last name, city, state or state abbreviation	**john smith minneapolis mn**
First name (or initial), last name, ZIP Code	**john smith 55415**
Last name, city, state abbreviation	**smith minneapolis mn**
Last name, ZIP code	**smith 55415**

 Narrow Your Search

The more details you provide about a person, the more targeted your Google Phonebook results will be. Searching for all the Smiths in Minneapolis will produce a higher number of results (most of them unwanted) than searching for all the John Smiths; searching for all the John Smiths in a particular ZIP Code will be much more effective than searching for all the John Smiths in an entire state.

1. From your web browser, go to the Google homepage, located at **www.google.com**.
2. In the search box, type **phonebook:** and the name of the person you're looking for, along with some geographical information (city, state, or ZIP code).
3. Click the **Search** button.
4. Google returns a Residential Phonebook search results page, as shown in Figure 2.5. The top matching names are listed here, along with each person's phone number, street address, and a link to a map of each address (via Google Maps).

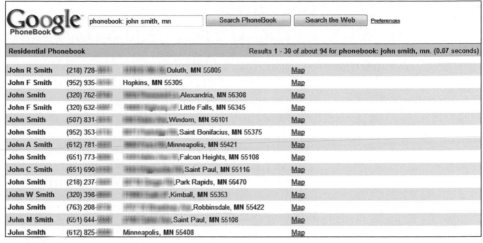

Figure 2.5 Results of a Google Phonebook search.

 Current Information

Because it takes so long to get change-of-address information into the system, Google Phonebook listings may not always be up to date. In addition, Google can only display names that are publicly available. If a person's phone number is unlisted, it won't be displayed. Also, it cannot locate cell phone numbers.

Activity 2.4

Searching by Phone Number

Once Google has captured name, address, and phone number information in its Phonebook database, it's an easy enough task to search that information in a variety of ways. One such approach, which you will use in this activity, is to do a reverse phone number lookup, where you enter a phone number and Google tells you who the number belongs to.

 Making Your Phone Number Private

If you'd rather not have your phone number available for everyone on the web, you can have your phone information removed from Google's database by following the instructions at **www.google.com/help/pbremoval.html**.

In this activity, you learn how to conduct a reverse phone number search.

1. From Google's homepage, enter a phone number into the search box. You must enter the full phone number, including area code. You can enter all 10 numbers in a row, without hyphens (like this: 9785551234), or use the standard hyphenated form (like this: 978-555-1234).

2. Click the **Google Search** button.

3. As long as the phone number is listed, Google now returns a single Phonebook result. If the number is unlisted, no Phonebook results are displayed.

Objective 3

Search for Scholarly Information

Google Scholar Google's database of scholarly articles and journals.

In addition to its main search index, Google keeps a database of scholarly journals and articles, called *Google Scholar*. Google Scholar enables students and researchers to conduct their research from the comfort of their dorm rooms, homes, and offices, without having to physically visit their university or local library.

Google Scholar is a comparable (and free) alternative to the expensive research databases offered by Elsevier, Thomson Reuters, and others. When you search Google Scholar, you receive a list of matching articles, journals, papers, theses, books, and the like, along with a brief summary of each item. Much of this information is available online free of charge; however, some is available online only for subscribers to a particular service, some is available online only for members of a particular library, and some is available only in printed format.

Activity 2.5

Searching Google Scholar

In this activity, you learn how to conduct a basic search of the Google Scholar database.

1. From your web browser, go to the Google Scholar homepage, located at **scholar.google.com** and shown in Figure 2.6.

Figure 2.6 The Google Scholar homepage.

2. Enter your query into the search box.

3. Click the **Search** button.

Activity 2.6

Conducting an Advanced Google Scholar Search

You can fine-tune your Google Scholar search by using the Advanced Scholar Search page. This lets you limit your search to specific authors, publications, or topic areas, as you will do in this activity.

1. From the Google Scholar homepage, click the **Advanced Scholar Search** link.

2. When the Advanced Scholar Search page appears, as shown in Figure 2.7, enter the keywords of your query into the shaded Find articles section. You can search for articles with *all the words,* an *exact phrase, at least one of the words*, or *without the words.* You can also select if the words appear only in the title or anywhere in the article.

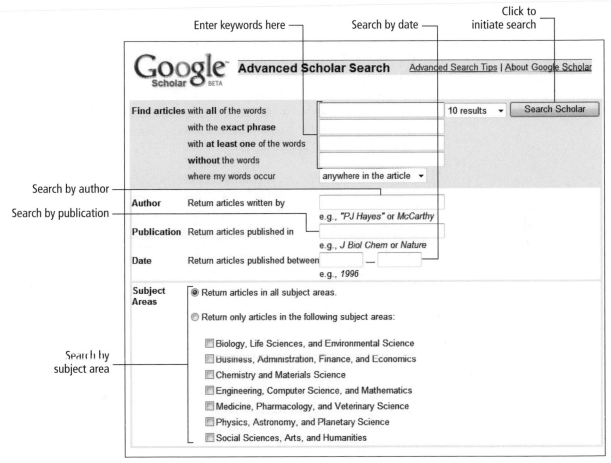

Figure 2.7 The Advanced Scholar Search page.

3. To find articles written by a specific author, enter the author's name into the Author box.

4. To find articles published in a specific publication, enter the publication's name into the Publication box.

5. To find articles published within a specified date range, enter the starting and ending years into the Date boxes.

6. To limit your search to a specific subject area (biology and life sciences, business and finance, and so on), go to the Subject Areas section and click those areas you want to search. (By default, Google Scholar searches all subject areas.)

7. Click the **Search Scholar** button to initiate your search.

Activity 2.7

Understanding Google Scholar Search Results

When you conduct a Google Scholar search, the results returned are limited primarily to scholarly articles, journals, theses, books, and more. Articles tend to make up the bulk of Google Search results. Figure 2.8 shows a typical Google Scholar search results page.

Figure 2.8 A typical Google Scholar search results page.

The information you see about a particular search result depends on what type of document it is. In this activity, you'll learn about the different types of results.

1. If a search result is for an article that is available for reading online, the title will be clickable. When you click the title, you're taken either to the full text of the

article or (if the article itself is available only via subscription) the article's abstract—that is, a brief description of the article. If the article is available for purchase via the British Library, a **BL Direct** link is displayed; click this link for purchase information.

2. If a search result is for an article *not* available online, the title will *not* be clickable and [CITATION] will appear beside the title. In this instance, you may be able to find the information you want by displaying the article's citations.

3. If a search result is for a book that is available in electronic form online, [BOOK] will appear beside the title and the title will be clickable. Click the title to view either the full text of the book or (if the book itself is available only via subscription) the book's abstract or title page and table of contents.

4. If a search result is for a book that is *not* available online, [BOOK] will appear beside the title and the title will *not* be clickable. You may see a **Library Search** link; click this link to find a library that carries a hard copy of the book.

5. If a search result is for a resource that is available in different formats—such as an article that was reprinted in multiple publications—Google tells you how many versions are available but consolidates them into one search result.

 Tip   **Look in Your Local Library**

If you're accessing Google Scholar from a university or research library, you may see a **FindIt @** link next to selected search results. Click this link to locate an electronic version of the work via your library's online resources.

Objective 4

Search for Books and Publications

There is a lot of great information on the web, but it pales in comparison to the amount of information available in printed books. For that reason, Google is working to create a global book repository, dubbed the ***Google Books Library Project***.

Google Books Library Project Google's global book repository that allows you to search the full text of any book ever published.

Google's ultimate goal with the Google Books Library Project is to let you search the full text of any book ever published and then provide the options of: reading that book online (for selected books, such as those that are in the public domain and are copyright free), purchasing the book (from selected booksellers), or finding out where you can borrow a copy of the book (from participating libraries). Google is now in the process of adding the contents of as many books as possible to its Google Books database, including both in-print and out-of-print titles; this book content is coming from both publishers and libraries.

 Note   **Book Industry Controversy**

The Google Books Library Project is not without controversy. Many publishers and authors object to having their books included in Google's database (even if it's just a listing or abstract) without any financial compensation. Other publishers and authors welcome the exposure that Google brings to hard-to-find or out-of-print books. Google claims that its Books Library Project works to promote the sale of printed books, especially through the included links to online booksellers. That said, most of the full-text books in Google's database tend to be older works with expired copyrights, thus avoiding most potential legal issues.

Activity 2.8

Searching Google Books

Google Book Search A method to locate books stored in the Google Books Library Project database.

You access the books in the Google Books Library Project via *Google Book Search*. In this activity, you'll learn how to conduct a basic book search.

1. From your web browser, go to the Google Book Search homepage, located at **books.google.com** and shown in Figure 2.9.

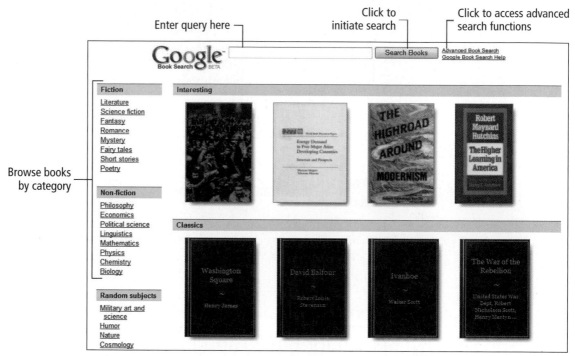

Figure 2.9 The Google Book Search homepage.

2. Enter your query into the search box—the book's title, the author, or keywords that describe the book's subject.

3. Click the **Search Books** button.

> **Tip** ★ **Browse the Bookshelves**
>
> You can also browse for books from the main Google Book Search page. Just click a category on the left and keep clicking until you find what you're looking for.

Activity 2.9

Conducting an Advanced Book Search

Google Book Search also offers an Advanced Book Search page, accessible when you click the Advanced Book Search link. This page offers many of the advanced search options you find on Google's regular Advanced Search page, as well as a few book-specific search options. In this activity, you will perform an advanced book search.

1. From the main Google Book Search page, click the **Advanced Book Search** link.

2. When the Advanced Book Search page appears, as shown in Figure 2.10, enter the keywords of your query into the shaded Find Results section. You can search for books that contain *all the words*, an *exact phrase*, *at least one of the words*, or *without the words*.

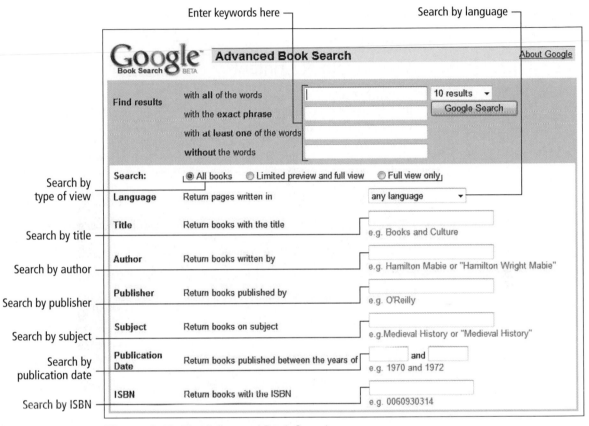

Figure 2.10 The Advanced Book Search page.

3. Not all books are available for online reading. To limit your search to those books that offer their full text for online reading, select the Full view only option. To limit your search to those that offer either full view or a limited preview, select the Limited preview and full view option. To limit your search to those books listed in library catalogs, select the Library catalogs option. To search all books, select the All books option.

4. To search for books written in a specific language, select a language from the Language list.

5. To search for a book by its title, enter your query into the Title box.

6. To search for works by a particular author, enter the author's name into the Author box.

7. To search for books by a particular publisher, enter the publisher's name into the Publisher box.

8. To search for books published within a particular time frame, enter the starting and ending years into the Publication Date fields.

9. If you know the book's ISBN (International Standard Book Number), enter that number into the ISBN box.

10. Click the **Google Search** button to initiate your search.

Activity 2.10

Viewing Book Content

After you initiate a Google book search, Google returns a list of matching books, like the one shown in Figure 2.11. You can display the results in Google's traditional list view or click the Cover View link to see a more visually appealing but less descriptive view of the results. In this activity, you will explore how to view book content.

Figure 2.11 The results of a Google book search.

Books in the search results list can have four different viewing options, depending on the book's copyright status and publisher/author wishes:

- **Full view** The full text of these books is available for reading online.

- **Limited preview** These books have only a limited number of pages available for reading online as a preview to the rest of the book. The full text of the book is not available for reading online.

Snippet A short excerpt from a book or article.

- **Snippet view** Similar to limited preview books, these books only offer a few small snippets of text for preview. *Snippets* show a few instances of the search term in context; the full text of the book is not available for reading online.

- **No preview available** For these books, no previews or snippets are available. Obviously, the full text of the books is also not available for reading online, although sometimes a marketing blurb or publisher's summary is posted.

In this activity, you learn how to navigate a book that is available in either limited preview or full view mode.

1. From the Google Book Search page, conduct a book search.

2. When the search results page appears, click the title of any book that is labeled Full view or Limited preview.

3. When the book page appears, like the one in Figure 2.12, click the **forward** (right arrow) button to advance to the next page. Alternately, you can click the **back** (left arrow) button to return to the previous page.

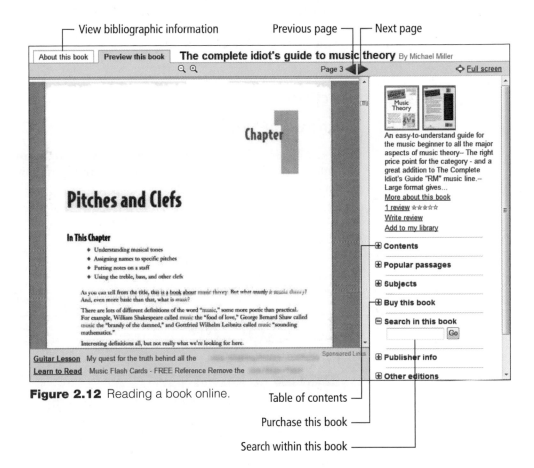

Figure 2.12 Reading a book online.

4. To view the book pages in full-screen mode, click the **Full screen** link. Click the **Exit full screen** link to return to normal view.

5. Click the **Contents** link to view the table of contents of the book. If the book is available for limited preview only, this may display only those chapters or sections available for preview.

6. To search for keywords or phrases within the book's text, enter your query into the Search in this book box and then click the **Go** button.

7. To purchase a copy of the book, click the **Buy this book** link and then click a link for a participating bookstore.

8. For more information, click the **About this book** tab to view a detailed description of the book, along with book details (publication date, page count, ISBN, and so forth).

All Books Are Not the Same

Not all of these options are available for all books, and the availability of information depends mainly on copyright restrictions. Many books simply let you see a preview or snippet, some brief bibliographical information, and a link or two to purchase the book online.

Objective 5

Search for News Articles

Google News Google's database of current and archived news headlines.

Google News is a news-gathering service that identifies, assembles, and displays the latest news headlines from more than 4,500 different news organizations. It also offers a comprehensive news archive search, with more than 200 years' worth of historical newspaper articles available.

Activity 2.11

Browsing News Articles

You get to Google News directly at **news.google.com** or by clicking the News link on any Google page. In this activity, you'll learn how to browse the articles presented on the Google News page.

1. From your web browser, go to the Google News homepage, located at **news.google.com** and shown in Figure 2.13.

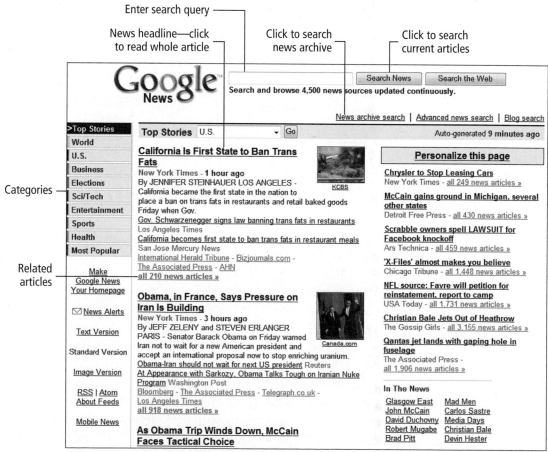

Figure 2.13 The Google News homepage.

2. Google News organizes its stories by category: Top Stories, World, U.S., Business, Sci/Tech, Entertainment, Sports, Health, and Most Popular. In addition, there are often temporary categories for current news events, such as Elections. The top three stories for each category are listed on each page, or you can click a category link on the left side of the page to view a full page of stories in that category.

3. For each story, Google News displays the article's headline, publication, date or time published, a brief synopsis, and possibly a related picture. To read a particular story in full on its originating website, click the story's headline.

4. To view stories related to a particular story, click the **All** *number* **news articles** link beneath that article.

Activity 2.12

Searching Current News Articles

With Google News, you can also search for stories about a particular topic. In this activity, you'll learn how to search by topic.

1. From the Google News homepage, enter one or more keywords into the search box at the top of the page.

2. Click the **Search News** button.

3. Google now displays a list of stories that match your query, as shown in Figure 2.14. To view the most recent stories, click one of the links in the Recent section on the left side of the page: Last hour, Last day, Last week, or Past month.

Filter by date

Figure 2.14 The results of a Google News search.

Activity 2.13

Searching the News Archive

By default, Google News uses the last 30 days' worth of articles in its search results. If you want to find news from 31 days to 200 years old, you can use Google's News Archive Search. In addition to finding recent—but not too recent—news headlines, it's also a great tool for learning about historical events. In this activity, you will learn how to search archived news articles.

1. From the Google News homepage, click the **News archive search** link.

2. From the News Archive Search page, shown in Figure 2.15, enter your query into the search box.

Figure 2.15 Searching Google's News Archive.

3. Click the **Search Archives** button to initiate your search.

4. From the search results page, narrow your search by clicking a date range in the Archives section on the left side of the page.

5. Alternately, click the **Timeline** link near the top of the page (or the **Show Timeline** button on the News Archive Search page) to display a timeline of matching articles, like the one shown in Figure 2.16.

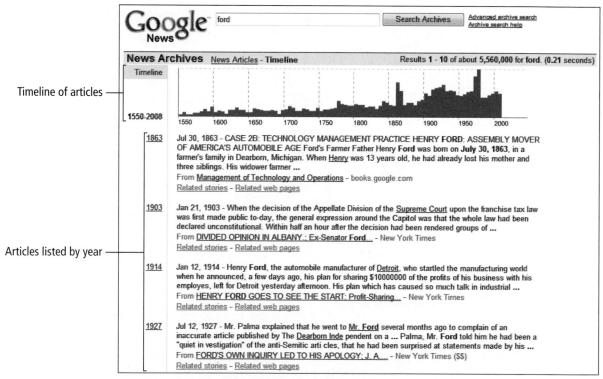

Figure 2.16 Viewing a Google News Archive Timeline.

Objective 6

Search for YouTube Videos

Google's *YouTube* is a video-sharing site that lets users upload and view all sorts of video clips online. The site is a repository for literally millions of movie clips, TV clips (both current and classic), music videos, how-to demonstrations, and home videos. The most popular YouTube videos quickly become *viral,* getting passed from one person to another person or group through email, links on other sites, and blogs on the web. If a YouTube video is particularly interesting, you'll see it pop up virtually everywhere, from television news shows to the front page of your favorite website.

Activity 2.14

Searching for Videos

To find a YouTube video to watch, you need to search for it. Because YouTube is part of the Google empire, it uses search conventions similar to those found on the main Google search site, as you will learn in this activity.

1. From your web browser, go to the YouTube homepage, located at **www.youtube.com** and shown in Figure 2.17.

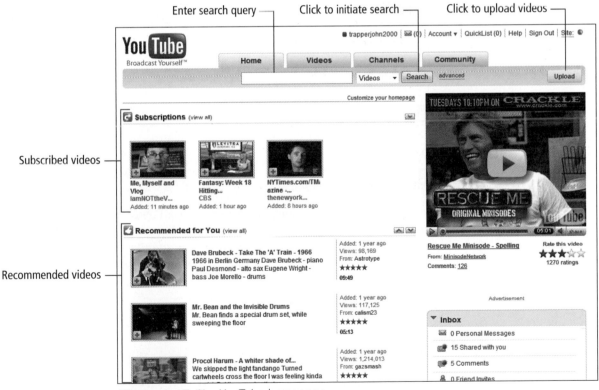

Figure 2.17 The YouTube homepage.

2. Enter your query into the search box.

3. Click the **Search** button.

4. YouTube now returns a list of videos that best match your search criteria, like the one shown in Figure 2.18. Click the video title or thumbnail to go to that video's page and start playback.

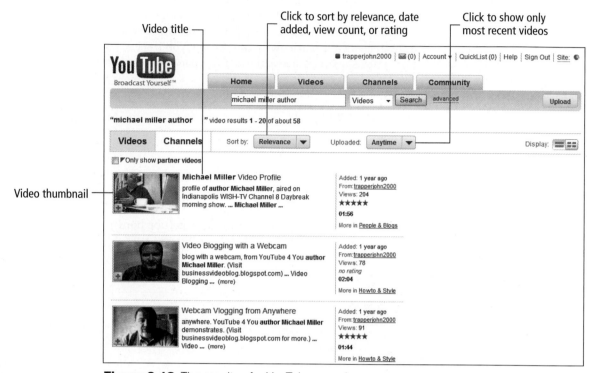

Figure 2.18 The results of a YouTube search.

Activity 2.15

Playing a Video

Playback To view a recorded video.

When you click a video's title or thumbnail on the search results page, you now see the page for that video. As you can see in Figure 2.19, a typical video page contains: a large video window for viewing or *playback*, information about the video, and various features that let you share and save the video. In this activity, you will learn how to play back a video.

View elapsed/total time

Adjust audio volume

View video full screen

Information about the video

Video playback window

Click to pause/play

Click to share video with others

Click to add video to your Favorites list

Figure 2.19 Playing a YouTube video.

In this activity, you'll learn how to play back YouTube videos.

> **Alert** **Playback Problems**
>
> Some large videos or videos played over a slow Internet connection may pause periodically after playback has started. This is due to the playback getting ahead of the streaming video download. If you find a video stopping and starting, just click the Play/Pause button to pause playback until more of the video has downloaded.

1. When you first access a video's page, the video should begin playback automatically. If it doesn't, click the **Play** button beneath the video.

2. To pause playback, click the **Pause** button. To resume playback, click the **Play** button.

3. To move forward and backward through the video, drag the slider control located beneath the video window. (This control also indicates how much of the video has downloaded; the slider fills with red as the video stream downloads.)

4. View the elapsed and total time for the video via the time display.

5. To control the sound level, either click the mute button (to completely mute the sound) or hover over the mute button to display the volume slider.

6. To view the video in full-screen mode, click the **full screen** button. To return to normal viewing mode, press the **Esc** key on your computer keyboard.

Activity 2.16

Saving Your Favorite Videos

When you view a video you really like, YouTube lets you save it in a Favorites list. This is kind of like the Favorites or Bookmarks list you have in your web browser. All your favorite videos are saved in a list that you can easily access for future viewing.

This activity shows you how to save a video to your Favorites list and then view the contents of that list.

Tip YouTube Accounts

While you can search for and view videos without logging into—or even having—a YouTube account, in order to access features such as a Favorites list or video uploading, you must sign up for a free YouTube account and be logged into your account.

1. From the video page, click the **Favorite** tab beneath the video player. The video is automatically added to your Favorites list.

2. To view your Favorites list, place your cursor over the **Account** link at the top of any YouTube page and then click **Favorites** from the drop-down menu.

3. This displays a list of all your favorite videos, as shown in Figure 2.20. Click any video to watch it again.

Figure 2.20 The videos in your Favorites list.

Activity 2.17

Sharing a Video Via Email

YouTube also lets you share with friends and family the videos you find. This activity shows you how.

1. From the video page, click the **Share** tab underneath the YouTube video player, then click the **more share options** link.

2. When the Share tab expands, scroll to the Send this video section, shown in Figure 2.21.

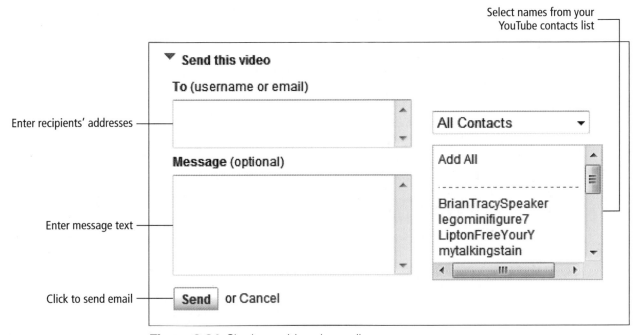

Select names from your YouTube contacts list

Enter recipients' addresses

Enter message text

Click to send email

Figure 2.21 Sharing a video via email.

3. Enter the email addresses of the intended recipients into the To box, separating multiple addresses with commas.

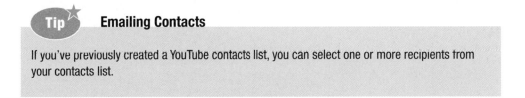

Tip

Emailing Contacts

If you've previously created a YouTube contacts list, you can select one or more recipients from your contacts list.

4. Enter a personal message into the Message box.

5. Click the **Send** button. In a few minutes, your recipients will receive an email message that contains a link to the selected video. To view the video, all a recipient has to do is click the video thumbnail in the message; this opens a web browser, accesses the YouTube site, and starts playing the video you shared.

Activity 2.18

Uploading Your Own Videos

YouTube is a video-sharing community, which means that in addition to viewing video, the YouTube site allows you to share with others the videos you create. The videos you share can be created with any digital video recording device, such as a camcorder or computer webcam.

Before you upload a video to YouTube, as you will learn to do in this activity, it must meet YouTube's file requirements. Make sure your video is formatted as follows:

- MPEG-4 format video with Divx, SVQ3, or Xvid codecs
- MP3 format audio
- 640 × 480 resolution
- Length of 10 minutes or less
- File size of 1GB or less

1. From any YouTube page, click the **Upload** button.

2. When the Video Upload page appears, as shown in Figure 2.22, enter a title for your video into the Title box.

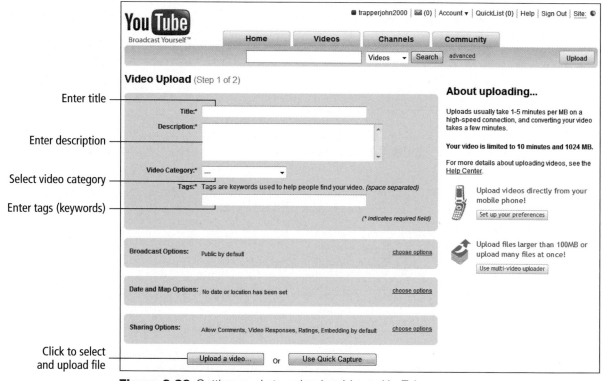

Figure 2.22 Getting ready to upload a video to YouTube.

3. Enter a description for the video into the Description box.

4. Select a category for the video from the Video Category list.

5. In the Tags box, enter one or more tags for the video, separating each tag by a space. *Tags* are keywords people use when searching; use as many tags as necessary to capture all possible search words.

6. To select whether the video is public or private, click the **Choose options** link in the Broadcast Options section.

Tag A label or keyword that describes the content of a YouTube video.

Tip ⭐ **Private Videos**

Use the private option when you're sharing home videos with friends and family.

7. To display when and where the video was recorded, click the **Choose options** link in the Date and Map Options section.

8. To determine whether you want to allow comments, links, and embedding, click the **Choose options** link in the Sharing Options section.

9. Click the **Upload a video** button.

10. When the next page appears, click the **Browse** button.

11. When the Choose File dialog box appears, navigate to and select the file you want, then click the **Open** button.

12. This loads the filename into the Select a Video to Upload box on the Video Upload page. Click the **Upload Video** button and YouTube starts uploading the video.

13. After you click the button, you need to be patient; it can take several minutes to upload a large video, especially over a slow Internet connection. There is additional processing time involved after the upload is complete, while YouTube converts the uploaded video to its own format and adds it to the YouTube database. When the video upload finishes, YouTube displays the Upload Complete page. To view your video, click the **My Videos** link on any YouTube page and then click the thumbnail for your new video.

Note **It Takes Time**

Videos you upload are not immediately available for viewing on YouTube. They must first be processed and approved by the site, which can take anywhere from a few minutes to a few hours.

Objective 7

Search for Locations and Directions

Google Maps Google's web-based mapping and directions service.

With *Google Maps,* you can generate maps for any given address or location, click and drag the maps to view adjacent sections, overlay map information on satellite images of the given area, view local traffic conditions, display nearby businesses as a series of pushpins on the map, and plot driving directions from one location to any other.

Activity 2.19

Searching for a Specific Address

As the name implies, Google Maps is all about the maps. In this activity, you will learn that all you have to do to display a map of a given location is enter information about that location into the top-of-page search box. Table 2.2 shows the different information you can enter to generate a map.

Table 2.2	Google Maps Address Formats	
Address Format	**Example**
city, state	indianapolis, in
ZIP	46204
address, city, state	101 e washington street, indianapolis, in
address, city, zip	101 e washington street, indianapolis, 46204
street intersection, city, state	e washington and n Pennsylvania, indianapolis, in *(can use the & sign instead of the word "and")*
street intersection, zip	e washington and n Pennsylvania, indianapolis, 46204 *(can use the & sign instead of the word "and")*
latitude, longitude	39.767, −86.156
airport code	LAX
subway station, country (in UK and Japan only)	paddington, uk

 Proper Formatting

In most instances, you don't need to spell out words like "east," "street," or "drive"; common abbreviations are okay, and you don't need to put a period after the abbreviation.

 Major Cities

For many major cities, Google Maps will accept just the city name. For example, entering **miami** gives you a map of Miami, Florida; entering **san francisco** displays a map of the city in California. If, on the other hand, you enter a city name that's fairly common (such as **greentown**—which appears in Indiana, Ohio, and several other states), Google will either display a map of the largest city with that name or provide a list of cities or matching businesses for you to choose from. In addition, you can't enter just a state name or abbreviation; while Google recognizes most cities, it doesn't recognize states or countries.

1. From your web browser, go to the Google Maps homepage, located at **maps.google.com** and shown in Figure 2.23.

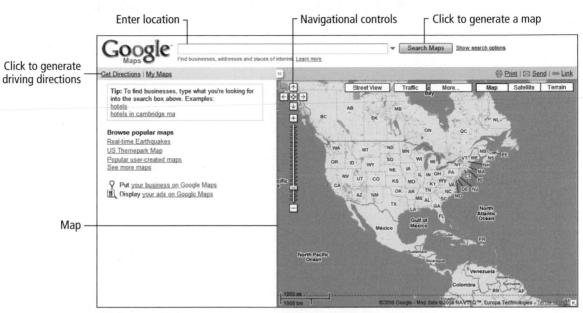

Figure 2.23 Getting ready to search Google Maps.

2. Enter the desired location into the search box.
3. Click the **Search Maps** button. A map of that location is now displayed on the page.

Activity 2.20

Navigating a Google Map

When you enter an address, Google displays a map of that address on the right side of the browser window. The address itself is listed in the Search Results tab on the left side of the window, and information about the address is displayed as a balloon overlaid on the main map. You can use the balloon information to set this address as your default location in Google Maps, to generate driving directions to or from this address, to initiate a search for nearby businesses, or to save this map in Google's My Maps.

Pan To navigate a map in a specific direction.

Using the navigation buttons and the mouse, you can *pan* (change the view of) the map. When using the navigation buttons, clicking repeatedly changes the view of the map yet again. You can also return to the original map results. In this activity, you learn how to navigate a Google map.

Tip **Display a Larger Map**

To display the map the full width of your browser window, click the "arrow" tab at the top left corner of the map. This hides the entire left-hand panel and expands the map to fill the space.

1. To pan west, click the **Pan left** button in the navigational controls or use your mouse to click and drag the map to the right.
2. To pan east, click the **Pan right** button in the navigational controls or use your mouse to click and drag the map to the left.

3. To pan north, click the **Pan up** button in the navigational controls or use your mouse to click and drag the map down.

4. To pan south, click the **Pan down** button in the navigational controls or use your mouse to click and drag the map up.

5. To zoom out to a wider area, click the − button in the navigational controls or drag the zoom slider down.

6. To zoom into a smaller area, click the + button in the navigational controls or drag the zoom slider up.

7. To display the map overlaid with a satellite image of the area, as shown in Figure 2.24, click the **Satellite** button. To return to the traditional map view, click the **Map** button.

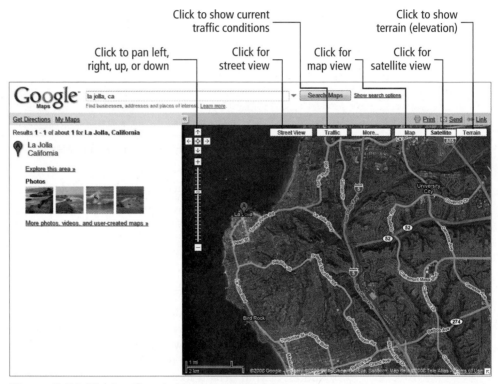

Figure 2.24 Viewing Google Maps in satellite view.

8. To return to the original map results, click the **Return to the last result** button in the center of the panning buttons.

9. To view street-level photographs (where available), click the **Street View** button.

10. To view current traffic conditions for major highways, click the **Traffic** button.

11. To print a copy of the current map view, click the **Print** link.

Street View Street-level photographs of a location in Google Maps.

Activity 2.21

Emailing a Map

Google lets you send copies of any map you generate to friends and family via email. This activity shows you how.

1. Create a map for the desired location.

2. Click the **Send** link.

3. This opens the Send window shown in Figure 2.25, with the URL for the map already entered into the Message box. Enter any additional message into this box.

4. Enter the recipient's email address into the To box.

5. Enter your email address into the From box.

6. Click the **Send** button.

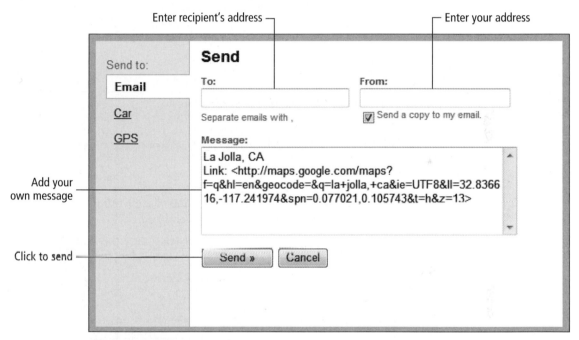

Figure 2.25 Emailing a link to a map you created.

Activity 2.22

Generating Driving Directions

In this activity, you will use Google Maps to generate driving directions from one location to another. It's a simple matter of entering two locations and letting Google get you from point A to point B (and even to points C and D).

1. From the Google Maps main page, click the **Get Directions** link.

2. The top of the left pane now changes to include two address boxes, as shown in Figure 2.26. Enter your starting location into the top (A) box.

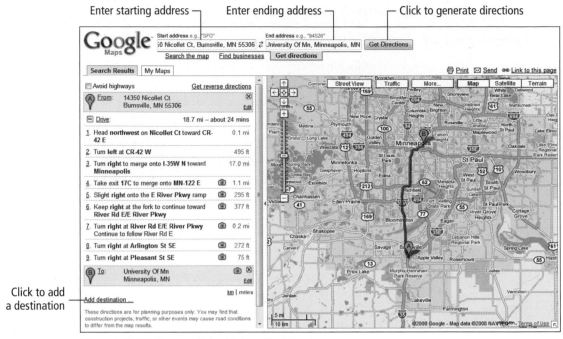

Figure 2.26 Generating driving directions.

3. Enter your ending location into the second (B) address box.

4. Click the **Get directions** button.

5. Google now generates turn-by-turn driving directions and maps your route. If you would like to change any section of your route, use your mouse to drag that section of the route to a different location.

6. To add another destination to your trip, click the **Add destination** link and enter the new location.

7. To print these directions, click the **Print** link.

Activity 2.23

Finding Nearby Businesses

As part of its Google Maps service, Google hosts a large database of local retailers. This lets you use Google Maps to search for retailers within any area or neighborhood or near any address. In this activity, you will learn how.

1. From the Google Maps homepage, enter your location into the search box.

2. Click the **Search Maps** button to display a map of your location.

3. Enter the business name or type of business you're looking for into the search box.

4. Click the **Search Maps** button.

5. Google now displays matching businesses pinpointed on the map and listed on the left side of the page, as shown in Figure 2.27. Click a business name or pinpoint to display an information balloon about the business.

6. This information balloon includes the business' address and phone number, as well as its website (if it has one). Links within the balloon let you read reviews about the business, generate driving directions, or display more information.

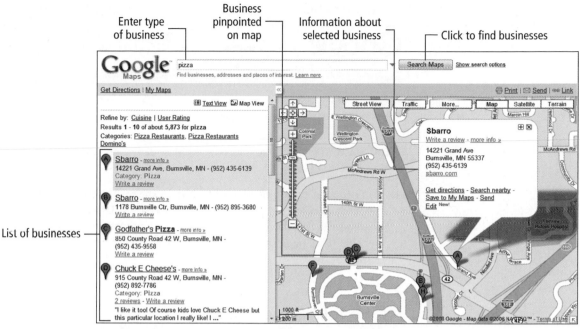

Figure 2.27 The results of a Google Maps business search.

 Note **Closest First**

Google Maps typically lists the closest businesses first and then expands its results geographically.

Objective 8

Search for Words and Definitions

Want to look up the definition of a particular word but don't want to bother pulling out the old hardcover dictionary? Not sure of a specific spelling? You can use Google as an online dictionary to look up any word you can think of. It's easy and there are two ways to do it.

Activity 2.24

Conducting a "What Is" Search

The first approach to looking up definitions is to use a little-known Google feature called a "what is" search. This activity shows how it works.

1. From the main Google search page, enter the keywords **what is** into the search box, followed by the word you want to define. (No question mark is necessary.) For example, to look up the definition of the word "defenestrate," enter **what is defenestrate**.

2. Click the **Google Search** button.

3. Google now returns a standard search results page, as well as a single web definition in a OneBox result at the top of the page. As you can see in Figure 2.28, this OneBox result includes a short definition of the word and two useful links. The result title is actually a link to other definitions of the word on the web. The **Definition in context** link displays an example of the word used in a sentence.

Enter "what is" query ─┐   Word link in statistics bar ─┐

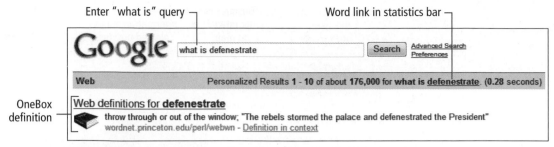

OneBox
definition

Figure 2.28 The special results of a "what is" definition search.

4. You can find even more useful results in the results page's statistics bar, where the word you searched for is displayed as a link. Click this link and Google displays the full dictionary definition of the word from the Answers.com website. This page includes a pronunciation of the word, as well as one or more definitions.

 Definitions from Answers.com

Answers.com (www.answers.com) offers all sorts of information, including—but not limited to—dictionary definitions. The sources of its definitions, such as *The American Heritage Dictionary*, are shown next to the definitions.

Activity 2.25

Searching the Google Glossary

Google Glossary Google's database of word definitions.

Even more definitions are available when you use the Google Glossary feature. *Google Glossary* is what Google calls it, but it's really just another advanced search operator that produces some very specific results, as you will learn in this activity.

1. From the main Google search page, enter the operator **define:** into the search box, followed by the word you want defined (with no spaces between). So, for example, if you want to define the word "defenestrate," enter the query **define:defenestrate**.

 Define a Phrase

If you want to define a phrase, use the **define:** operator, but put the phrase in quotation marks. For example, to define the phrase "peer to peer," enter the query **define: "peer to peer"**. Without the quotation marks, Google will only define the first word in the phrase.

2. Click the **Google Search** button.

3. Google now displays a special definitions page, as shown in Figure 2.29. This page includes all the definitions for the word that Google found on the web; click a link to view the full definition.

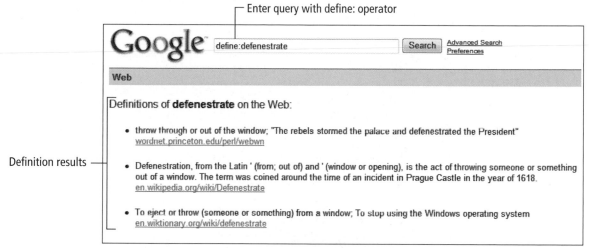

Enter query with define: operator

Definition results

*Definitions of **defenestrate** on the Web:*

- *throw through or out of the window; "The rebels stormed the palace and defenestrated the President"*
  wordnet.princeton.edu/perl/webwn

- *Defenestration, from the Latin ' (from; out of) and ' (window or opening), is the act of throwing someone or something out of a window. The term was coined around the time of an incident in Prague Castle in the year of 1618.*
  en.wikipedia.org/wiki/Defenestrate

- *To eject or throw (someone or something) from a window; To stop using the Windows operating system*
  en.wiktionary.org/wiki/defenestrate

Figure 2.29 Results of a search using the **define:** operator.

Alert   **Use the Operator, Not the Word**

If you enter the keyword **define**—and not the **define:** operator—with a space between it and the word you want defined, Google returns the same results as if you entered a "what is" query.

Objective 9

Use Google as a Calculator

Here's something few Google users know: You can use Google as a calculator to solve various types of mathematical equations, right from the basic search box.

Activity 2.26

Performing Basic Calculations

In this activity, you will use Google as a calculator. All you have to do is enter your equation or formula into the search box and then click the Google Search button. Just make sure you use the proper operators, as detailed in Table 2.3. Also make sure you leave spaces between all numbers and operators, and separate calculations with parentheses as necessary.

1. From Google's main search page, enter the equation into the search box.

2. Click the **Google Search** button.

3. The results of the equation are shown in a Calculator OneBox listing at the top of the results page, as shown in Figure 2.30.

Table 2.3	Google's Basic Calculator Functions		
Function	**Operator**	**Example**	**Result**
Addition	+ *or* plus *or* and	2 + 1	3
Subtraction	− *or* minus	2 − 1	1
Multiplication	X *or* × *or* times	2 × 1	2
Division	/ *or* over *or* divided by	2 / 1	2

Enter equation

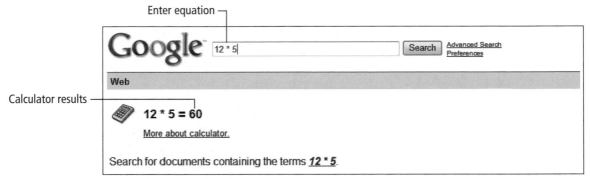

Calculator results

Figure 2.30 Results of a calculation.

 Tip **Multiple Operations**

Google also lets you string multiple operations together. For example, if you want to calculate 12 times 5 divided by 4, enter **12 * 5 / 4**. You can also create nesting equations by using appropriately placed parentheses. Following mathematical rules, calculations in parentheses and using exponents are done first; then the calculations work from left to right, multiplying and dividing first and then adding and subtracting. So, to divide the sum of 4 plus 3 by the sum of 5 plus 2, enter **(4 + 3) / (5 + 2)**.

Activity 2.27

Performing Advanced Calculations

Google's calculator can also handle more advanced calculations, trigonometric functions, inverse trigonometric functions, hyperbolic functions, and logarithmic functions, as you will learn in this activity.

This activity demonstrates just a few of Google's advanced mathematic functions.

1. To calculate percentages, enter **x% of y**. For example, to calculate twenty percent of the number ten, enter **20% of 10**.

2. To calculate square roots, use the **sqrt** operator, followed by the number in parentheses. For example, to calculate the square root of 16, enter **sqrt(16)**.

3. To calculate exponents (raising a number to a power), enter the number, followed by the ^ operator, followed by the exponential factor. For example, to raise the number four by the power of two, enter **4^2**.

4. To calculate factorials, enter the number, followed by the ! operator. For example, to calculate the factorial of 10, enter **10!**.

5. To calculate the cosine of a number, enter the **cos** operator, followed by the number in parentheses. For example, to calculate the cosine of 100, enter **cos(100)**.

Objective 10

Use Google to Find Constants and Conversions

In addition to performing calculations, Google also knows a variety of mathematical and scientific constants. It also knows units of measure and can convert numbers from one unit to another from the basic search box.

Activity 2.28

Looking Up the Values of Constants

What constants does Google know? It's a long list, starting with pi, Avogadro's Number, and Planck's Constant. Google also knows the radius of the Earth, the mass of the sun, the speed of light, the gravitational constant, and a lot more.

To return the value of a constant, simply enter that constant into the Google search box and then click the **Google Search** button, as you will do in this activity. Google returns the value of the constant in a OneBox result, like the one shown in Figure 2.31, as well as links to other search results.

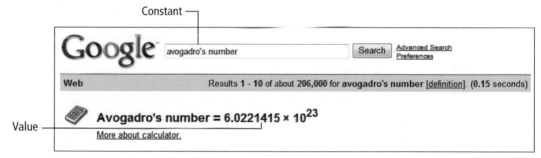

Figure 2.31 Using Google to display the value of a constant—in this example, Avogadro's Number.

In this activity, you'll learn how to look up some of the more popular constants.

1. To display the value of pi, enter the query **pi**.

2. To display the value of Avogadro's number, enter the query **avogadro's number**.

3. To display the value of an Astronomical Unit, enter the query **astronomical unit**.

4. To display the value of the speed of light, enter the query **speed of light**.

5. To display the value of the radius of the Earth, enter the query **radius of earth**.

Activity 2.29

Converting Units of Measure

In this activity, you will use Google's calculator to convert units of measure, such as miles and meters, furlongs and light years, and seconds and fortnights. Table 2.4 lists some of the categories of measurements and the units into which you can convert them using Google.

Table 2.4	Google's Units of Measure	
Type of Measurement	**Units**
Currency	U.S. dollars (USD), Australian dollars (AUD), Canadian dollars, British pounds (GBP, pounds), Euros
Mass	Grams (g), kilograms (kg), pounds (lbs), grains, carats, stones, tons, tones
Distance (length)	Meters (m), kilometers (km), miles, feet (ft), Angstroms, cubits, furlongs, nautical miles, smoots, light years
Volume	Gallons, liters (l), pints, quarts, teaspoons, tablespoons, cups
Area	Square miles, square kilometers, square feet, square yards, acres, hectares
Time	Days, hours, minutes, seconds (s), months, years, centuries, sidereal years, fortnights
Electricity	Volts, amps, ohms, henrys
Power	Watts, kilowatts, horsepower (hp)
Energy	British thermal units (BTU), joules, ergs, foot-pounds, calories, kilocalories (kcal)
Temperature	Degrees Fahrenheit, degrees Celsius
Speed	Miles per hour (mph), kilometers per hour (kph), kilometers per second, knots
Data	Bites, bytes, kilobytes (KB), megabytes (MB), gigabytes (GB), terabytes (TB)
Quantity	Dozen, baker's dozen, gross, great gross, score, googol
Numbering systems	Decimal, hexadecimal (hex), octal (Oo), binary, roman numerals

The key to using the Google calculator as a converter is to express your query using the proper syntax. Enter the first unit of measure, followed by the word "in," followed by the second unit of measure. A general query looks like this: **x firstunits in secondunits**; a typical result is shown in Figure 2.32.

Query ⌐

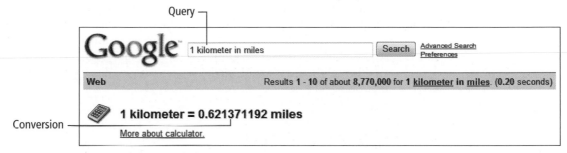

Conversion ⌐

Figure 2.32 Using Google to convert units of measure.

In this activity, we examine some examples of Google's conversion function.

1. To find out how many feet equal a meter, enter the query **1 meter in feet**.

2. To find out how many teaspoons are in a cup, enter the query **1 cup in teaspoons**.

3. To find out the current value in euros of 100 U.S. dollars, enter the query **100 usd in euros**.

4. To convert 72 degrees Fahrenheit to Celsius, enter the query **72 degrees Fahrenheit in Celsius**.

5. To convert 500 miles to kilometers, enter the query **500 miles in kilometers**.

Summary

In this chapter, you learned how to use Google for various types of nontraditional searches. You learned how to obtain quality results from the human-edited Google Directory. You searched for addresses and phone numbers. Using Google Scholar, you searched for information in scholarly journals, books, and news articles. You learned how to search YouTube for videos and Google Maps for locations and directions. This chapter also introduced you to other features of Google's main search page, including displaying word definitions, performing mathematic equations, displaying constants, and converting units of measure.

Key Terms

Assessments

Multiple Choice

1. Which of the following is true?
   (a) The Google Directory can only be browsed, not searched.
   (b) The Google Directory is assembled by human editors.
   (c) The Google Directory is larger than the Google Search Index.
   (d) The Google Directory contains results found by GoogleBot software.

2. Which of the following queries is most likely to generate the most targeted Google Phonebook results?
   (a) marcia hernandez 02101
   (b) marcia hernandez boston
   (c) m hernandez boston
   (d) marcia hernandez boston ma

3. Google Scholar lets you fine-tune your results with the following parameter(s):
   (a) date
   (b) publication
   (c) author
   (d) all of the above

4. Which of the following is true?
   (a) The Google Book Search database contains every book ever published.
   (b) The Google Book Search database contains only books with full-text viewing.
   (c) The Google Book Search database obtains all of its content from the books' publishers.
   (d) The Google Book Search database contains both in-print and out-of-print books.

5. Google News contains _____.
   (a) current news articles only
   (b) historical news articles only
   (c) both current and historical news articles
   (d) articles from only the top dozen news organizations

6. YouTube is _____.
   (a) a video-sharing community
   (b) a site to watch the latest viral videos
   (c) a site for uploading your own videos
   (d) all of the above

7. Which of the following is *not* a view in Google Maps?
   (a) Street View
   (b) 3-D Virtual View
   (c) Satellite View
   (d) Terrain View

8. To display the definition of the word "cumbersome," enter this query:
   (a) word:cumbersome
   (b) dictionary:cumbersome
   (c) define:cumbersome
   (d) cumbersome

9. To calculate the value of 42 divided by the sum of 3 plus 5, enter this query:
   (a) 42 / 3 + 5
   (b) 42 / (3 + 5)
   (c) (42 / 3) + 5
   (d) − 42 / (3 + 5)

10. To convert ten gallons to liters, enter this query:
    (a) 10 gallons in liters
    (b) 10 gallons = liters
    (c) liters = 10 gallons
    (d) how many liters in 10 gallons

Fill in the Blank

Write the correct word in the space provided.

1. The Google Directory contains _____ listings than the normal Google search index.
2. To look up who belongs to a given phone number, perform a _____ phone number lookup.
3. In Google Scholar, an article not available online displays the word _____ next to the title.
4. In Google Book Search, a _____ book presents only selected pages for reading online.
5. By default, Google News keeps _____ days' worth of articles in its database; older articles can be found using News Archive Search.
6. When you find a YouTube video you like, you can save it in your _____ list.
7. To pan east on a Google Map, use your mouse to click and drag the map to the _____.
8. To display the definition of a word, use either a "what is" search or the _____ operator.
9. To calculate the square root of 25, enter the query _____.
10. Numbers such as pi, Avogadro's Number, and the speed of light are called _____.

Skills Review

1. Use the Google Directory to browse for web pages about hiking.
2. Search Google for your home street address.
3. Use Google Scholar to search for articles about prehistoric birds.
4. Use Google Book Search to search for books by Ernest Hemingway.
5. Search Google News for archived stories about the Apollo space program.
6. Search YouTube for videos of fast cars.
7. Use Google Maps to generate driving directions from your home to your school.
8. Use Google to define the word "largesse."
9. Use Google to calculate the sum of 7 plus 5.
10. Use Google to calculate the value of the speed of sound.

CHAPTER 3

Using Gmail

Objectives

By the end of this chapter you will be able to:

1. Sign Up for a Gmail Account

2. Read Email Messages

3. Send Email Messages

4. Send and Receive File Attachments

5. Manage Messages

6. Manage Gmail Contacts

As part of its suite of online applications, Google offers a web-based email service, called **Gmail**. You can use Gmail to send and receive email from any computer with an Internet connection. Your messages are stored on Google's servers, so they're always accessible no matter where you are.

Gmail Google's web-based email service.

Objective 1

Sign Up for a Gmail Account

Gmail is a free service; anyone can establish an account for no charge. In addition, because it's web-based, there's no software to download. You access Gmail on the Internet, using Mozilla Firefox, Internet Explorer, or any other web browser.

Activity 3.1

Signing Up for a Gmail Account

If you already have a Google account, that account serves as your Gmail account. When you go to the main Gmail page, just enter your Google account username and password and you're ready to go. If you don't yet have a Google account, it's easy to sign up for a new Gmail account. This activity shows you how.

1. From your web browser, go to mail.google.com.

2. Click the **Sign up for Gmail** link.

3. When the Create an Account page appears, as shown in Figure 3.1, enter your first name and last name into the First name and Last name boxes.

Figure 3.1 Creating a new Gmail account.

4. Enter the username you'd like to use into the Desired Login Name box, then click the **check availability!** button. If that name is available, Google tells you so, and you can proceed to the next step. If the name you chose isn't available, Google suggests some options; select one of the options or enter a new username.

5. Enter your desired password into the Choose a password box, then enter it again into the Re-enter password box.

 Create a Strong Password

To create a stronger password, create a longer password. You can also strengthen your password by including letters, numbers, and special characters. (Google will tell you how strong your password is as you type it.)

6. Click the **Remember me on this computer** checkbox only if you are using a personal computer; do not click this if you are using a shared or lab computer.

7. If you want Google to track your online activities to better fine-tune your search results, click the **Enable Web History** checkbox.

8. Select a security question from the Security Question list, then enter the answer to that question into the Answer box.

9. Enter a secondary email address (your home or school address) into the Secondary email box, to be used in case you ever have problems accessing your Gmail account.

10. Confirm your location in the Location list; United States is the default location.

11. Type the appropriate characters into the Word Verification box; this helps to prevent automated software from signing up for accounts (typically for spam purposes).

12. Read the terms and conditions, then click the **I accept. Create my account.** button. Google now creates your account and assigns you the requested email address in the form of *username*@gmail.com.

Activity 3.2

Getting to Know the Gmail Interface

Once you sign up for your Gmail account, you are assigned your email address and you have access to the Gmail Inbox page, shown in Figure 3.2. This activity takes you on a tour of the Gmail interface.

1. From your web browser, go to **mail.google.com**.

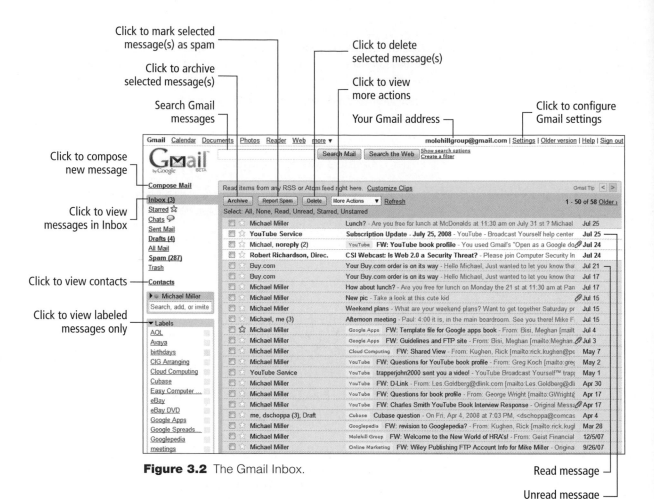

Click to mark selected
message(s) as spam

Click to archive
selected message(s)

Search Gmail
messages

Click to compose
new message

Click to view
messages in Inbox

Click to view contacts

Click to view labeled
messages only

Click to delete
selected message(s)

Click to view
more actions

Your Gmail address

Click to configure
Gmail settings

Read message

Unread message

Figure 3.2 The Gmail Inbox.

> **Note**
>
> **Sign In First**
>
> If you're prompted to sign in, enter your Gmail or Google username and password.

2. When the main Gmail page appears, click the **Inbox** link to view the messages in your Inbox. This is where all of your received messages are stored, unless you delete or relocate them.

3. To switch to another view of your messages, click the appropriate links at the left, top, or bottom of the page. For example, to view all your sent mail, click the **Sent Mail** link on the left; to view only unread messages, click the **Unread** link at the top or bottom of the page.

4. Each message is listed with the message's sender, the subject of the message, a short snippet from the first line of the message, and the date or time the message was sent. Unread messages are listed in bold; once a message has been read, it is displayed in normal, nonbold text with a blue-shaded background. If you've assigned a label to a message (which you will learn to do later in this chapter), the label appears in green before the message subject. To view a message, click that message in the Inbox.

5. To perform an action on a message or group of messages, click the checkbox for the message(s) and then click one of the buttons at the top or bottom of the list. For example, to archive a message, click the checkbox for that message, then click the *Archive* button.

Archive To store old or inactive messages.

Note   **More Actions**

Additional actions are available by clicking the More Actions list arrow. From this list, you can mark a message as read or unread, add or remove a star from a message, or apply a label to a message.

Objective 2

Read Email Messages

Google lets you read individual messages in your Inbox or groups of messages organized into conversations.

 Tip   **Refresh Your Inbox**

To display recently received messages, you can refresh your Inbox by clicking the **Refresh** link.

Activity 3.3

Reading Messages

You read the messages you receive in the same web browser you use to view the Gmail Inbox. In this activity, you learn how to read an individual message.

1. From your web browser, go to mail.google.com and sign into your Gmail account.

2. When the Gmail homepage appears, click the **Inbox** link.

3. Unread messages are displayed in bold; read messages are nonbold with a shaded blue background. To read a message, click the message's title.

4. The full text of the message is displayed on a new page, as shown in Figure 3.3. To return to the Inbox, click the **Inbox** link.

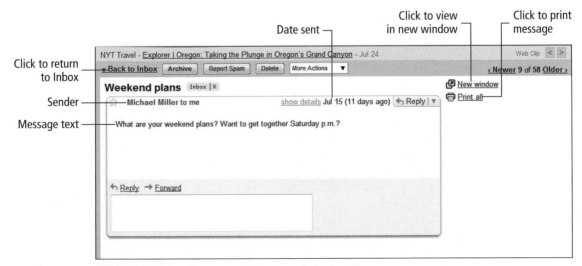

Figure 3.3 Reading an email message in Gmail.

Activity 3.4

Viewing Conversations

Conversation A group of
related email messages.

One of the unique things about Gmail is that all related email messages are grouped together in what Google calls *conversations*. A conversation might be an initial message and all the replies (and replies to replies) to that message. A conversation could also be all the daily emails from a single source with a common subject, such as messages you receive from a mailing list to which you have subscribed.

A conversation is noted in the Inbox list by a number in parentheses after the sender name(s). If a conversation has replies from more than one person, more than one name is listed. In this activity, you learn how to view the messages in a conversation.

1. From the Gmail Inbox, click the message title for the conversation you want to view.

2. The conversation now appears in your web browser. As you can see in Figure 3.4, only the most recent message is displayed in full. To view the text of any previous message in the conversation, click that message's subject.

3. To expand all the messages in a conversation, click the **Expand all** link. All the messages in the conversation are now stacked on top of each other, with the text of the newest message fully displayed.

Click to view all messages
in the conversation

Previous message

Most recent message

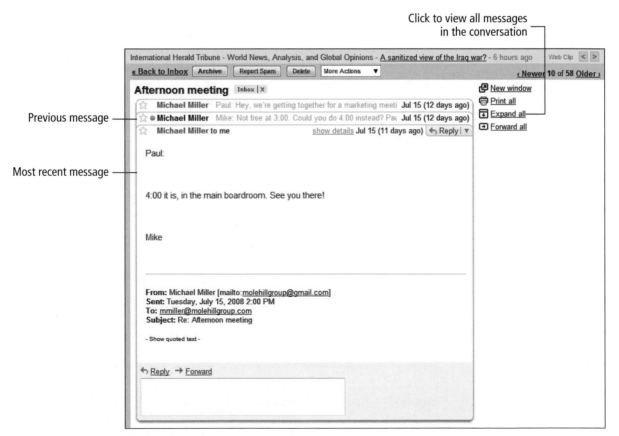

Figure 3.4 Viewing a conversation.

Objective 3

Send Email Messages

Sending messages is every bit as easy in Gmail as receiving them. You can quickly and easily reply to any message you've received or compose and send a completely new message.

Activity 3.5

Replying to Messages

Whether you're reading a single message or a conversation, it's easy to send a reply, as you will do in this activity:

1. In the original message, click the **Reply** button. This expands the message to include a reply box, like the one shown in Figure 3.5.

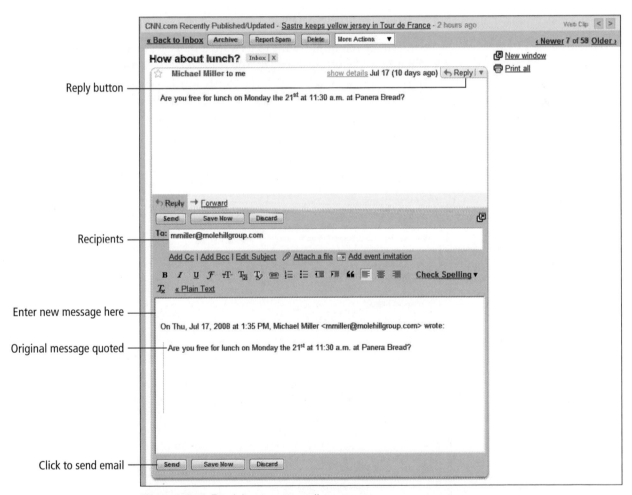

Figure 3.5 Replying to an email message.

 Replying to Multiple Recipients

If a conversation has multiple participants, you can reply to all of them by clicking the **Reply** button arrow and then clicking **Reply to all**.

Send Email Messages   77

2. The subject is the same, but the prefix Re: is added to indicate to the sender that you are replying to a message. The text of the original message is already quoted in the reply. Add your new text above the original text.

3. The original sender's address is automatically added to the To line. Click the **Send** button to send the message.

 Changing Your Mind

If you change your mind about replying to a message, click the **Discard** button to abandon the current reply. If you want to save a draft of your message before sending it, click the **Save Now** button; you can retrieve the draft message later by clicking the **Drafts** link on the left side of the page.

Activity 3.6

Forwarding Messages

Sometimes you might want to forward a message to a third party, instead of simply replying to the original sender. You learn how to do this in this activity.

1. In the original message, click the **Reply** button arrow, then click **Forward**. This expands the message to include a Forward box, shown in Figure 3.6. The subject is the same, but the prefix Fwd: is added to indicate to the sender that you are forwarding a message.

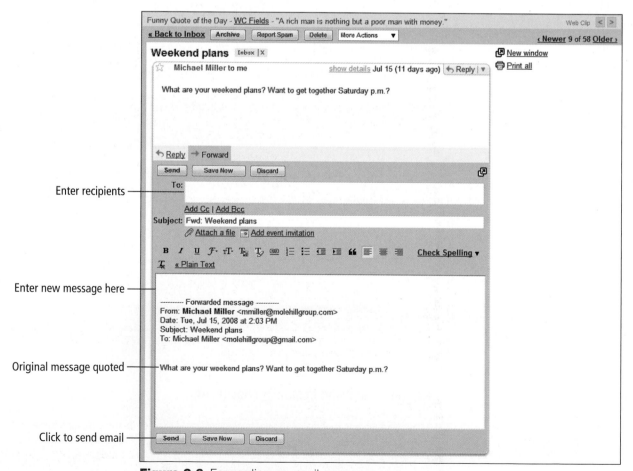

Figure 3.6 Forwarding an email message.

2. Add the recipient's email address to the To box.

3. Enter your cover message into the main message box.

4. Click the **Send** button.

Activity 3.7

Composing and Sending New Messages

Creating a new message from scratch isn't much more difficult than replying to a pre-existing message. In this activity, you learn how to compose and send a new message.

 Add Event Information

If you and your recipient both use Google Calendar, you can add event information for your calendars in your new email message. Click the **Add event invitation** link and Gmail prompts you for details about the event; the recipient is then invited to the event as part of the email message.

1. From any Gmail page, click the **Compose Mail** link.

2. When the Compose Mail page appears, as shown in Figure 3.7, enter the recipient's email address into the To box. Separate multiple recipients with commas.

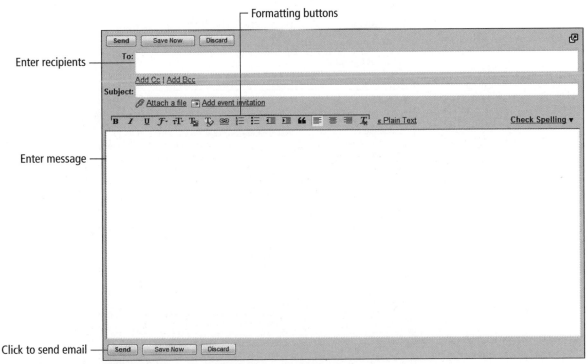

Figure 3.7 Composing a new email message.

 Cc and Bcc

You can cc (carbon copy) and bcc (blind carbon copy) additional recipients by clicking the **Add Cc** and **Add Bcc** links. This expands the message to include Cc or Bcc boxes, into which you enter the recipients' addresses. A cc sends the message to the copied recipients and allows display of their addresses to the main recipients; a bcc hides the addresses of copied recipients.

3. Enter a subject for the message into the Subject box. While a subject is optional, it is preferable because it allows you to create conversations and tags and alerts the recipient to the message content. You will be prompted to add a subject if you leave it blank.

4. Enter the text of your message into the large message text box. Use the formatting buttons (bold, italic, font, and so forth) to enhance your message as desired.

5. When you're done composing your message, click the **Send** button.

 Spell Check

Gmail provides spell checking for all your outgoing messages. Click the **Check Spelling** link, then accept or reject suggested spelling changes throughout your document.

Activity 3.8

Adding a Signature to Your Messages

Signature Personalized text that appears at the bottom of an email message.

A *signature* is personalized text that appears at the bottom of an email message. Signatures typically include the sender's name and contact information.

If you want to add a signature to the bottom of all your email messages, you don't have to manually enter that signature every time you send a message. Instead, you can configure Gmail to automatically add the signature. In this activity, you learn how.

1. From any Gmail page, click the **Settings** link at the top of the page.

2. When the Settings page appears, as shown in Figure 3.8, click the **General** tab if necessary.

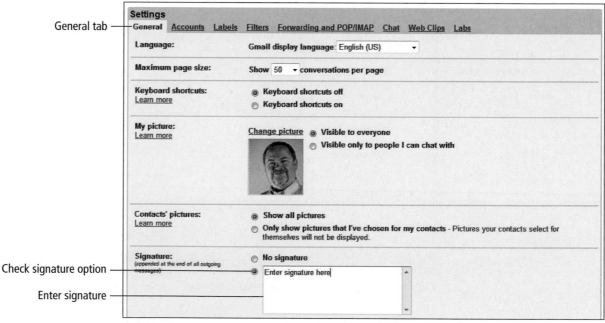

Figure 3.8 Creating a new email signature.

3. Scroll down to the Signature section and click the second option button (below No Signature).

4. Enter your signature into the large text box.

5. Click the **Save Changes** button.

 Note **No Signature**

If you prefer not to include a signature, check the **No signature** option button on the Settings page.

Objective 4
Send and Receive File Attachments

Attachment A file that is sent along with an email message.

One of the key features of Gmail is its capability to store large amounts of data. You can use this feature to email files to yourself for backup purposes. You can send and receive files as *attachments* to your email messages.

Alert ! **No Program Files**

Executable program file A computer file that contains a software program.

While Gmail lets you send Word documents, Excel spreadsheets, MP3 music files, JPG picture files, and the like, it won't let you send any *executable program files* (files that have an .exe extension). You can't even send .exe files when they're compressed into .zip files. Gmail blocks the transmittal of *all* .exe files in an attempt to prevent potential computer viruses.

Activity 3.9
Attaching Files to Outgoing Messages

Gmail lets you attach files to any message you're sending. In this activity, you learn how to attach a file to a Gmail message.

1. Use Gmail to compose a new message.

2. From the new message page, click the **Attach a file** link.

3. When the Choose file or File Upload dialog box opens, navigate to and select the file you want to attach and then click the **Open** button.

4. The file you selected now appears under the Subject box on the new message page, as shown in Figure 3.9. To attach another file to this same message, click the **Attach another file** link; otherwise, compose and send your message.

File attachment ——

Click to add another file

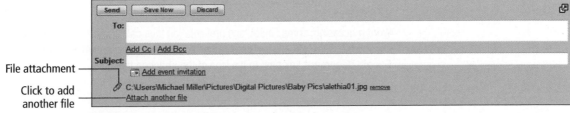

Figure 3.9 A file added to an outgoing message.

Activity 3.10

Opening or Viewing Attached Files

What do you do if someone sends you a file attached to an email message? First, make sure that you're expecting the attachment, to be certain that it's not a virus tagging along for the ride. If you're confident that it's a legitimate attachment from someone you know and trust, you can opt to either view the attachment (ideal for photos) or save the attachment to your hard drive.

When you receive a message with an attachment, you see a paper clip icon next to the message subject/snippet in your Inbox. In this activity, you learn how to view or open that attached file.

1. From the Google Inbox, click the message to open it. If the attached file is a picture, it is displayed below the message text, as shown in Figure 3.10; otherwise, the filename appears below the text.

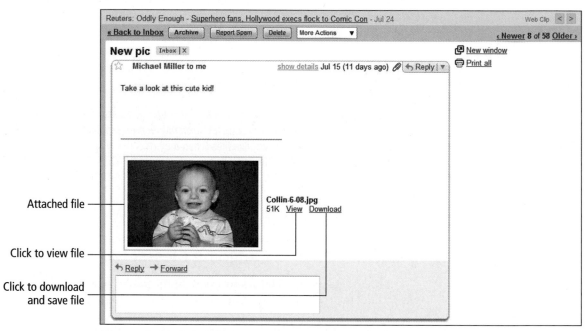

Attached file ——

Click to view file ——

Click to download and save file ——

Figure 3.10 A .jpg file attached to a Gmail message.

2. Different types of files have different viewing options. For example, photos are viewed full-size in a separate web browser window, and Word files can be viewed as HTML documents to avoid opening them in a word processor. To view the file, click the **View** or **View as HTML** link to open the file in a new window.

 Note   **Google Documents**

Word processing, spreadsheet, and presentation files can also be opened as Google-format documents, compatible with Google Docs applications. This option is presented as an **Open as a Google document** link next to the icon of the attached file.

3. To save the file to your hard disk, click the **Download** link. When the File Download dialog box appears, click the **Save** button, select a location for the file, then click the **Save** button in the Save As dialog box.

Objective 5

Manage Messages

Unlike many other email services, Gmail doesn't use folders to organize your messages. Instead, Gmail uses searches to find the messages you want—not a surprise, given Google's search-centric business model. In addition, Gmail lets you tag each message with one or more labels. *Tagging* is a way of creating virtual folders; you can search and sort your messages by any tag label.

Tagging Creates virtual folders, which you can use to search and sort messages by any tag label.

Activity 3.11

Deleting Messages

You can delete messages from either your Inbox or an open message window. When you delete a message, it is moved to the Trash. Messages stay in the Trash for 30 days; after that, they're permanently deleted. In this activity, you will learn both ways to delete a message.

1. To delete a message from your Inbox, click the message checkbox, then click the **Delete** button, as shown in Figure 3.11.

2. To delete an open message, click the **Delete** button.

Click to delete selected message

Click to view previously deleted messages

Check to select message to delete

Figure 3.11 Deleting a message from the Gmail Inbox.

 Alert! **Deleting Conversations**

Because Gmail organizes your email messages into conversations, it's easy to mistakenly delete an entire conversation instead of just a single message. Take care to select only the message within a conversation that you want to delete.

 Tip **Viewing Deleted Messages**

You can view the messages in the Trash by clicking the **Trash** link in the left column of the page. You can then undelete any message by checking it and clicking the **Move to Inbox** button, or remove it permanently by clicking the **Delete Forever** button.

Activity 3.12

Searching Your Inbox

As noted previously, Gmail organization is based on Google's search model. To find a specific message in your crowded Inbox, you have to search for it.

For most users, Gmail's basic search feature will quickly and easily find the messages they're looking for. In this activity, you learn how to search your Inbox for messages.

1. Enter one or more keywords into the search box at the top of any Gmail page.

2. Click the **Search Mail** button.

 No Automatic Stemming

Unlike Google's web search, a Gmail search doesn't offer automatic stemming, which means that it doesn't recognize matches to partial strings, plurals, misspellings, and the like. If you search for **dog**, Gmail won't recognize **dogs**, **dogged**, or **doggy**.

3. Gmail now returns a search results page, like the one shown in Figure 3.12. This page lists messages in which the queried keywords appear anywhere in the message—in the subject line, in the message text, or in the sender or recipient lists. Click a message to read it.

Enter query ⌐   ⌐ Click to search Inbox messages

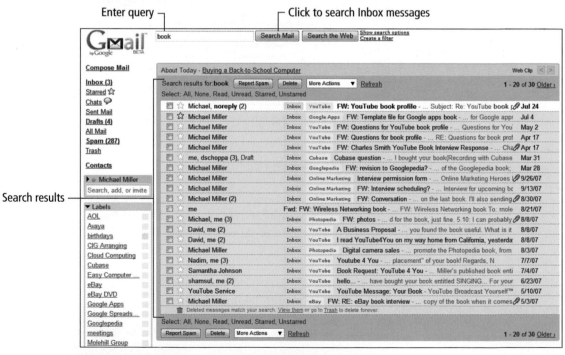

Figure 3.12 Viewing the results of a Gmail search.

Activity 3.13

Using Gmail's Search Options

The more messages in your Inbox, the more you'll need to fine-tune your mail searches. Gmail uses checkboxes to help you with advanced search functions. You will learn how to do this in this activity.

1. From your Gmail Inbox, click the **Show search options** link (next to the search buttons). The top of the Gmail page expands to display the Search Options panel, shown in Figure 3.13.

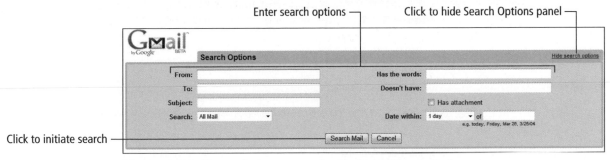

Enter search options ⌐   Click to hide Search Options panel ⌐

Click to initiate search ⌐

Figure 3.13 Fine-tuning your search with Gmail Search Options.

2. To search for messages from a particular sender, enter that person's name into the From box.

3. To search for messages to a particular recipient, enter that person's name into the To box.

4. To search the subject lines of messages only, enter a query consisting of one or more keywords into the Subject box.

5. To search the text of messages, enter a query consisting of one or more keywords into the Has the words box.

6. To exclude messages that contain one or more words, enter those words into the Doesn't have box.

7. To search for messages that contain attached files, click the **Has attachment** checkbox.

8. To search for messages by date, select a range from the Date within list and then enter a date in the of box. For instance, to search for all messages within a week of July 15, 2009, select 1 week from the Date within list, then enter July 15, 2009 in the of box.

9. To search only specific types of messages (starred, unread mail, and so forth) or for messages with a specific tag, select the search criteria from the Search list.

10. Click the **Search Mail** button to initiate the search.

Activity 3.14

Starring Important Messages

Star A means of identifying selected email messages.

If you find a message that you think is more important than other messages, you can *star* the message. In Gmail, starring is the same as the flagging feature found in other email services and programs. You will learn to star messages in this activity.

1. From the Gmail Inbox, identify the message you want to star.

2. Click the empty star next to that message. Once clicked, the star appears in solid yellow, as shown in Figure 3.14.

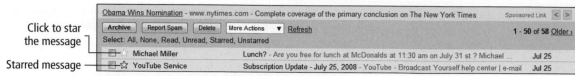

Click to star the message
Starred message
Obama Wins Nomination - www.nytimes.com - Complete coverage of the primary conclusion on The New York Times
Sponsored Link
Archive
Report Spam
Delete
More Actions
Refresh
1 - 50 of 58 Older ›
Select: All, None, Read, Unread, Starred, Unstarred
Michael Miller
Lunch? - Are you free for lunch at McDonalds at 11:30 am on July 31 st ? Michael ...
Jul 25
YouTube Service
Subscription Update - July 25, 2008 - YouTube - Broadcast Yourself help center | e-mail
Jul 25

Figure 3.14 Starred messages in the Gmail Inbox.

> **Tip — Displaying Starred Messages**
>
> The advantage of starring messages is that Gmail lets you display only starred messages by clicking the **Starred** link above the Inbox list.

Activity 3.15

Applying Labels

Label A keyword or tag that describes an email message.

Another way to organize your Gmail messages is to tag each message with a descriptive ***label***.

You can assign one or more labels to every message in your Inbox. Once labeled, you can then recall all messages that share a given label—similar to opening a folder. This is done from the Labels box at the bottom left of the Inbox window, as shown in Figure 3.15. To view all messages with the same label, just click the label name in the Labels box and Gmail displays all the messages that share that label.

Label
Labels
AOL
Avaya
birthdays
CIG Arranging
Cloud Computing
Cubase
Easy Computer ...
eBay
eBay DVD
Google Apps
Google Spreads...
Googlepedia
meetings
Molehill Group
NEW HOUSE
New York Times
Online Marketing
Photopedia
photos
YouTube
Edit labels

Figure 3.15 Gmail's Labels box.

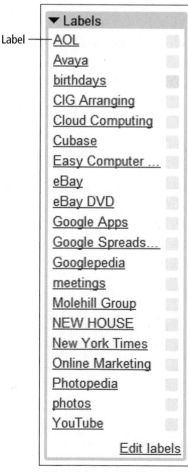

In this activity, you learn how to assign a label to one or more messages in your Inbox.

1. In the Gmail Inbox, click the checkboxes for the messages you want to share the same label.

2. Click the **More Actions** list arrow, then click **New label**. (Or, if you've already created a label, select it from the list.)

3. If a dialog box opens, enter the label you want to apply to the selected message(s).

 Deleting Labels

To delete a label, click the **Edit labels** link in the Labels box, click the **Remove label** link, then click **OK** in the dialog box that opens.

Activity 3.16

Archiving Old Messages

If you receive a lot of emails, your Inbox will get very large very quickly. This is particularly so with Gmail, as you can't store messages from the Inbox into folders.

When your Inbox becomes too cluttered with messages, Gmail lets you archive older messages. When you archive a message, it moves out of the Inbox into a larger store called All Mail. Because your Gmail searches include the All Mail messages, one strategy is to archive all messages after you've read them, thus freeing up the Inbox for only your most recent messages.

In this activity, you learn how to archive messages.

1. From the Gmail Inbox, click the checkboxes for the messages you want to archive, as shown in Figure 3.16.

Click to archive selected message(s)

Check to select message

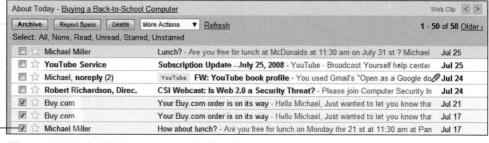

Figure 3.16 Archiving messages in Gmail.

2. Click the **Archive** button. The messages you marked are now removed from the Inbox but remain accessible from the All Mail link or whenever you perform a Gmail search.

 Unarchiving Messages

You can return archived messages to the Inbox by clicking the **All Mail** link, clicking the checkboxes for the message(s) you want to move, then clicking the **Move to Inbox** button.

Activity 3.17

Filtering Incoming Mail

Filter An action that is applied to email messages, such as automatic deletion or starting.

Another way to organize your messages is to specify what happens to them when they arrive in your Inbox by creating a *filter*. Gmail lets you create up to 20 filters that identify certain types of incoming messages and then handle them in a specified manner.

For example, you can create filters that apply a label to all messages with certain words in the subject line, star all messages from a particular contact, or forward all messages from one sender to another recipient. You can also specify that messages from a particular sender or with a particular subject be deleted automatically.

Gmail lets you choose from seven different actions for your filters:

- Skip the Inbox (automatically archive the message)
- Mark as read
- Star it
- Apply the label (choose from a list or create a new label)
- Forward it to (a specified email address)
- Delete it
- Never send it to Spam

In this activity you learn how to create an email filter.

1. From the Gmail Inbox, click the **Create a filter** link (next to the search buttons).

2. The Create a Filter panel now appears at the top of the Inbox page, as shown in Figure 3.17. Enter the search criteria to identify which messages you want the filter applied to, then click the **Next Step** button.

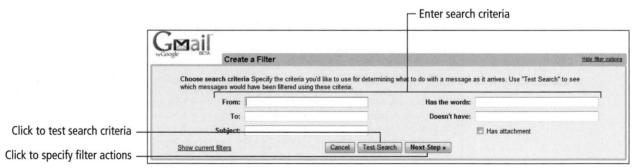

Figure labels: "Enter search criteria", "Click to test search criteria", "Click to specify filter actions"

Figure 3.17 Specifying which messages the new filter will apply to.

3. When the next page appears, as shown in Figure 3.18, select the action you want the filter to initiate. You can apply multiple actions if you wish.

4. Click the **Create Filter** button. All future messages that match your search criteria (as well as matching messages already in your Inbox) will now have the specified action performed on them.

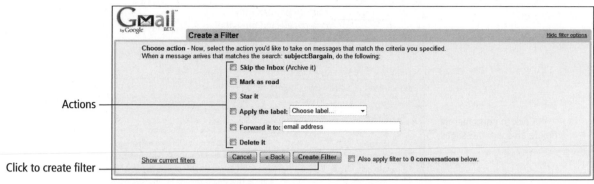

Actions

Click to create filter

Figure 3.18 Specifying the action you want the filter to apply.

 Viewing Filters

To view all your current filters (as well as to edit or delete selected filters), click the **Settings** link at the top of the Gmail Inbox page, then click the **Filters** tab.

Activity 3.18

Blocking Spam Messages

Gmail offers several features designed to reduce the amount of unsolicited commercial email messages—called *spam*—that you receive in your Inbox. These features are applied automatically.

Spam Unsolicited commercial email.

 Defining Spam

Spam is any commercial message that you didn't request or opt into. By this definition, emails from a merchant you previously purchased from are not spam, while unwanted advertisements selling herbal remedies and financial "get rich quick" schemes are. Gmail tries to identify spam based on content and keywords but doesn't always catch it all—and Gmail sometimes identifies legitimate messages as spam!

Google starts by applying a variety of internal spam filters to identify spam as it enters the Gmail system, thus blocking it from appearing in users' Inboxes. In most cases, you never see the spam because Google blocks it before it ever gets to you.

If spam makes it past Google's main filter, the message appears in the Spam section of your Inbox. Like the Trash, spam is deleted after 30 days.

In this activity, you learn how to view your spam messages.

1. From your Gmail Inbox, click the **Spam** link. Gmail now displays all the messages previously marked as spam, as shown in Figure 3.19. Click any message to view its contents.

2. It's possible for Google to route an occasional legitimate message to your Spam list. If you find a non-spam message in this list, click the message check box and click the **Not Spam** button. This moves the message out of the Spam list back into your Inbox.

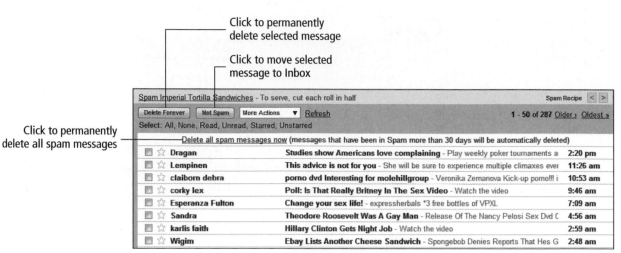

Figure 3.19 Viewing messages in Gmail's spam list.

3. To permanently delete an individual message from your spam list, click the message check box, then click the **Delete Forever** button.

4. To permanently delete all messages from your spam list, click the **Delete all spam messages now** link.

Objective 6

Manage Gmail Contacts

Contact A listing of information about a person, including name, email address, and more.

Every email program or service offers some sort of address book or list of your most frequent correspondents, called *contacts*. Gmail's Contacts list lets you store contact information (including but not limited to email addresses) for thousands of people.

Activity 3.19

Adding a New Contact

Before you can use your contacts in Gmail, you have to add people to your contact list. In this activity, you learn how to add a new contact.

1. Click the **Contacts** link on the left side of any Gmail page.

2. When the Contacts page appears, click the **New Contact** button.

3. The right panel of the Contacts page now displays a series of boxes, as shown in Figure 3.20. Enter the person's name, email address, phone number, street address, and instant messaging name into the appropriate boxes.

Click to add a
single contact

Click to add a
contact group

Enter information
about new contact

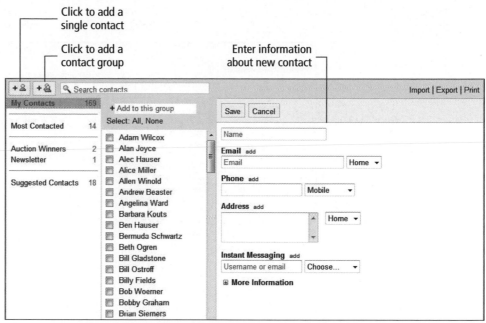

Figure 3.20 Adding a new Gmail contact.

 Note **Optional Information**

All the information requested for a contact is optional. You can add as much or as little information as you like about any of your contacts.

4. To enter any additional information about this person— title, company, and notes—click the plus sign next to **More Information** and enter any necessary information.

5. Click the **Save** button to create the contact.

Activity 3.20

Displaying Contacts

In addition to using Gmail's contacts list to send email messages, you can also view the information about a contact at any time in order to delete, edit, or review it. You will view contact information in this activity.

1. Click the **Contacts** link on the left side of any Gmail page.

2. When the Contacts page appears, as shown in Figure 3.21, your contacts are shown in the middle panel. Select a contact to display that person's information in the right panel.

3. To edit a selected contact, click the **Edit** button.

4. To delete a selected contact, click the **Delete contact** button.

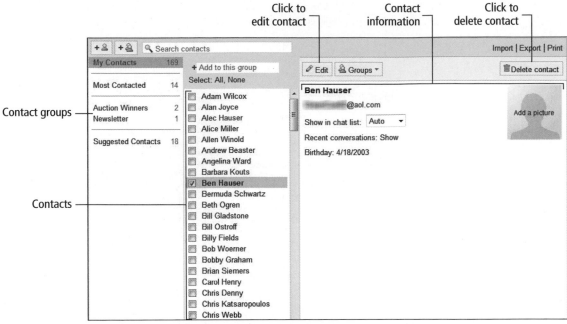

Click to edit contact   Contact information   Click to delete contact

Contact groups

Contacts

Figure 3.21 Viewing your Gmail contacts.

 Tip | **Displaying Contact Groups**

The Contacts page also displays any contact group you've created. To view the contacts in a specific group, select the group from the left panel. Select **My Contacts** to redisplay all your contacts.

Activity 3.21

Searching for Contacts

If you have a lot of contacts in your Contacts list, you may need to search for the ones you want to use. In this activity, you learn how to do this.

1. Click the **Contacts** link on the left side of any Gmail page.

2. When the Contacts page appears, enter a name or partial name into the Search contacts box at the top of the page.

3. Gmail displays matching contacts as you type your query. These contacts are displayed in the contacts pane below the search box. Click a contact name to display that person's information.

Activity 3.22

Creating a Contact Group

Contact group A collection of Gmail contacts, used to create email mailing lists.

Most email programs let you create mailing lists that contain multiple email addresses, which make it easier to send bulk mailings to groups of people. Gmail also offers a mailing list feature, which it calls *contact groups*. When you want to send a message to all members of a group, you only have to select the group name—not every contact individually.

In this activity, you learn how to create a contact group.

1. From the Gmail Inbox page, click the **Contacts** link.

2. When the Contacts page appears, click the **New Group** button.

3. A pop-up window appears, prompting you for the name of the group. Enter the group name, then click the **OK** button.

 Enable Pop-Ups

To display the group name pop-up window, you must either disable your web browser's pop-up blocker or choose to allow scripted windows.

4. The Contacts page is now updated with the new group. Select the group name from the left group pane; the Contacts page changes to show the contacts in this group.

5. Enter the contacts you want included in this group into the Add to this group box; use commas to separate names.

 Another Way to Add Contacts

To add contacts to a group from your My Contacts list, click the check boxes for the contacts you want to add, click the **Groups** button, then select the name of the contact group.

Activity 3.23

Sending a Message to a Contact or Contact Group

The whole point of creating contacts and contact groups is to make it easier to send email messages without having to memorize email addresses. In this activity, you will send a message to a contact or group.

1. From the Gmail Inbox page, click the **Compose Mail** link.

2. When the new message appears, enter the name of a contact or group into the To box. When you enter the group name, Gmail automatically replaces it with the email addresses of all the individual contacts in that group.

3. Complete and send your message.

 Auto Complete

If you start to enter the name of an individual contact into the To: box, Gmail automatically displays all contacts that start with the first letter(s) you've typed. Click a contact name from this list to select it.

Summary

In this chapter, you signed up for a Gmail account. You received and read messages in your Inbox. You replied to and forwarded these messages, and composed and sent new messages. You attached a file to an outgoing message and viewed and saved a file attached to an incoming message. You deleted, starred, and filtered messages in your Inbox. You also created contacts and contact lists and sent messages to these contacts.

Key Terms

Assessments

Multiple Choice

1. Which of the following is true?
   (a) Gmail is a feature of Microsoft Outlook.
   (b) Gmail is a web-based email service.
   (c) Gmail costs $9.95 per month.
   (d) Gmail requires you to download a software program.

2. Gmail uses _____ to organize email messages
   (a) labels
   (b) folders
   (c) hierarchical directories
   (d) all of the above

3. A conversation is:
   (a) an instant message session saved as an email message.
   (b) a message sent to a contact group.
   (c) a private message sent to a single member of a contact group.
   (d) a series of related messages grouped together.

4. "Bcc" stands for:
    (a) blind carbon copy.
    (b) blind copy contact.
    (c) before content copy.
    (d) bring cranberry cake.

5. The _____ filetype *cannot* be attached to a Gmail message.
    (a) .jpg
    (b) .doc
    (c) .exe
    (d) .pdf

6. Which of the following is true?
    (a) Gmail never permanently deletes old messages.
    (b) Spam messages are automatically deleted.
    (c) You can only delete the message you're reading.
    (d) Deleted messages are stored in the Trash.

7. Which of the following is *not* an action you can apply to an email filter?
    (a) Star the message.
    (b) Mark the message as spam.
    (c) Apply a label to the message.
    (d) Delete the message.

8. _____ is mandatory information for a new contact.
    (a) Name
    (b) Email address
    (c) Phone number
    (d) None of the above

9. Which of the following is *not* true?
    (a) Gmail applies spam filters before messages arrive in your Inbox.
    (b) Messages in your Spam list can be restored to your normal Inbox.
    (c) Gmail is 100 percent effective in blocking spam messages.
    (d) You can permanently delete messages in your Spam list.

10. To send an existing message to a different recipient, use the _____ Gmail function.
    (a) Reply
    (b) Forward
    (c) Cc:
    (d) Star

Fill in the Blank

Write the correct word in the space provided.

1. A _____ is a block of personalized text that appears at the bottom of an email message.
2. Unsolicited commercial email is called _____ .
3. To send a file via email, you _____ the file to a message.

4. Unlike other email applications, Gmail does not use _____ to organize received messages.

5. To help identify like messages, you can assign unique _____ to your email messages.

6. A _____ is a collection of contacts, like a mailing list.

7. Archived email messages are stored in the _____ list.

8. A _____ identifies specific messages and applies an action to those messages.

9. To permanently delete messages from the Trash, click the _____ button.

10. To perform an advanced search of your Gmail Inbox, click the _____ link.

Skills Review

1. Compose and send an email message to a friend or relative.
2. Forward an email message you've received to another person.
3. Compose a new email message and carbon copy a second recipient to the message.
4. Create a new "friends" label and apply it to appropriate messages in your Inbox.
5. Display those messages with the "friends" label.
6. Identify an older message in your Inbox and archive it to the All Mail list.
7. Star three messages that you think are important.
8. Create a filter that automatically deletes all messages with the subject "Get rich quick."
9. Find a digital photo on your computer and send it via email to a friend or relative.
10. Create a new contact group named "Friends" and add your closest friends to the group.

CHAPTER 4

Using Google Calendar

Objectives

By the end of this chapter you will be able to:

1. Create a New Calendar

2. View Your Calendars

3. Add New Events

4. Share Your Calendar with Others

Like most Google apps, Google Calendar is a web-based application accessible from any web browser using any computer attached to the Internet. This allows you to keep track of your schedule and appointments wherever you are, even if you're away from home, school, or work. All you have to do is log onto the **Google Calendar** website from any web browser, and all your appointments and schedules are displayed. You enter your appointments—Google calls them *events*—directly into the calendar, which you can display in daily, weekly, or monthly views and share with others.

Google Calendar Google's web-based calendar application.

Event An appointment or other scheduled item in Google Calendar.

Objective 1

Create a New Calendar

Google Calendar lets you easily set up multiple private and public calendars in just a few steps.

Activity 4.1

Setting Up a Basic Calendar

Setting up your first calendar is easy, as you'll learn in this activity.

1. From your web browser, go to **calendar.google.com** and sign into your Google account if necessary. If this is your first time using Calendar, enter the necessary information, including your name, time zone, and location.

2. Google Calendar displays your default calendar, as shown in Figure 4.1. The name of this calendar is shown in the Calendars panel on the left of the page.

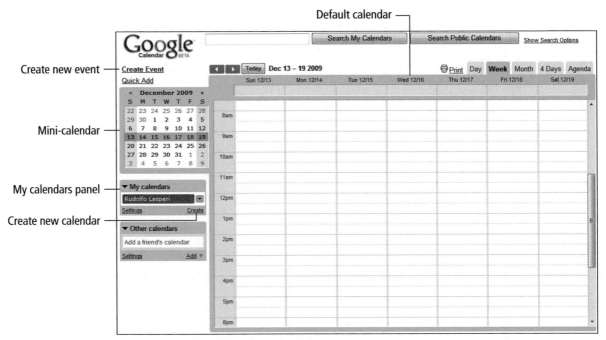

Figure 4.1 The default Google Calendar.

 Creating a Google Account

In order to use Google Calendar, you must have a Google account. Click the **Create an account** button and enter the appropriate information to create your account.

Activity 4.2

Setting Up Multiple Calendars

One of the key features of Google Calendar is the ability to create and manage multiple calendars. For example, you might want to create one calendar with work events and another with social events.

In this activity, you learn how to create a new calendar.

1. From the main Google Calendar page, click the **Create** link.

2. When the Create New Calendar page appears, as shown in Figure 4.2, enter the calendar's name into the Calendar Name box.

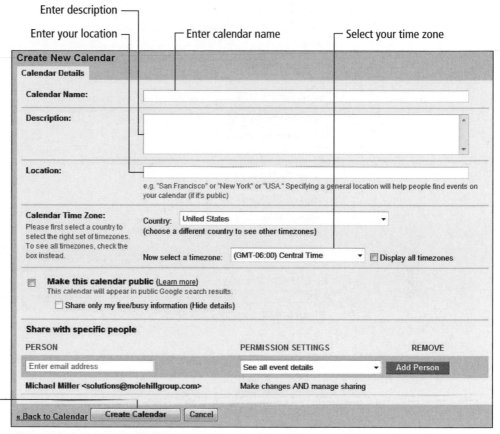

Figure 4.2 Creating a new calendar.

3. Enter a short description of the calendar into the Description box.

4. Enter your location (city and state) into the Location box.

5. Select your time zone from the Calendar Time Zone list.

6. Click the **Create Calendar** button. Your new calendar is now listed in the Calendars box on the left side of the Google Calendar page, under My Calendars.

Objective 2

View Your Calendars

The main Google Calendar page is where you can display your calendars in several different views.

Activity 4.3

Using Different Views

Google Calendar lets you view your calendar in several different ways. In this activity, you will learn how to view your calendar by day, week, month, the next 4 days, or in a special events-only agenda view.

1. To view a full-month calendar, as shown in Figure 4.3, click the **Month** tab.

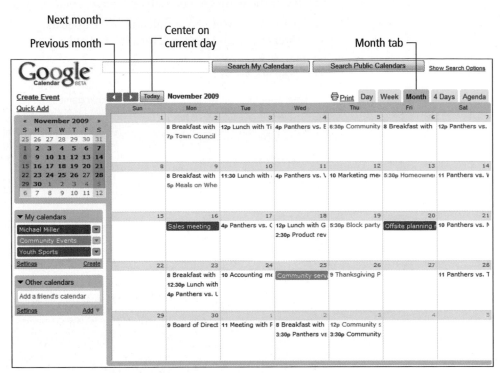

Figure 4.3 Google Calendar month view.

2. To view a weekly calendar, as shown in Figure 4.4, click the **Week** tab.

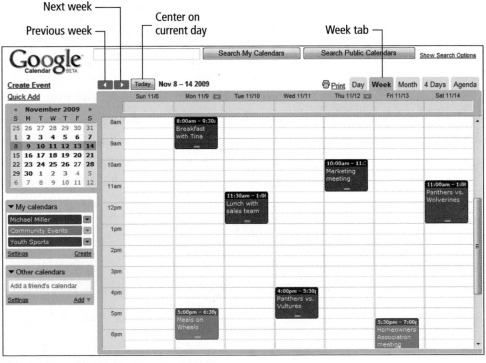

Figure 4.4 Google Calendar week view.

3. To view a daily calendar, as shown in Figure 4.5, click the **Day** tab.

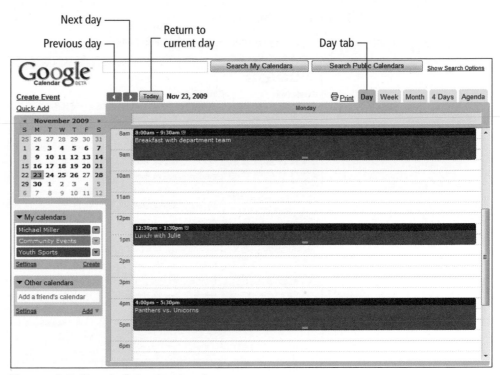

Figure 4.5 Google Calendar day view.

4. To view a calendar for the next four days, as shown in Figure 4.6, click the 4 **Days** tab.

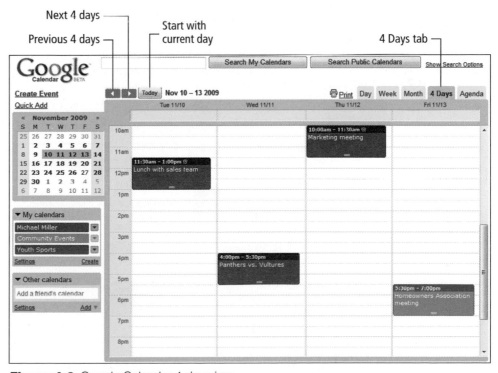

Figure 4.6 Google Calendar 4-day view.

5. To view a list of upcoming events, as shown in Figure 4.7, click the **Agenda** tab.

Figure 4.7 Google Calendar agenda view.

6. For each view, you can move backward and forward in time by clicking the left and right arrow buttons at the top right of the calendar. After you have changed the time period being viewed, click the **Today** button to shift the view of the calendar to center around the current date.

7. To view details about a specific event in a pop-up window, as shown in Figure 4.8, click that event in the calendar. To close the pop-up window, click the **Close** button in the top right corner of the balloon.

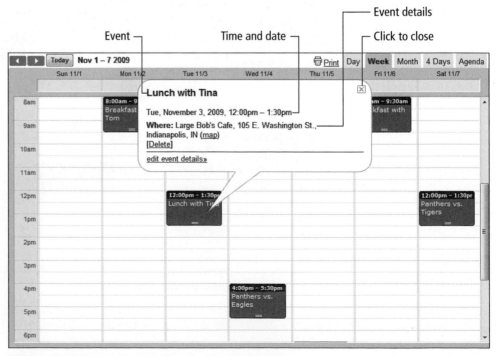

Figure 4.8 Details about a Google Calendar event.

Activity 4.4

Viewing Multiple Calendars

All of the calendars you create are listed in the My calendars box on the left side of the Google Calendar page. The main calendar on the Google Calendar page can display any single calendar individually or multiple calendars simultaneously; it all depends on which calendar(s) you check in the Calendars box. You will learn how to display multiple calendars in this activity.

1. To display the events for a specific calendar, click that calendar in the My calendars box, as shown in Figure 4.9. The calendar name will now be displayed with a colored background.

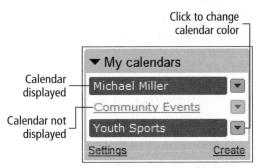

Figure 4.9 Selecting which calendars to display.

2. To remove a calendar from the main display, click on the calendar name in the My calendars box. The calendar name will now be displayed as a simple text link.

3. Events for each calendar are color coded in the main calendar. To change the color for a given calendar, click the list arrow next to that calendar in the My calendars box and select a different color.

Objective 3

Add New Events

All the items scheduled on your calendar—meetings, appointments, etc. —are called events. An event can include all sorts of information, including date, time, location, and the like.

Activity 4.5

Adding an Event to Your Calendar

Google provides several ways to add events to your calendar. In this activity, you'll learn the easiest way to add an event directly to your calendar.

Tip ⭐ **Another Way to Add an Event**

You can also add an event by clicking the **Create Event** link in the upper-left corner of the Google Calendar page.

1. From the main Google Calendar page, click the hour or the day on your calendar for which you'd like to create an event. If you add an event to a daily or weekly calendar, click and drag to select the entire time frame of the event. To create a multi-day event in month view, drag to select the days of the event.

2. A new event balloon opens, like the one shown in Figure 4.10. Enter the name of the event into the What box.

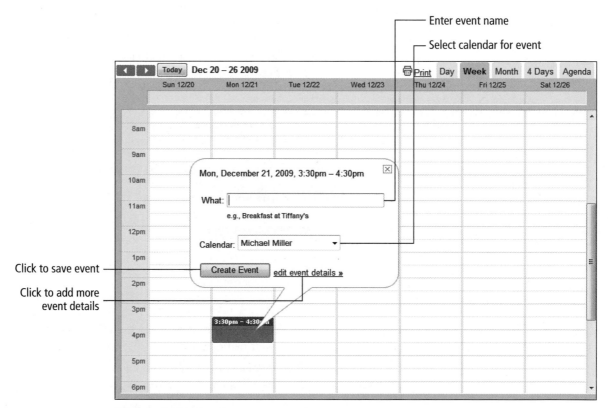

Figure 4.10 Creating a new event.

3. Click the **Calendar** list arrow, then select the calendar to which this event belongs.

4. To add more information about the event, click the **edit event details** link to display the event details page shown in Figure 4.11.

Click to save event

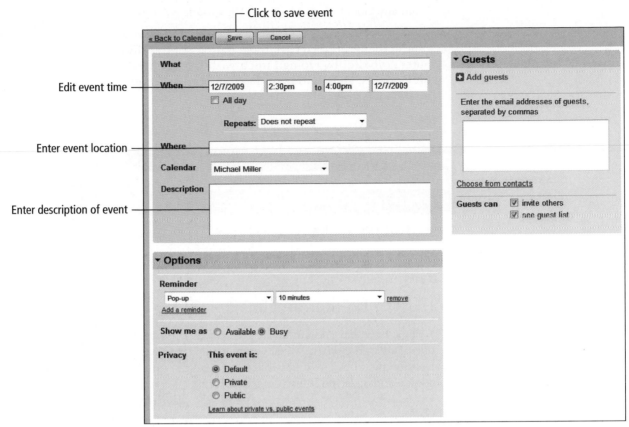

Edit event time

Enter event location

Enter description of event

Figure 4.11 Entering more detailed event information.

5. Add any additional details about the event, such as location (in the Where box), description, etc. If you've added this event to a monthly calendar, you should also enter the time of the event (in the When box). If you want this event to repeat, select an option from the Repeats list.

6. Click the **Save** button to add the event to the selected calendar.

 Note **Recurring Events**

If you have a recurring event, select the appropriate option from the Repeats list. You can designate an event to repeat: daily; every weekday (Monday through Friday); every Monday, Wednesday, and Friday; every Tuesday and Thursday; weekly; monthly; and yearly.

 Tip **Map an Event**

When you include location information about an event, Google Calendar includes a Map link in that event's information. Click the **Map** link to view a Google Map of that event's location.

Activity 4.6

Adding an Event via Quick Add

An even easier way to add an event is by using Google Calendar's Quick Add feature, which you'll learn how to do in this activity. Quick Add interprets the information you type and creates an appointment that you can edit or save.

1. From any Google Calendar, click the **Quick Add** link or type the letter **Q**.

2. The Quick Add entry box displays, as shown in Figure 4.12. Enter the name and time of the event, then click the + button or press the **Enter** key on your computer keyboard. By typing **Lunch with George at noon Monday at McDonalds**, Quick Add translates the text and enters the event, time, date, and location information.

Click to add event ⌐

Enter event details ─

Figure 4.12 Using Quick Add to add an event.

Activity 4.7

Adding an Event from Gmail

Integrated applications Two or more applications that are designed to work together.

Google Calendar and Gmail are *integrated applications*, meaning that you can use one to affect the other. When you're reading a Gmail message that contains information pertaining to a possible event, you can quickly add that event to your Google Calendar, as you'll learn in this activity.

1. Open a Gmail message in your Gmail account. Click the **Add to calendar** link, or click the **More Actions** list arrow, then click **Create event**.

2. A New Event window opens, as shown in Figure 4.13. Google fills in as much information as it can figure out about the event. Add or correct the information as necessary.

3. Click the **Save Changes** button to add the event to your Google Calendar.

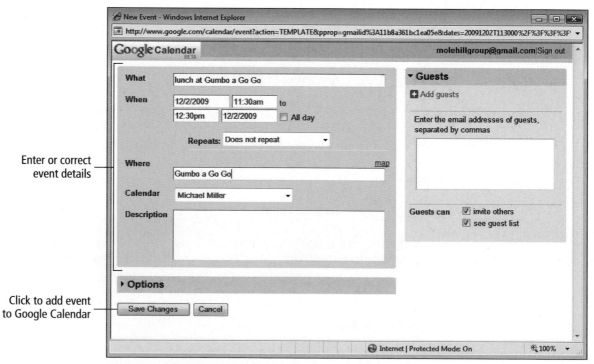

Figure 4.13 Finalizing event information.

Unblocking Pop-Up Windows

Depending on your security settings, you may not be able to see pop-up windows such as the New Event window. If an alert appears at the top of your browser window, click it, then instruct the browser to temporarily accept pop-ups. Before you modify your security settings, you should verify that the site is valid, and if you are in a lab setting, check with your technical support person.

Activity 4.8

Inviting Others to an Event

When you first create an event, you have the option of inviting guests to the event. You can also invite guests to an event after it's been created, as you'll learn in this activity

1. With your calendar open, click an event on your calendar, then click **edit event details**.

2. When the event details page appears, click the **Add guests** link.

3. This expands the Guests panel, as shown in Figure 4.14. Enter the email addresses of your guests into the text box; separate multiple addresses with commas.

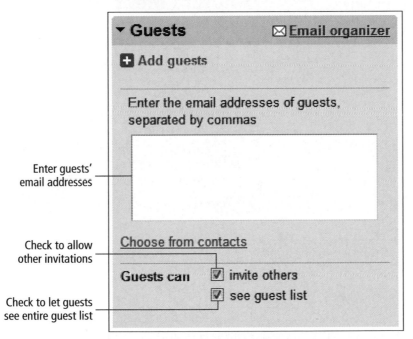

Enter guests' email addresses

Check to allow other invitations

Check to let guests see entire guest list

Figure 4.14 Inviting guests to an event.

 Suggested Contacts

Calendar will search for contacts you have saved in your Gmail account while you type guests' names. If Calendar finds a match to the characters you have typed, press the **Enter** key to accept the suggested name, or keep typing to enter a new name.

4. If you want your guests to be able to invite other guests to the event, click the **invite others** checkbox. If you don't want additional guests to be invited, deselect the checkbox.

5. If you want your guests to see who else was invited to the event, click the **see guest list** checkbox. If you want your guest list to remain private, deselect the checkbox.

6. Click the **Save** button.

7. Google Calendar now displays a dialog box asking if you're ready to send the invitations. Click the **Send** button to do so.

8. Google now sends invitations to all the guests you added, like the one shown in Figure 4.15. (The exact invitation seen depends on which program or device the recipient is using.) Each invitation includes links for the guest's response—Yes, No, or Maybe. When a guest clicks one of these links, a Submit Response web page opens. The guest's response is then automatically entered into the event in your Google Calendar, as shown in the Guests section of the event page.

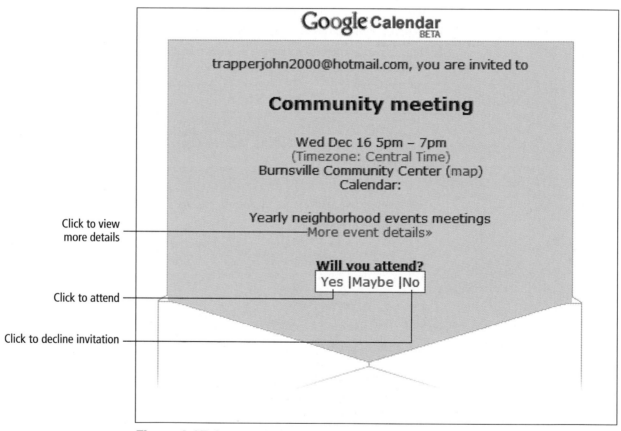

Figure 4.15 An event invitation sent via Gmail.

Objective 4

Share Your Calendar with Others

So far in this chapter, you have worked with private calendars that can only be viewed by the person who created them. You can make your calendar public and enable it to be viewed and edited by others, as you specify.

Activity 4.9

Creating a Public Calendar

A public calendar is one that can be viewed—but not necessarily edited—by anyone on the web. When a calendar is public, it can be searched for via Google's web search and appear in Google's search results. It's a great way to disseminate information about public events such as sports teams or community groups.

As you'll learn in this activity, you can make your calendar public when you first create it.

1. From the main Google Calendar page, click the **Create** link.
2. When the Create New Calendar page appears, enter the calendar's name, description, location, and other information as normal.
3. Click the **Make this calendar public** checkbox.
4. If you want to hide the details of your events on your calendar, click the **Share only my free/busy information** checkbox. This allows others to see when you are available and unavailable but does not tell them details about your events.
5. Click the **Create Calendar** button.

 View Your Calendar's URL

To view the URL of a public calendar, click the list arrow next to the calendar in your Calendars list, then click **Calendar settings**. In the Calendar Address section, click on any of the XML, iCal, or HTML icons. The calendar's URL now appears in a pop-up window.

Activity 4.10

Sharing Your Calendar with Specific People

When you make your calendar public, anyone can search for it via Google's web search. If you'd rather share your calendar with only a select group of people, such as your department at work or your family, Google Calendar offers that option and allows you to give them permission to add or edit events on the calendar, as you will do in this activity.

1. From the main Google Calendar page, click the **Create** link.
2. When the Create New Calendar page appears, enter the calendar's name, description, location, and other information as normal.
3. In the Share with specific people section, shown in Figure 4.16, enter the email address of the first person you want to have access to your calendar.

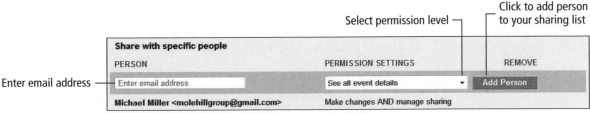

Figure 4.16 Sharing your calendar with others.

4. Click the **Permission Settings** list arrow, then specify what type of access you want this person to have: Make changes *and* manage sharing (add and edit events and invite others to share the calendar); Make changes to event (add and edit events but not invite others to share); See all event details (but not add or edit events); or See only free/busy (hide details—without editing).

5. Click the **Add Person** button.

6. Repeat steps 3 to 5 to share your calendar with additional people.

7. Click the **Create Calendar** button to save this calendar and notify the people you added. Each person will receive an email with the URL of your calendar; they can then access the calendar with the permission level you selected.

 Google Account Required

Anyone sharing your calendar must have a Google account. If they don't currently have an account, they're prompted to create one.

Summary

In this chapter, you learned how to create Google Calendars and displayed calendars in month, week, day, and custom views. You added events to your calendars and invited others to an event. You also learned how to make a calendar public or share it with others you specify.

Key Terms

Assessments

Multiple Choice

1. Which of the following is true?
   (a) Google Calendars are stored on your computer's hard disk.
   (b) Google Calendar is accessible from any computer with an Internet connection.
   (c) Google Calendar is only for office use.
   (d) All of the above.

2. By default, the Google Calendars you create are _____.
   (a) private
   (b) public
   (c) shared with your Gmail Contacts list
   (d) none of the above

3. Google Calendar's Quick Add feature lets you:
   (a) quickly invite a person to share your calendar.
   (b) quickly create a new calendar.
   (c) quickly display holidays on your calendar.
   (d) quickly create a new event with a line of descriptive text.

4. Which of the following is *not* true?
   (a) You can add events directly from Gmail messages.
   (b) You can add events by selecting a day or time on a calendar.
   (c) You can add events by typing them directly into a calendar.
   (d) You can add events by clicking the Create Event link.

5. Google Calendars can be displayed by _____.
   (a) day
   (b) week
   (c) month
   (d) all of the above

6. When you select a calendar in the Calendars list, the following happens:
   (a) Events for that calendar are displayed in the main calendar.
   (b) The calendar name is displayed as a text link.
   (c) The calendar name is displayed with a colored background.
   (d) (a) and (c).

7. When you choose to make a calendar public, the following happens:
   (a) Anyone can add new events to the calendar.
   (b) Only users with a Google account can add new events to the calendar.
   (c) The calendar can show up in Google search results.
   (d) Only users in your Gmail contacts list can add new events to the calendar.

8. Which of the following is true?
   (a) When you include location information for an event, a Map link is displayed.
   (b) When you include a hotel or restaurant name for an event, a logo for that hotel or restaurant is displayed.
   (c) When you invite others to an event, those people's photos are displayed.
   (d) When you include location information for an event, driving directions are displayed.

9. When you invite someone to an event, the following happens:
   (a) The event automatically appears on that person's Google Calendar.
   (b) The person receives an invitation to the event via email.
   (c) The person is automatically added to your Gmail contacts list.
   (d) A special calendar is created in your Google Calendar just for that person.

10. Which of the following is *not* an option for sharing a calendar?
    (a) See all event details only—cannot edit or add events.
    (b) Edit events only—cannot add new events.
    (c) Make changes to events—can add and edit events.
    (d) Make changes and manage sharing—can add and edit events *and* invite others to share.

Fill in the Blank

Write the correct word in the space provided.

1. To shift a calendar view to center around the current date, click the _____ button.
2. An appointment on your calendar is called a(n) _____.
3. A(n) _____ calendar can be searched for via Google web search.
4. To add an event by typing a short text description, click the _____ link.
5. To add a new calendar, click the _____ link.
6. To view a list of upcoming events, click the _____ tab.
7. When creating an event, enter location information into the _____ box.
8. To specify a recurring event, select the appropriate option from the _____ list.
9. When you invite someone to an event, they receive notice of the event via _____.
10. Events for each calendar you create are assigned their own unique _____.

Skills Review

1. Create a new private calendar named School Events.
2. Change the default color of the School Events calendar to green.
3. For the School Events calendar, add an event titled Study Group for 7:00 p.m. next Wednesday.
4. Invite two friends to the Study Group event.
5. Display the next four days on your calendar.
6. Create a new calendar named Public Calendar and make it public.
7. Create a new calendar named Shared Calendar and share it with two of your friends; make sure your friends can add and edit events but not invite others to share the calendar.
8. Display only upcoming events for your calendars.
9. Add an event called Road Trip to your main calendar, with the location of San Diego, CA; then display a map for this event.
10. Choose not to display the School Events calendar on your main calendar.

CHAPTER 5

Using Google Docs

Objectives

By the end of this chapter you will be able to:

1. Create and Save New Documents

2. Import and Export Word Documents

3. Enter and Edit Text

4. Format Text

5. Format Paragraphs

6. Create Bulleted and Numbered Lists

7. Work with Images

8. Insert Links and Comments

9. Create a Table

10. Proof and Print Your Document

11. Share and Collaborate

Google Docs is a suite of applications designed for home, business, and educational use. It consists of the Google Docs word processor, Google Spreadsheets spreadsheet program, and Google Presentations presentation application. The Google Docs applications share many of the key features found in similar programs in the Microsoft Office suite (Word, Excel, and PowerPoint), including menus and toolbars.

Google Docs differs from Microsoft Office in that it is web based. The application and all your documents reside on Google's servers, not on your computer. This lets you access your applications and documents from any computer connected to the Internet and collaborate with other users located anywhere in the world.

Google Docs
Google's suite of online applications; also, the word processing application within the Google Docs suite.

In this chapter, you will learn to use the word processing application in Google Docs, which also goes by the name of Google Docs. In later chapters, you will learn how to use Google Docs' spreadsheet and presentation applications.

Objective 1

Create and Save New Documents

Word processor An application used to create letters, memos, reports, and other text-based documents.

Google Docs is the name of both Google's suite of online applications and its word processing application. A **word processor**, such as Google Docs, is used to create various types of text-based documents, including letters, memos, reports, and newsletters.

To use Google Docs, you need a Google account. When you log on to your Google account, you see the main Google Docs page shown in Figure 5.1. This is the homepage for the three Google Docs applications—word processing, spreadsheets, and presentations. All of your previously created documents are listed on this page. This is also where you create new documents.

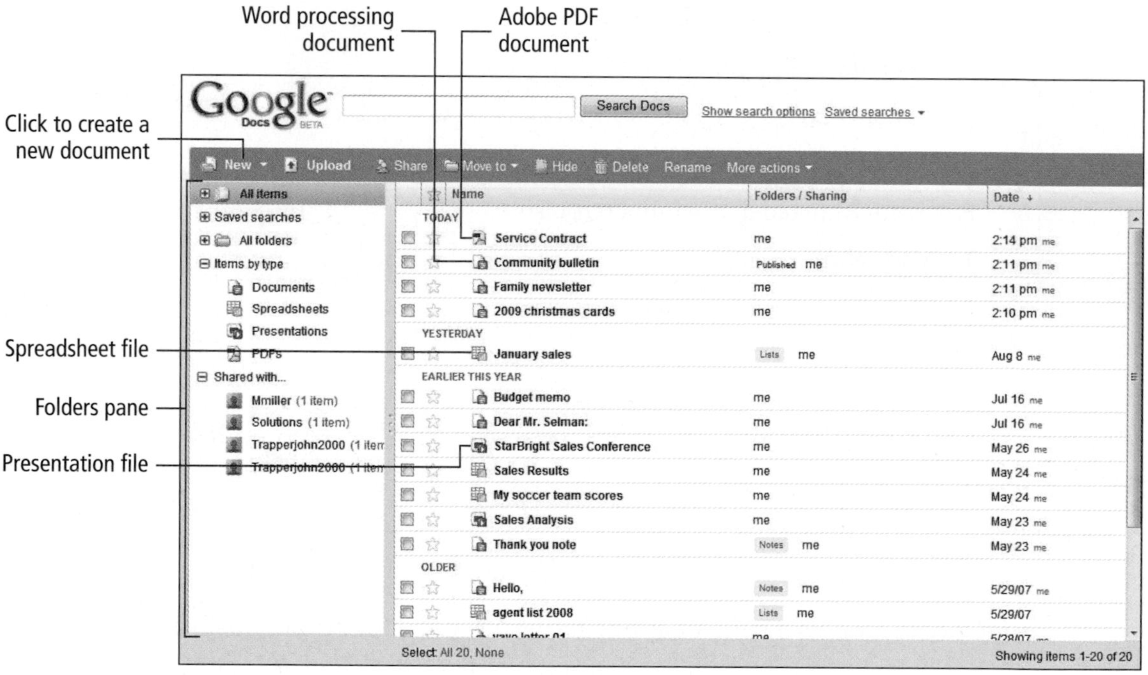

Word processing document — Adobe PDF document

Click to create a new document

Spreadsheet file

Folders pane

Presentation file

Figure 5.1 The main page for all Google Docs applications.

At the top of the window is a toolbar that contains buttons you can use to manage files or create new ones. The left pane on this page is where you organize your documents. You can see the results of saved searches, store files in folders, view documents by type (word processing documents, spreadsheets, presentations, or PDFs), and display documents shared with specific people.

 Tip **New Folders**

To create a new folder, click the **New** button, then click **Folder**. Position the insertion point over the words New Folder in the main editing window, click, and then type the name of the new folder. To move a document to a folder, click the checkbox next to the document, click the **Move to** button, click the folder you want to add it to, then click the **Move to folder** button.

The documents stored within the selected folder are displayed in the main part of the window. Word processing documents are noted with a document icon, spreadsheets have a spreadsheet icon, presentations have a slide icon, and PDF documents have an Adobe PDF icon.

Tip   Adobe PDF

Adobe's ***Portable Document Format (PDF)*** file format is a common way to distribute noneditable documents electronically. Using a free program called Adobe Acrobat Reader, which most users have installed, PDF files can be viewed, printed, and shared without having access to the program in which the file was created. If you don't have Adobe Acrobat Reader installed on your computer, you can download it for free from www.adobe.com.

Portable Document Format (PDF) Adobe Acrobat Reader program files that can be viewed, printed, and shared without having access to the program in which the file was created.

Activity 5.1

Creating a New Document

In this activity you learn how to create a new blank word processing document.

1. Go to the main Google Docs page (**docs.google.com**). Log into your account if necessary.

2. Click the **New** button, then click **Document**. A new document opens in a new browser window.

Activity 5.2

Creating a New Document from a Template

Template A pre-designed selection of text, formatting, and graphics, used to create a new document, spreadsheet, or presentation.

Placeholder Text in a template that indicates the type of information to include and a sample page layout.

Alternately, you can create a new document based on a predesigned template. A *template* is a combination of text styles, document formatting, and graphics to which you can add your own text, graphics, and numbers. Templates contain *placeholder* text, which indicates the type of information you want to include and gives you a sample page layout. In this activity, you learn how to create a new document based on a predesigned template.

Tip   Template Quick Starts

Templates are great for getting a head start on a specific type of document or project. Google includes templates for calendars, photo albums, invoices, letterheads, business cards, business plans, budgets, and more.

1. From the main Google Docs page, click the **New** button, then click **From template**.

2. Google opens a new Templates Gallery window. You can search or browse the gallery for document, spreadsheet, and presentation templates. To view document templates, click the **Documents** link, as shown in Figure 5.2.

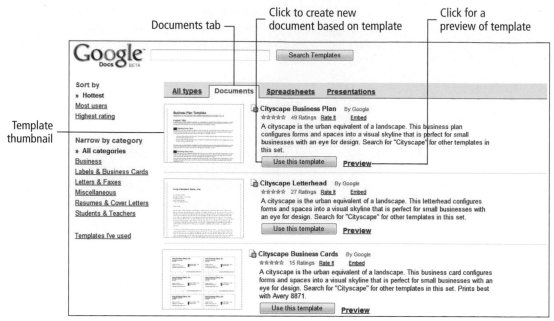

Figure 5.2 Browsing Google Docs' Templates Gallery.

3. When you find the template you want to use, click the **Use this template** button to open a new browser window that contains a blank document based on the template, as shown in Figure 5.3.

4. Replace the placeholder text of the template with your own text.

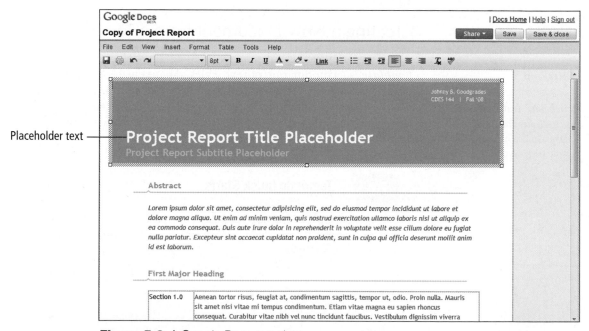

Figure 5.3 A Google Docs template.

Activity 5.3

Saving a Document

After you create a new document, you need to save the file. When you first save a file, you must do it manually. After this first save, Google automatically resaves the file every time you make a change to the document. This means that you only have to save the document once; Google saves all further changes automatically.

In this activity, you learn how to save a newly created document file.

1. From within the document window, click the **Save** button, as shown in Figure 5.4, or press **Ctrl+S** on the keyboard. Google now saves the document and names it according to the first few words of text. For example, if you had entered the text "Dear Mr. Selman:", your file would automatically be named **Dear Mr. Selman:**.

Click to save file

Click and select Rename to rename saved file

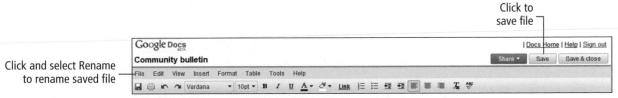

Figure 5.4 Saving a Google Docs file.

2. To rename a document, open it, click **File** on the menu bar, then click **Rename**. When the pop-up window opens, type the new document name, then click **OK**.

 Note   **Unblocking Pop-Up Windows**

Depending on your security settings, you may not be able to see pop-up windows. If an alert appears at the top of your browser window, click it, then instruct the browser to temporarily accept pop-ups. Before you modify your security settings, you should verify that the site is valid, and if you are in a lab setting, check with your technical support person.

Activity 5.4

Opening an Existing Document

Once you've created and saved a document, you can reopen it for editing at any time. In this activity, you learn how to open an existing document.

1. From the main Google Docs page, click the **Documents** link in the left pane under Items by type to view all of your word processing documents. As shown in Figure 5.5, word processing documents are identified by a letter icon.

Click to open document in new window

Click to view only word processing documents

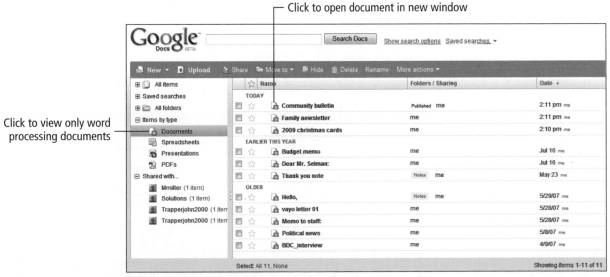

Figure 5.5 Opening a Google Docs file.

2. Click the document's name to open the file in a new browser window.

 Tip **Working Offline**

The document file you save isn't stored on your computer's hard disk. Instead, the file is stored by default on Google's servers, which means you must be connected to the Internet to access it. However, if you're not connected to the Internet, Google lets you edit your documents *offline*. To do this, you have to install the Google Docs Offline application. Click the **Offline** link at the top of the Google Docs homepage, then click the **Get Google Gears Now** button. Follow the simple onscreen instructions to download and install the program. Once Google Gears has been installed, you can open the offline version of Google Docs by entering docs.google.com into your web browser or by clicking the Google Docs shortcut on your desktop. If you're not connected to the Internet, you'll open the offline version of Google Docs; if you are connected to the Internet, you'll open the normal online version. Whenever you're online, Google Docs automatically synchronizes the files stored on your computer with those stored online so that both locations contain the document version that was most recently edited. (You can also work offline when using Google's Chrome web browser, which has Google Gears built in.)

Offline When you're not connected to the Internet.

Objective 2

Import and Export Word Documents

If you or your colleagues use Microsoft Word as a word processor, you can import your Word documents into Google Docs for online editing and collaboration. You can also save your Google Docs documents as Microsoft Word files on your hard disk.

Activity 5.5

Importing a Word Document

Google Docs lets you upload your Microsoft Word documents so they can be stored on the web and edited with the web-based Google Docs application. In this activity you learn how to import a Word file into Google Docs.

1. From the Google Docs main page, click the **Upload** button.

2. When the Upload a File page appears, as shown in Figure 5.6, click the **Browse** button.

3. When the Choose file dialog box appears, locate and select the file you want to upload, then click the **Open** button.

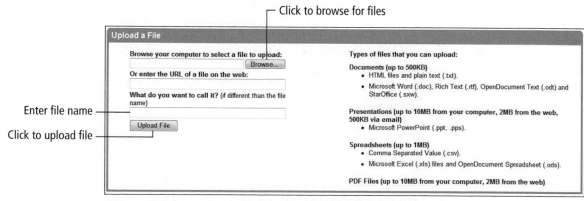

Figure 5.6 Importing a file into Google Docs.

4. When the Upload a File page reappears, enter a name for the uploaded file into the **What do you want to call it?** box if necessary.

5. Click the **Upload File** button. The file now opens in Google Docs for editing.

 Note **File Upload Limits**

You can import word processing files in the following formats: Microsoft Word (.doc), Rich Text Format (.rtf), OpenDocument Text (.odt), StarOffice (.sxw), plain text (.txt), and HTML (.htm or .html). Files must be 500KB or less in size. When this book was printed, Google did not support files created with the latest version of Microsoft Word, Word 2007 (.docx).

Activity 5.6

Exporting a Google Document to Word Format

By default, all the documents you work with in Google Docs are stored on Google's servers. You can, however, download files from Google to your computer's hard drive to work with them in Microsoft Word. In this activity, you learn how to export a Google document to Microsoft Word.

 Note **Other Ways to Export**

Google also lets you export your document as a PDF file, an OpenOffice file, a plain text or Rich Text Format file, and as an HTML file for use on the web.

1. From within the current document window, click **File** on the menu bar, point to **Download file as**, then click **Word**, as shown in Figure 5.7.

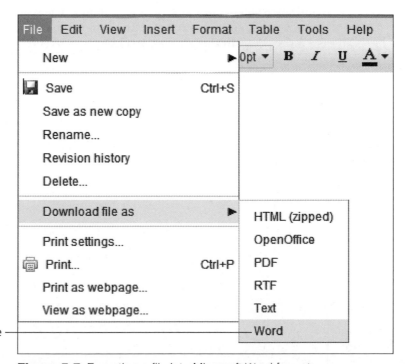

Click to export file

Figure 5.7 Exporting a file into Microsoft Word format.

2. When the File Download dialog box appears, click the **Save** button.

3. When the Save As dialog box appears, select a location for the downloaded file, rename it if necessary, and then click the **Save** button. The Google Docs file is now saved in .doc format to your hard disk. You can now open it with Microsoft Word and edit it as you would any Word document.

 Alert ! **Don't Get Out of Sync**

Unlike Google Docs files, which will automatically synchronize online and offline versions if you've installed the Google Docs Offline application, whatever changes you make to a file from within Microsoft Word affect only the downloaded file, not the copy of the document that still resides on the Google Docs site. To reimport the Word file to Google Docs, go to the main Google Docs page and use the Upload function. When you reimport a file, Google Docs saves it as a new document file rather than saving it over the previous version.

Objective 3

Enter and Edit Text

Editing documents in Google Docs is much the same as editing documents in Microsoft Word or any other word processing program. You enter text using your computer's keyboard. You then edit and format the text using the menu bar, toolbar, and keyboard shortcuts.

Activity 5.7

Entering Text

When you create a new Google Docs document, like the one in Figure 5.8, a big blank space appears in a new browser window. The space above the blank area has a menu bar and toolbar, which contain buttons and commands that you can use to edit and format text. In this activity, you learn how to enter text into this new document.

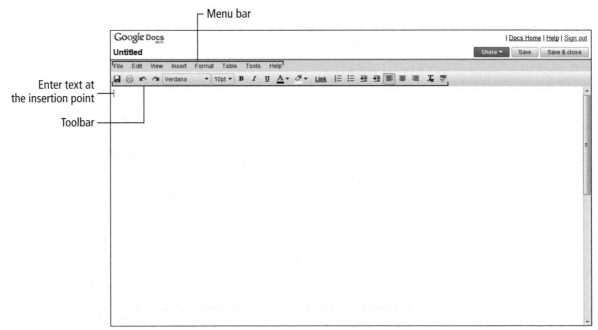

Figure 5.8 Entering text into a Google Docs document.

1. Click in the blank area of the document window to position the insertion point.

2. Use your computer keyboard to type text at the insertion point. The insertion point moves to the right, along with the text you enter.

Activity 5.8

Editing Text

Editing To make changes to correct mistakes or to rephrase text, including deleting characters or selections of text, inserting additional text, and moving and copying text.

Clipboard A Windows storage area for cut or copied text or images that you can paste into a new location.

Cut To remove text from a document and store it on the Clipboard so that it can be moved to a new location.

Copy To store text onto the Clipboard so that it can be inserted into a new location and still remain in the original location.

Paste To transfer text or images from the Clipboard into a new location in a document.

Making changes—to correct mistakes or to rephrase text if you change your mind about how to say something—is called *editing*. Editing includes deleting characters or selections of text, inserting additional text, and moving and copying text.

Google Docs, like all Windows-based applications, uses a common Windows *Clipboard*, which stores text or images in order for you to paste them into a new location or document. You can cut or copy text to the Clipboard to move it to a new location (*cut*) or insert the same text in multiple locations (*copy* and *paste*).

You will learn how to position the insertion point and select and edit text in this activity.

1. Use your mouse or the arrow keys on your keyboard to move through the text until you find the text you want to edit.

2. To select one word at a time, as shown in Figure 5.9, either press and hold the **Shift** key while pressing the forward or back arrow keys on your keyboard or double-click within a word.

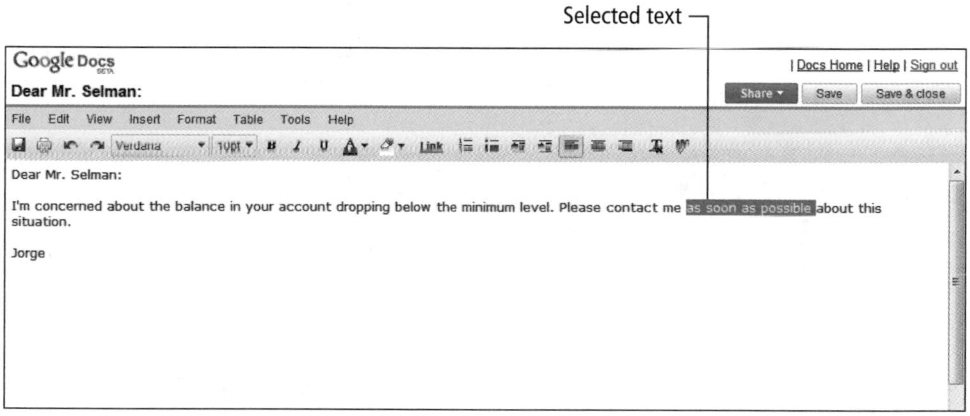

Figure 5.9 Selecting a block of text to edit.

3. To insert text at a given point, position the insertion point, then begin typing. The text you enter will be inserted before the next character in your document and will push the remaining text to the right, or down, in the document.

4. To delete the character positioned before the insertion point, press the **Backspace** key on your keyboard.

5. To delete a selected piece of text, press the **Delete** key on your keyboard.

6. To copy a selected piece of text, click **Edit** on the menu bar, then click **Copy**.

7. To move a selected piece of text, click **Edit** on the menu bar, then click **Cut**.

8. To paste text that has been cut or copied to the Clipboard, position the insertion point at the new location in the document, click **Edit** on the menu bar, then click **Paste**. Text that has been cut or copied can be pasted to more than one location.

Tip **Keyboard Names**

Depending on your keyboard size or manufacturer, the labels and locations of your keys may vary slightly. Some keyboards use abbreviations or only lowercase names for common keys. For instance, while your key may be labeled *delete* or *DEL*, the key is still called the *Delete* key. Other common abbreviated key names are CTRL (Control) and ESC (Escape).

Tip **Undo Edits**

To undo any edits you've made, click **Edit** on the menu bar, then click **Undo** or press **Ctrl+Z** on your keyboard.

Objective 4

Format Text

Google Docs lets you format your text in a number of different ways. Table 5.1 details the formatting options, all available from the Google Docs toolbar:

Table 5.1—Google Docs Formatting Options		
Formatting	**Instructions**	**Keyboard shortcut**
Apply bold	Click the Bold button	Ctrl+B
Apply italics	Click the Italic button	Ctrl+I
Apply underlining	Click the Underline button	Ctrl+U
Change the font type	Click the Font button and select a new font	
Change the font size	Click the Font size button and select a new size	
Change the font color	Click the Text Color button, then click a color from the gallery	
Highlight text	Click the Text Background Color button, then click a color from the gallery	
Indent a paragraph	Click the Increase Indent button	
Move an indented paragraph to the left	Click the Decrease Indent button	
Left align a paragraph	Click the Left Justify button	Ctrl+L
Right align a paragraph	Click the Right Justify button	Ctrl+R
Center a paragraph	Click the Center Justify button	Ctrl+E
Remove the formatting	Click the Remove Formatting button	

Activity 5.9

Bolding and Italicizing Text

The most common types of text formatting are bold and italics, both used to emphasize specific words or sentences. In this activity, you learn how to apply both types of text formatting.

1. Use the mouse or keyboard arrow keys to select the text you want to format.

2. To apply bold to the selected text, as shown in Figure 5.10, click the **Bold** button on the toolbar or press **Ctrl+B** on your keyboard.

3. To italicize the selected text, click the **Italic** button on the toolbar or press **Ctrl+I** on your keyboard.

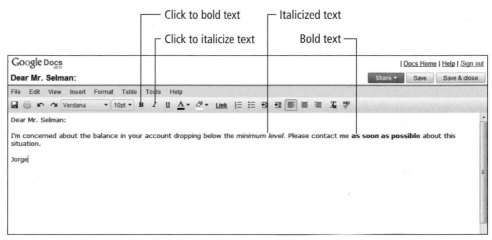

Figure 5.10 Bolding and italicizing text.

 Avoid Underlining

Back in the days of typewriters, underlined text was used to format a book title, as typewriters were unable to italicize text. Now, underlining is associated with hyperlinked text. Avoid using underlining to emphasize text, as the reader may try to click it.

 Format While Typing

You can also apply bold and italics while typing. Press the keyboard shortcut or click the button on the toolbar to turn on bold or italics, then continue typing; the text you type will now be bold or italic. To turn off the formatting, press the keyboard shortcut or click the button on the toolbar again.

Activity 5.10

Changing Font, Font Size, and Font Color

font A typeface in which letters and characters share similar size, shape, and other characteristics.

A *font* is a particular typeface in which letters and characters share similar size, shape, and other characteristics. Each font has its own look and personality, and it can be enhanced or modified by changing the size or color. In this activity, you learn to change the font, the font size, and the font color.

1. Use the mouse or keyboard arrow keys to select the text you want to change.

2. To change the font, as shown in Figure 5.11, click the **Font** button on the toolbar and select the font from the list.

Click to change font size

Click to change font

Click to change font color

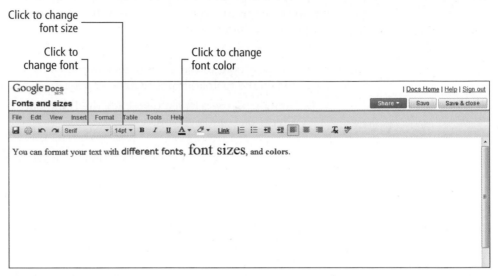

Figure 5.11 Changing font, font size, and font color.

3. To change the font size, click the **Font size** button on the toolbar and select the size from the list.

4. To change the font color, click the **Text Color** button on the toolbar and select the color from the gallery.

 Available Fonts

Google Docs offers the following font options: Sans Serif, Serif, Wide, Narrow, Comic Sans MS, Courier New, Garamond, Georgia, Tahoma, Trebuchet MS, Verdana, and Wingdings. All fonts are available in 8-, 10-, 12-, 14-, 18-, 24-, and 36-point sizes.

Objective 5

Format Paragraphs

As previously discussed, text formatting changes the look of individual characters, words, and sentences. Google Docs also offers various types of paragraph formatting which change the position and layout of the text in your document by modifying the indentation and alignment.

Activity 5.11

Indenting a Paragraph

You may want to indent specific paragraphs to draw attention to the text. For example, you can indent a paragraph that contains a long quote, as shown in Figure 5.12. In this activity, you learn how to change paragraph indentation.

Click to decrease indent — ┌ Click to increase indent

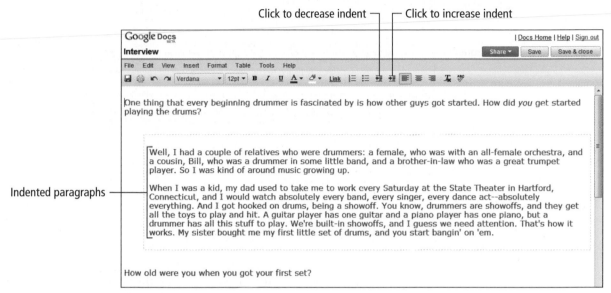

Indented paragraphs —

Figure 5.12 Indenting a selected paragraph.

1. Position the insertion point anywhere within the paragraph you wish to indent.

2. Click the **Increase Indent** button on the toolbar to indent the paragraph to the right. Click the button again to increase the indent.

3. To move the paragraph back to the left, click the **Decrease Indent** button on the toolbar.

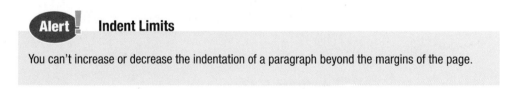

Alert! **Indent Limits**

You can't increase or decrease the indentation of a paragraph beyond the margins of the page.

Activity 5.12

Changing Paragraph Alignment

Google Docs also lets you change the alignment of individual paragraphs. You can align a paragraph to the left margin or right margin, center the paragraph, or justify it to space it evenly between the margins. When you align to left, right, or center, the opposite margin is ragged. When you justify a paragraph, space is added between words to make both the left and right margins line up neatly, as shown in Figure 5.13. In this activity, you learn how to change the alignment of selected paragraphs.

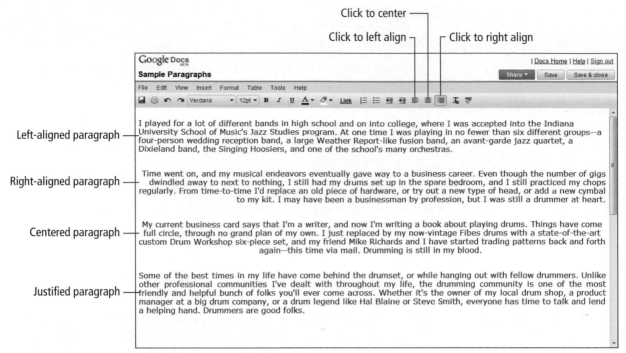

Figure 5.13 Changing paragraph alignment.

1. Position the insertion point anywhere within the paragraph you wish to align.

2. To left align the paragraph, click the **Left** Justify button on the toolbar.

3. To right align the paragraph, click the **Right** Justify button on the toolbar.

4. To center the paragraph, click the **Center** Justify button on the toolbar.

5. To justify the paragraph, click **Format** on the menu bar, point to **Align**, then click **Justified**.

 Default Alignment

By default, all paragraphs in new documents are left aligned.

Activity 5.13

Applying Heading Styles

If your document includes multiple sections, you may want to introduce each section with its own heading. Google Docs includes heading styles that are preformatted using font sizes and formatting such as bold. As shown in Figure 5.14, you can apply three levels of headings, labeled H1 (largest) to H3 (smallest). In this activity, you learn how to apply these heading styles to the headings in your document.

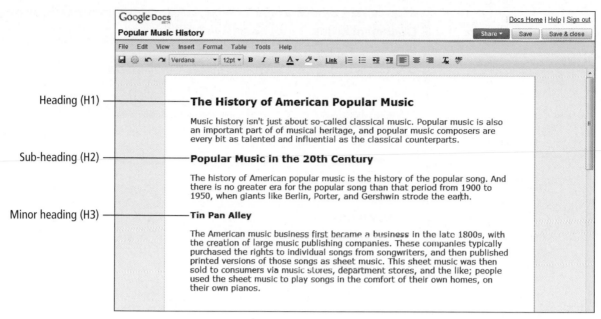

Heading (H1)

Sub-heading (H2)

Minor heading (H3)

Figure 5.14 Headings used to introduce sections in a document.

1. Enter the text for your section heading.

2. Position the insertion point anywhere on the section heading line.

3. Click **Format** on the menu bar, then click **Heading (H1), Sub-heading (H2),** or **Minor heading (H3).**

Activity 5.14

Changing Line Spacing

Line spacing The space between lines of text.

You can change the look of your document by changing the *line spacing*—literally, the space between lines of text. While most types of documents are best presented with the default single-line spacing, other types of documents, such as manuscripts and school reports, require more space between lines. Google Docs lets you change the line spacing for all paragraphs using the same font style. In this activity, you learn how to change line spacing.

1. From your open document, click **Edit** on the menu bar, then click **Document styles.**

2. When the Document styles dialog box appears, as shown in Figure 5.15, click the **Font** list arrow, then click the font style for the text that you wish to change.

3. Click the **Line-spacing** list arrow, then select new spacing. The default Normal spacing is slightly more than 1 line. You can also select Single spaced, 1.5 spaced, Double spaced, and Triple spaced.

4. Click the **OK** button to apply the desired line spacing to the selected paragraphs formatted with the selected font.

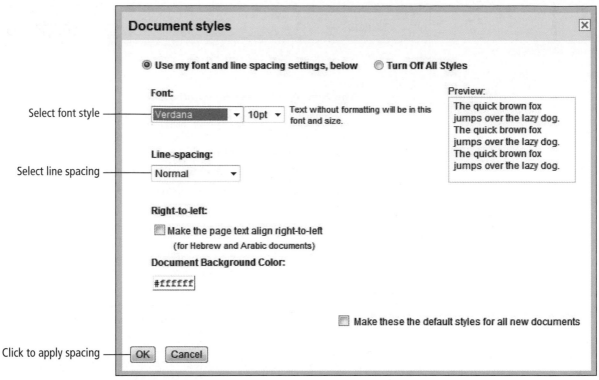

Select font style ——

Select line spacing ——

Click to apply spacing ——

Figure 5.15 Changing line spacing for a given font style.

Activity 5.15

Adding Header and Footer Text

Many types of documents, such as reports, require that information about the document be placed on all pages. Text objects that appear at the top of every page and contain the same information on every page are called *headers* (top of page) and *footers* (bottom of page). Headers and footers may include the document's title, page number, or the author's name. In this activity, you learn how to add headers and footers to your documents.

1. From your open document, click **Insert** on the menu bar, then click either **Header** or **Footer**.

2. A text object is inserted at the top (header) or bottom (footer) of your document, as shown in Figure 5.16. Enter the text for your header or footer into this text object; the header/footer text you enter will be repeated on every page of your document.

Header A text object that appears at the top of every page, including the document's title, page number, or the author's name.

Footer A text object that appears at the bottom of every page, including the document's title, page number, or the author's name.

Header text object ——

The History of American Popular Music

Music history isn't just about so-called classical music. Popular music is also an important part of of musical heritage, and popular music composers are every bit as talented and influential as the classical counterparts.

Figure 5.16 Adding a header to a document.

Activity 5.16

Inserting a Page Break

To control the flow of text in a document, Google Docs lets you insert your own manual page breaks. In this activity, you learn how to insert a page break into your document.

1. Position the insertion point at the start of the paragraph or line that you want to appear at the top of the next page.

2. Click **Insert** on the menu bar, then click **Page break (for printing)**. A double dotted line now appears in your document where the page break will occur, as shown in Figure 5.17.

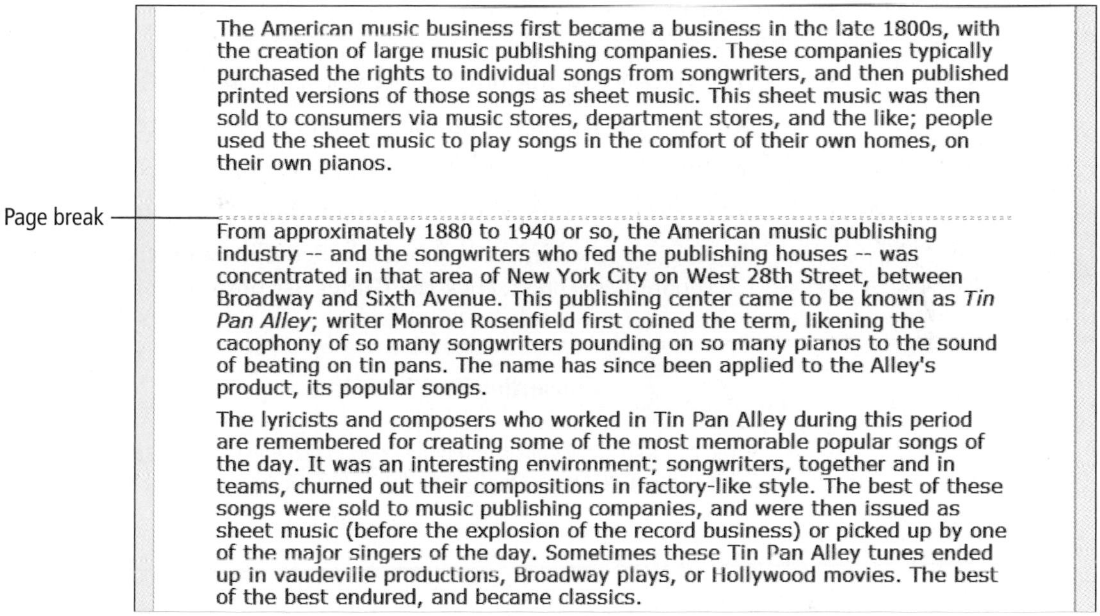

Page break —

The American music business first became a business in the late 1800s, with the creation of large music publishing companies. These companies typically purchased the rights to individual songs from songwriters, and then published printed versions of those songs as sheet music. This sheet music was then sold to consumers via music stores, department stores, and the like; people used the sheet music to play songs in the comfort of their own homes, on their own pianos.

From approximately 1880 to 1940 or so, the American music publishing industry -- and the songwriters who fed the publishing houses -- was concentrated in that area of New York City on West 28th Street, between Broadway and Sixth Avenue. This publishing center came to be known as *Tin Pan Alley*; writer Monroe Rosenfield first coined the term, likening the cacophony of so many songwriters pounding on so many pianos to the sound of beating on tin pans. The name has since been applied to the Alley's product, its popular songs.

The lyricists and composers who worked in Tin Pan Alley during this period are remembered for creating some of the most memorable popular songs of the day. It was an interesting environment; songwriters, together and in teams, churned out their compositions in factory-like style. The best of these songs were sold to music publishing companies, and were then issued as sheet music (before the explosion of the record business) or picked up by one of the major singers of the day. Sometimes these Tin Pan Alley tunes ended up in vaudeville productions, Broadway plays, or Hollywood movies. The best of the best endured, and became classics.

Figure 5.17 Inserting a manual page break.

Objective 6

Create Bulleted and Numbered Lists

Some types of text are best presented in list format. For example, if you're listing a collection of items that can appear in any order, use a *bulleted list*. If you're describing how to do something in a step-by-step fashion, use a *numbered list*.

Bulleted list A list of items that can appear in any order.

Numbered list A list of items that must appear in a certain order.

Activity 5.17

Creating a Bulleted List

In this activity, you will create a bulleted list, like the one in Figure 5.18.

Click to create bulleted list ⌐

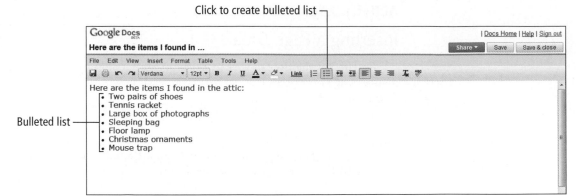

Figure 5.18 Creating a bulleted list.

1. Type the first line or item that you want bulleted.

2. Click the **Bullet list** button. This turns the first item into the first bullet.

3. Press **Enter**, then type the second line or item; it is bulleted also.

4. Continue to press **Enter** and type additional line items for your bulleted list.

5. When you've finished with the bulleted list and wish to resume entering normal (nonbulleted) text, click the **Bullet list** button again or press **Enter** twice.

 Converting Text to Lists

You can also apply bullets and numbering to text you have already typed. Select the text, then click either the **Bullet list** or **Numbered list** button on the toolbar.

Activity 5.18

Creating a Numbered List

Numbered lists, like the one in Figure 5.19, are used to present items in a specific order, such as directions. In this activity, you learn how to create a numbered list in Google Docs.

Click to create numbered list ⌐

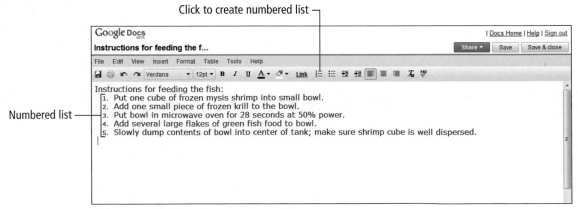

Figure 5.19 Creating a numbered list.

1. Type the first line of your numbered list.

2. Click the **Numbered list** button. The number 1 appears at the beginning of the line.

3. Press **Enter** and type the second line. The number 2 appears at the beginning of the line.

4. Continue to press **Enter** and type additional line items for your numbered list. The numbering continues in order.

5. When you've finished with the numbered list and wish to resume entering normal (non-numbered) text, click the **Numbered list** button again or press **Enter** twice.

Objective 7

Work with Images

Documents such as a reports, newsletters, or personal letters can be enhanced with photographs or other images to add visual interest or to present a graphic to support the text. Google Docs allows you to easily add images to a document.

Activity 5.19

Inserting an Image into Your Document

Google Docs lets you add pictures to any word processing document, like the one shown in Figure 5.20. In this activity, you learn how to upload image files stored on your hard disk or point to images stored on any public website.

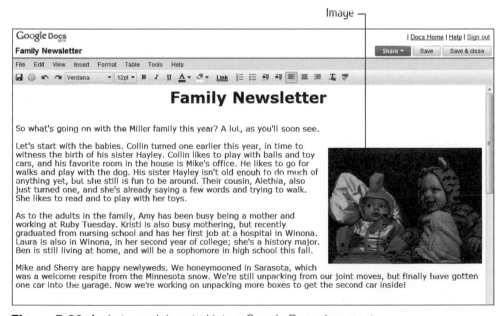

Figure 5.20 A photograph inserted into a Google Docs document.

Note **Image File Formats**

Google Docs lets you insert .jpg, .gif, .png, and .bmp format images up to 2MB in size.

1. From within the open document, position the insertion point where you want the image to display.

2. Click **Insert** on the menu bar, then click **Picture**.

3. When the Insert Image dialog box appears, as shown in Figure 5.21, click the **From this computer** option button to upload an image from your hard drive or from a network folder to which you have access.

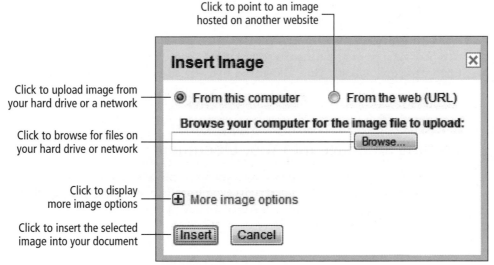

Figure 5.21 Inserting a picture into a document.

4. Click the **Browse** button to open the Choose file dialog box.

5. Navigate to and select the file you want to upload, then click the **Open** button.

6. Click the **Insert** button. The image is now uploaded to Google Docs and displayed in your document.

 Note **Images from the Web**

You can insert any image hosted on a public website. Click the **From the web (URL)** option button and enter the URL for the image (including the filename and file extension) into the Enter image web address box. Images you find on the Internet may be protected under copyright laws; use only those images for which you have the proper rights.

Activity 5.20

Configuring an Image

While you're inserting an image, you can change how it is displayed in the document by specifying the size, alignment, and position in regard to text. In this activity, you learn how to configure the image display.

1. From within the open document, position the insertion point where you want the image to display.

2. Click **Insert** on the menu bar, then click **Picture**.

3. In the Insert Image dialog box, click the **Browse** button, select an image, then click the **Open** button.

4. Click the **More image options** link to expand the Insert Image dialog box, as shown in Figure 5.22.

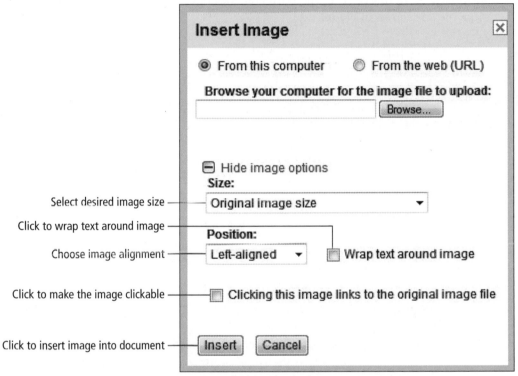

Figure 5.22 Configuring an image.

5. To change the size of the image in the document, click the **Size** list arrow, then click an option. You can choose the actual size (Original image size), a specific number of pixels (Custom size), fill the page (Fit page width), or choose a general size (Thumbnail, Small, Medium, Large, or Extra large).

6. To specify the **position** of the image on the page, click the **Position** list arrow, then click one of the following: Left-aligned, Centered, or Right-aligned.

7. By default, the image is positioned on its own line, with text above and below it. To wrap the text around the edge of a picture, click the **Wrap text around image** checkbox.

8. To display a link to the original image file (at its original size) below the picture in the document, click the **Clicking this image links to the original image file** checkbox.

9. Click the **Insert** button to insert the picture.

Objective 8

Insert Links and Comments

Google Docs also lets you include links to other web pages to make your documents interactive when viewed online. You can also insert comments about the document when editing a document collaboratively with other users.

Activity 5.21

Inserting a Web Link

Anchor text The text that accompanies a link to another web page.

Inserting links to other web pages—to the source of a quotation, for instance—can provide the reader of your document with additional information in the form of related articles or documentation. The text that is used to create the link is called the ***anchor text***. In this activity, you learn how to add a clickable link in a document, like the one shown in Figure 5.23.

Link to another web page ⌐

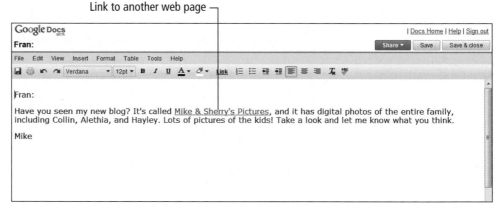

Figure 5.23 A clickable link in a Google Docs document.

1. In a document, use the mouse or arrow keys to select the text you want to use for the link.

2. Click the **Add or remove link** button on the toolbar or press **Ctrl+K** to open the Insert Link dialog box, as shown in Figure 5.24. The selected text is shown in the Text box. If you edit the text in the Text box, it will change the text in the document.

3. Enter the URL you want to link to into the URL box.

4. If you want to display a ScreenTip that appears when a user hovers over the anchor text, enter that text into the Flyover box.

5. If you want the link to open in a new browser window, click the **Open link in new window** checkbox.

6. Click the **Insert** button to create the link in your document.

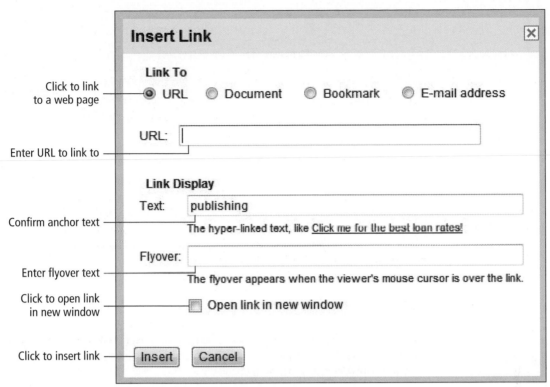

Click to link to a web page

Enter URL to link to

Confirm anchor text

Enter flyover text

Click to open link in new window

Click to insert link

Figure 5.24 Inserting a link into a document.

 Note **Other Types of Links**

These instructions show you how to link to a specific web page. In the Insert Link dialog box, you can also choose to link to other web-based Google Docs documents, insert a bookmark to another location in the document, or create a link to an email address.

Activity 5.22

Inserting a Comment

When collaborating with other users to edit or create a Google Docs document, you can insert comments that the other users can view but that don't affect the text. For instance, you can add a comment that asks a question about someone's edit or asks another user to verify a fact or figure in the document. This activity shows you how to insert a comment.

1. From within the open document, position the insertion point where you wish the comment to appear.

2. Click **Insert** on the menu bar, then click **Comment** or press **Ctrl+M** to insert a new comment, as shown in Figure 5.25; the words *type here* are selected.

3. Type your comment into the comment field to replace the *type here* text.

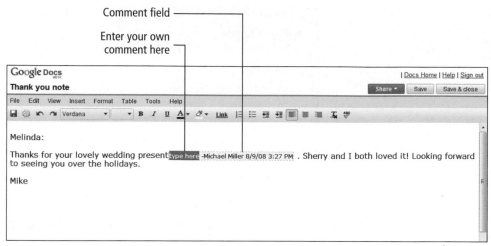

Figure 5.25 Inserting a comment into a document.

 Onscreen Comments

By default, comments are displayed only onscreen, not when the document is printed. You can choose to print the comments along with the document in the Print Settings dialog box. You will learn to print documents later on in Chapter 5.

Objective 9

Create a Table

Table Information displayed in a grid, organized in rows and columns, to help readers distinguish complex data.

Tables display information in a grid. The table format, with individual cells organized in rows and columns, helps readers distinguish complex data.

Activity 5.23

Creating a Table

In this activity, you learn how to create a basic table in your document, like the one shown in Figure 5.26. Once you've created the table, you can then insert text into the table's cells, as well as format various elements of the table.

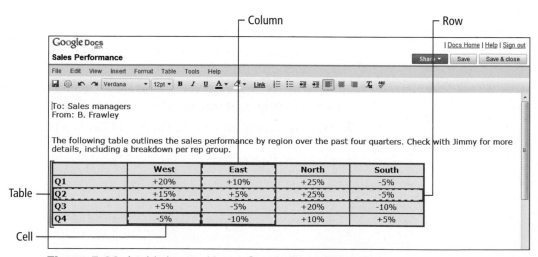

Figure 5.26 A table inserted into a Google Docs document.

1. In your open document, position the insertion point where you want the table to appear.

2. Click **Insert** on the menu bar, then click **Table** to open the Insert Table dialog box, shown in Figure 5.27.

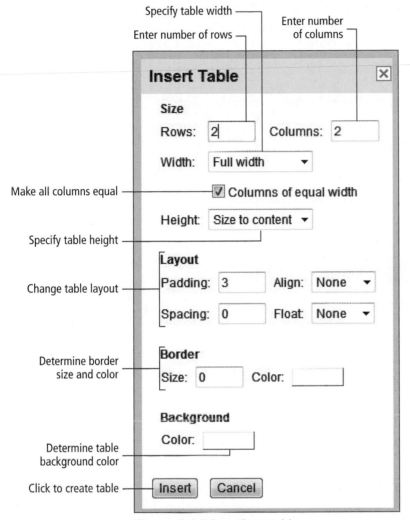

Figure 5.27 Inserting a table.

3. Enter the number of rows for the table into the Rows box.

4. Enter the number of columns for the table into the Columns box.

5. Determine the total width of the table by clicking the **Width** list arrow and selecting from the following: Full width (table is the full width of the page); Size to content (the more data in the table, the wider it is); Pixels (enter the desired width in pixels); or Percent (enter the desired width as a percent of the total page width).

6. If you want all columns in the table to be of equal size, check the **Columns of equal width** checkbox.

7. To add space between the cell text and the surrounding cell border, enter a value (in pixels) into the Padding box. The larger the value, the more space around the text.

8. To add space between individual cells, enter a value (in pixels) into the Spacing box.

9. To align the table on the page, click the **Align** list arrow and select Left, Center, or Right. Note that this only works when a table does not take up the full width of the page.

10. To have text wrap around a smaller table, click the **Float** list arrow and select either Left (to align the table to the left and have text wrap to the right) or Right (to align the table to the right and have text wrap to the left).

11. To add a border to the table, enter a value (in pixels) into the Border Size box, then click the **Border Color** box to select a border color.

12. To add a colored background to the table, click the **Background Color** box and select a color.

13. Click the **Insert** button to create the table.

Activity 5.24

Entering Table Text

After you've created a table, you can enter text into the table's cells, as you will do in this activity.

> **Tip** **Navigating in a Table**
>
> Press the **Tab** key to move to the next cell in the row, or, if you're at the furthest cell to the right, to the first cell in the next row. If the insertion point is in the last cell in the table, pressing the Tab key creates a new row. Press **Shift+Tab** to move one cell backwards in the row or to the last cell in the previous column. Use the up and down arrow keys to move between rows. Use the left and right arrow keys to move between blank cells or between characters in a cell that contains data.

1. Position the insertion point into top left cell in the table, as shown in Figure 5.28.

Start entering text here

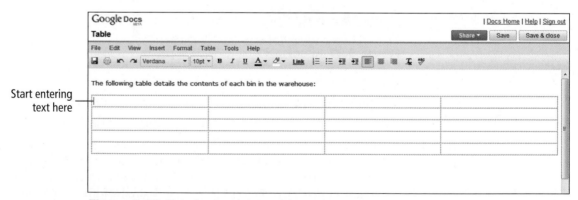

Figure 5.28 Entering text into a table.

2. Type the text for that cell.

3. Press the **Tab** key to move to the next cell in the table, then enter the text for that cell.

4. Repeat step 3 until you've filled all the cells in the table.

Activity 5.25

Modifying a Table

At any time after you've created a table, you can change the entire table at once, a row, a column, or individual cells. You can also change the order of, insert, and delete columns and rows in the table, as you'll learn in this activity.

 Note **Formatting Table Text**

You format the text in the table's cells using the same skills you use to format text in a document that is not part of a table.

1. To format the entire table, position the insertion point anywhere in the table, click **Table** on the menu bar, then click **Modify table properties** to open the Change Table dialog box shown in Figure 5.29. Make the appropriate changes, then click the **Change** button.

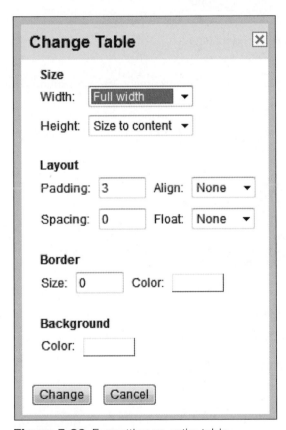

Figure 5.29 Formatting an entire table.

2. To format the height, alignment, or background color of a row, position the insertion point in any cell in that row, click **Table** on the menu bar, then click **Modify row properties**. When the Change Row dialog box appears, as shown in Figure 5.30, make the appropriate changes, then click the **Change** button.

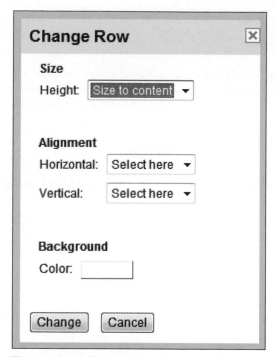

Figure 5.30 Formatting a row.

3. To format the width, alignment, or background color of a column, position the insertion point in any cell in that column, click **Table** on the menu bar, then click **Modify column properties**. When the Change Column dialog box appears, as shown in Figure 5.31, make the appropriate changes, then click the **Change** button.

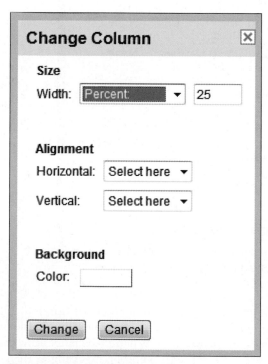

Figure 5.31 Formatting a column.

4. To format the size, alignment, or background color of an individual cell, position the insertion point within that cell, click **Table** on the menu bar, then click **Modify cell properties**. When the Change Cell dialog box appears, as shown in Figure 5.32, make the appropriate changes, then click the **Change** button.

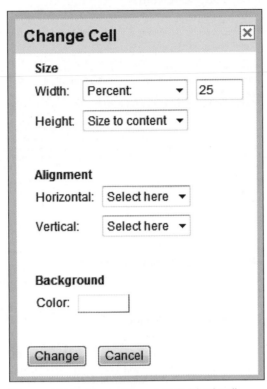

Figure 5.32 Formatting an individual cell.

5. To insert a row into your table, position the insertion point in the row above or below where you want the new row to appear, click **Table** on the menu bar, then click **Insert row above** or **Insert row below**.

6. To insert a column into your table, position the insertion point in the column to the left or right of where you want the new column to appear, click **Table** on the menu bar, then click **Insert column on the right** or **Insert column on the left**.

7. To delete an entire row from your table, position the insertion point anywhere in that row, click **Table** on the menu bar, then click **Delete row**.

8. To delete an entire column from your table, position the insertion point anywhere in that column, click **Table** on the menu bar, then click **Delete column**.

Objective 10

Proof and Print Your Document

Activity 5.26

Checking Your Spelling

Before you print or distribute your document, you should read through it to make sure that you haven't made any mistakes, then use the spell checker to check your spelling. In this activity, you learn how to spell check your document.

1. From within an open document, click the **Check Spelling** button on the toolbar.

2. Google Docs checks your document and highlights those words that are either misspelled or not in its built-in dictionary. Click a highlighted word to see a list of suggested spellings, as shown in Figure 5.33, then select a suggested word to replace the misspelled word.

Misspelled word

Suggested replacements

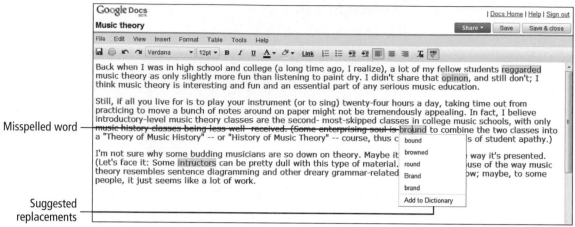

Figure 5.33 Spell checking a document.

Note **Adding New Words**

Sometimes Google's spell checker doesn't know a legitimate word, such as a name or an industry-specific term, and identifies that word as being misspelled. To add a word to the spell checker's dictionary, click a highlighted word, then click **Add to Dictionary**.

Activity 5.27

Printing a Document

Printing Creating a hard copy printout of your document.

Printing creates a hard copy printout of your document. In this activity, you learn how to print a Google Docs document.

1. From within the open document, click the **Print** button on the toolbar or press **Ctrl+P** to print the document with the default printer and printer settings.

2. To specify printing options—such as printing only a section of the document or printing to a printer other than your default printer—click **File** on the menu bar, then click **Print** or press **Ctrl+P**. When the Print dialog box appears, as shown in Figure 5.34, select the desired options, then click the **OK** button.

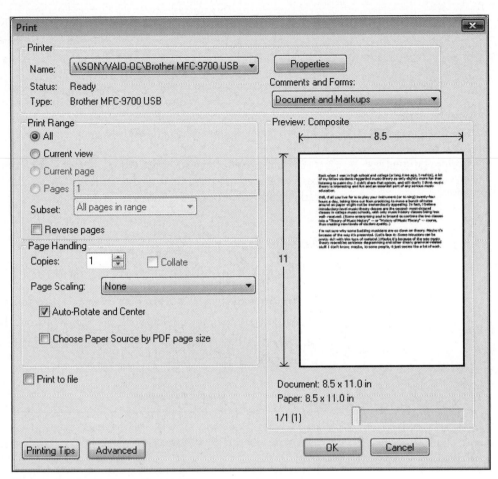

Figure 5.34 Printing a document.

3. To specify print settings such as page orientation or to include comments in the printed manuscript, click **File** on the menu bar, then click **Print settings**. When the Print Settings dialog box appears, as shown in Figure 5.35, select the desired options, then click the **OK** button.

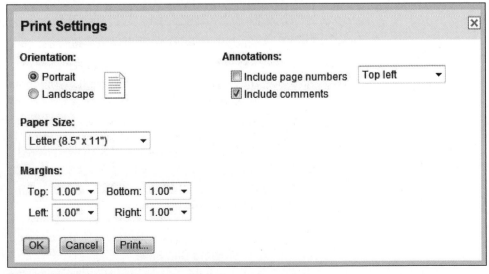

Figure 5.35 Configuring print settings.

Objective 11

Share and Collaborate

Collaborate To share a document with others online for viewing or editing as a group to create a finished document.

What makes Google Docs different from other word processing programs, is the ability to share a document with others for online viewing or collaborative editing. You can share documents online with anyone who has a Google account. When you share documents, you can *collaborate* or edit as a group to create a finished document.

There are two ways to share Google Docs documents online: you can choose to have others view a document without the ability to edit or to allow others to collaboratively edit the document online.

Activity 5.28

Inviting Other Users to View Your Document

In this activity, you'll learn how to share a view-only (read-only) document.

1. From your open document, click the **Share** button, then click **Share with others**.

2. When the Share this document page appears, as shown in Figure 5.36, check the **as viewers** option button.

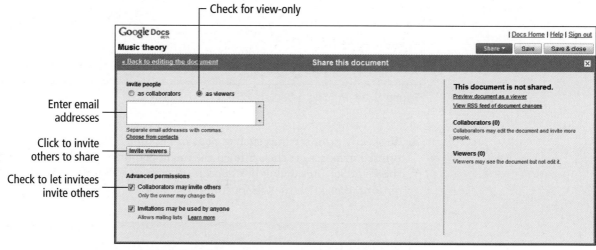

Figure 5.36 Getting ready to share a document.

3. Enter the email addresses of the people with whom you want to share this document into the Invite people box. Separate addresses with commas.

4. If you want the invitees to be able to invite others to view your document, click the **Collaborators may invite others** checkbox. Leave this checkbox unselected to limit the invitees to the ones you have selected.

5. Click the **Invite viewers** button. Your recipients now receive an email invitation that contains a link to the document. Clicking this link opens the document in a new browser window.

 Viewers Can Save

Anyone invited as a viewer can navigate throughout the entire file and also save that file to their personal Google Docs online storage area or as a file to their own computer.

Activity 5.29

Inviting Other Users to Collaborate

With Google Docs, you can collaborate on documents with other users in real time over the Internet. Your collaborators need to have Google accounts and be invited by you to share the document. In this activity, you learn how to invite others to collaborate on an online document.

1. From your open document, click the **Share** button, then click **Share with others**.

2. When the Share this document page appears, click the **as collaborators** option button.

3. Enter the email addresses of the people with whom you want to share this document into the Invite people box. Separate addresses with commas.

4. If you want the invitees to be able to invite others to view your document, click the **Collaborators may invite others** checkbox. Leave this checkbox unselected to limit the invitees to the ones you have selected.

5. Click the **Invite collaborators** button. Your recipients now receive an email invitation that contains a link to the document; clicking this link opens the document in a new browser window.

 Collaborators Can Edit

Anyone invited as a collaborator can edit the file in their web browsers. Google Docs lets multiple users edit the document at the same time, so you can have an entire group working together in real time. You can also get alerts when a document you have shared is changed by another user.

Summary

In this chapter, you learned how to create and save new documents, as well as to import and export documents from and to Microsoft Word. You learned how to enter, edit, and format text and paragraphs. The chapter included information on how to create bulleted and numbered lists and insert images, links, and comments into your documents. You practiced creating and formatting a table, as well as proofing and printing your document. Finally, you learned how to use Google Docs' unique web-based features to share and collaborate with others online.

Key Terms

Assessments

Multiple Choice

1. Which of the following is true?
    (a) Google Docs is an online word processor.
    (b) Google Docs is a suite of online applications.
    (c) Google Docs competes with Microsoft Office.
    (d) All of the above.

2. When spell checking a document, do the following:
   (a) Click a misspelled word to see a list of suggested corrections.
   (b) Right-click a misspelled word to see a list of suggested corrections.
   (c) Double-click a misspelled word to see a list of suggested corrections.
   (d) Press Alt+I to ignore a misspelling.

3. Google Docs lets you create the following types of lists:
   (a) bulleted.
   (b) numbered.
   (c) un-numbered.
   (d) (a) and (b).

4. Which of the following is true?
   (a) Google Docs includes only three font families: Serif, Sans Serif, and Proportional.
   (b) Google Docs documents can only be edited when you're connected to the Internet.
   (c) Google Docs lets you insert only .jpg-format image files.
   (d) Google Docs offers only three type sizes: Small, Regular, and Large.

5. To apply bold to selected text, do the following:
   (a) Press Ctrl+B.
   (b) Click Format on the menu bar, then click Bold.
   (c) Click Edit on the menu bar, then click Bold.
   (d) All of the above.

6. Which of the following *cannot* be inserted into a Google Docs document?
   (a) web link
   (b) video file
   (c) comment
   (d) digital photograph

7. When creating a table, you can format which of the following elements?
   (a) individual cells
   (b) rows and columns
   (c) entire table
   (d) all of the above

8. What happens when you click File on the menu bar, then click Print?
   (a) Your document is printed on your default printer.
   (b) Your document is saved, printed, and closed.
   (c) The Print dialog box opens so you can select the parts of the document to print.
   (d) You're asked to select your default printer.

9. Google Docs can import word processing documents in the following formats:
   (a) WordPerfect (.wpd).
   (b) Google Docs (.gdx).
   (c) Microsoft Word (.doc).
   (d) all of the above.

10. Which of the following features differentiates Google Docs from Microsoft Word?
    (a) the ability to share and collaborate online
    (b) the ability to format both text and paragraphs
    (c) the ability to insert web links
    (d) the ability to create documents from predesigned templates

Fill in the Blank

Write the correct word in the space provided.

1. All Google Docs documents are stored on the _____.
2. Most formatting options are selected by clicking buttons on the _____.
3. To delete a selected piece of text, press the _____ key.
4. To cancel the most recent edit, click Edit on the menu bar, then click _____.
5. To make both sides of a paragraph align evenly, you must _____ the text.
6. To present a series of step-by-step instructions, create a _____ list.
7. The text that accompanies an embedded web link is called the _____ text.
8. To italicize a selected piece of text, press the _____ keys.
9. A _____ is a predesigned combination of text styles and formatting.
10. A table consists of a grid of _____ and columns.

Skills Review

1. Create a new, blank document and name it **sample document** 1.
2. In the first line of this document, type the title **Neighborhood Newsletter**. Format the title as 36-point Sans Serif bold, centered on the page.
3. Beneath the title, enter enough text into this new document to fill two printed pages. Format the text as 12-point Serif, not bold, left aligned.
4. Cut the second paragraph from your document and paste it at the end of the document.
5. Near the top of what would be the second page, insert a photograph. Format the photograph as Small, left aligned, with word wrap enabled.
6. Indent the paragraph directly after the photograph and italicize the entire paragraph.
7. Insert a table after the indented paragraph; the table should have 3 columns and 5 rows. Format the table so that it has a thin (1-point) blue border and a light blue background. Enter data into the table, then format the data to your liking.
8. Spell check your document and make the necessary corrections.
9. Save and then print your document.
10. Share your document as view-only with three of your friends or colleagues.

CHAPTER 6

Using Google Spreadsheets

Objectives

By the end of this chapter you will be able to:

1. Create and Save New Spreadsheets

2. Import and Export Excel Spreadsheets

3. Enter and Edit Data

4. Format Text and Numbers

5. Work with Ranges and Sort Data

6. Work with Formulas, Functions, and Gadgets

7. Chart Your Data

8. Print, Share, and Collaborate

Google Spreadsheets is the spreadsheet application in the Google Docs suite. Google Spreadsheets includes many of the features found in Microsoft Excel and other software-based spreadsheet programs, including formulas, functions, and charts. A ***spreadsheet***, like a table, organizes data in rows and columns, but spreadsheets also allow you to perform complex calculations and analysis. You can use Google Spreadsheets to organize numbers and text to create budgets, financial comparisons, and more.

Google Spreadsheets The spreadsheet application within the Google Docs suite.

Spreadsheet A program that organizes data in rows and columns and allows you to perform complex calculations and analysis.

Objective 1

Create and Save New Spreadsheets

To use any Google Docs application, you need a Google account. When you log on to your Google account, you see the main Google Docs page shown in Figure 6.1. This is the homepage for all three Google Docs applications, including Google Spreadsheets. All of your previously created documents are listed on this page. This is also where you create new documents.

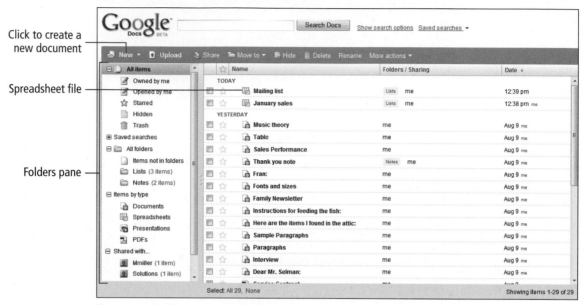

Click to create a new document

Spreadsheet file

Folders pane

Figure 6.1 The main page for all Google Docs applications.

At the top of the window is a toolbar that contains buttons you can use to manage files or create new ones. The left pane on this page is where you organize your documents. You can see the results of saved searches, store files in folders, view documents by type (word processing documents, spreadsheets, presentations, or PDFs), and display documents shared with specific people.

 New Folders

To create a new folder, click the **New** button, then click **Folder**. Position the insertion point over the words New Folder in the main editing window, then type the name of the new folder. To move a document to a folder, click the checkbox next to the document, click the **Move to** button, click the folder you want to add it to, then click the **Move to folder** button.

The documents stored within the selected folder or filter are displayed in the main part of the window. Spreadsheet files are identified by a spreadsheet icon.

Activity 6.1

Creating a New Spreadsheet

In this activity, you will learn how to create a new, blank spreadsheet.

1. Go to the main Google Docs page, **docs.google.com**. Log into your account if necessary.

2. Click the **New** button, then click **Spreadsheet**. A new spreadsheet opens in its own window on your desktop.

Activity 6.2

Creating a New Spreadsheet from a Template

Template A pre-designed selection of text, formatting, and graphics, used to create new document, spreadsheet, or presentation.

Placeholder Text in a template that indicates the type of information to include and a sample page layout.

You can also create a new spreadsheet based on a predesigned template. A *template* is a combination of text styles, document formatting, and graphics to which you can add your own numbers, text, and graphics. Many templates contain *placeholder* text, which indicates the type of information you want to include and gives you a sample page layout; others let you simply start entering data by filling in the blanks. In this activity, you learn how to create a new spreadsheet based on a predesigned template.

Note **Unblocking Pop-Up Windows**

Depending on your security settings, you may not be able to see pop-up windows. If an alert appears at the top of your browser window, click it, then instruct the browser to temporarily accept pop-ups. Before you modify your security settings, you should verify that the site is valid, and if you are in a lab setting, check with your technical support person

Tip **Template Quick Starts**

Templates are great for getting a head start on a specific type of spreadsheet project; Google includes templates for invoices, business plans, budgets, and more.

1. From the main Google Docs page, click the **New** button, then click **From template**.

2. Google opens a new Templates Gallery window. You can search or browse the gallery for document, spreadsheet, and presentation templates. To view spreadsheet templates, click the Spreadsheets link, as shown in Figure 6.2.

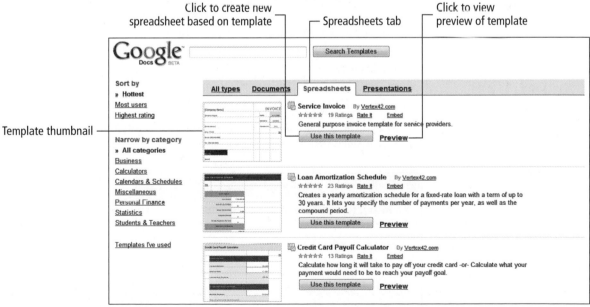

Figure 6.2 Browsing Google Docs' Templates Gallery.

3. When you find the template you want to use, click the **Use this template** button to open a new browser window that contains a spreadsheet based on the template, as shown in Figure 6.3.

4. Fill in the necessary blanks in the template or replace any placeholder text with your own text.

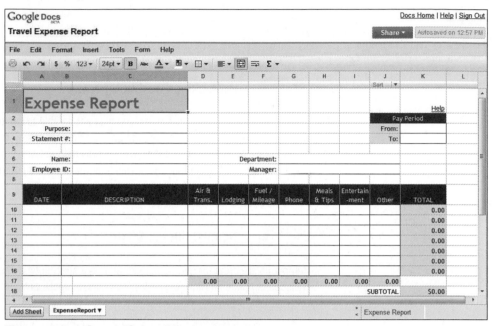

Figure 6.3 A Google Spreadsheets template.

Activity 6.3

Saving a Spreadsheet

Template files are saved automatically when created. After you create a new, blank spreadsheet, you need to save the file. When you first save a file, you must do so manually and give the file a name. After this first save, Google automatically resaves the file every time you make a change to the spreadsheet. In essence, this means that you only have to save the spreadsheet once; Google saves all further changes automatically.

In this activity, you learn how to save a newly created spreadsheet file.

1. From within the spreadsheet window, click the **Save** button at the top right of the screen or press **Ctrl+S** on the keyboard.

2. When the dialog box appears, as shown in Figure 6.4, enter a name for the spreadsheet into the Save spreadsheet as box.

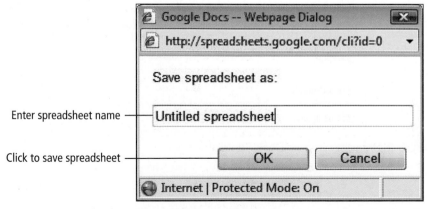

Enter spreadsheet name

Click to save spreadsheet

Figure 6.4 Saving a new spreadsheet for the first time.

3. Click the **OK** button. The spreadsheet is now saved on Google's servers and you don't have to bother resaving it at any future point.

Activity 6.4

Opening an Existing Spreadsheet

After you've saved a spreadsheet, reopening it is easy, as you'll learn in this activity.

1. From the main Google Docs page, click the **Spreadsheets** link in the left pane under Items by type to view all of your spreadsheet files. As you can see in Figure 6.5, spreadsheet documents are identified by a green spreadsheet icon.

2. Click the spreadsheet's name to open the file in a new browser window.

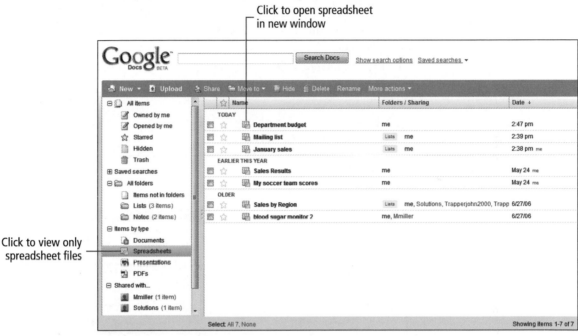

Figure 6.5 Opening a spreadsheet file.

 Tip   **Working Offline**

The spreadsheet file you save isn't stored on your computer's hard disk. Instead, the file is stored by default on Google's servers, which means you must be connected to the Internet to access it. However, if you're not connected to the Internet, Google now makes it possible for you to edit your spreadsheets *offline*. To do this, you have to install the Google Docs Offline application. Click the **Offline** link at the top of the Google Docs homepage, then click the **Get Google Gears Now** button. Follow the simple onscreen instructions to download and install the program. Once Google Gears has been installed, you can open the offline version of Google Docs by entering docs.google.com into your web browser or by clicking the Google Docs shortcut on your desktop. If you're not connected to the Internet, you'll open the offline version of Google Docs; if you are connected to the Internet, you'll open the normal online version. Whenever you're online, Google Docs automatically synchronizes the files stored on your computer with those stored online so that both locations contain the document version that was most recently edited. (You can also work offline when using Google's Chrome web browser, which has Google Gears built in.)

Offline When you're not connected to the Internet.

Objective 2

Import and Export Excel Spreadsheets

If you or your colleagues use Microsoft Excel as a spreadsheet program, you can import your Excel spreadsheets into Google Spreadsheets for online editing and collaboration. You can also save your Google Spreadsheets files as Microsoft Excel (.xls) files on your hard disk.

Activity 6.5

Importing an Excel Spreadsheet

Google Spreadsheets enables you to upload your Microsoft Excel spreadsheets so they can be stored on the web and edited with the web-based Google Spreadsheets application. In this activity, you learn how to import an Excel file into Google Spreadsheets.

1. From the Google Docs main page, click the **Upload** button.

2. When the Upload a File page appears, as shown in Figure 6.6, click the **Browse** button.

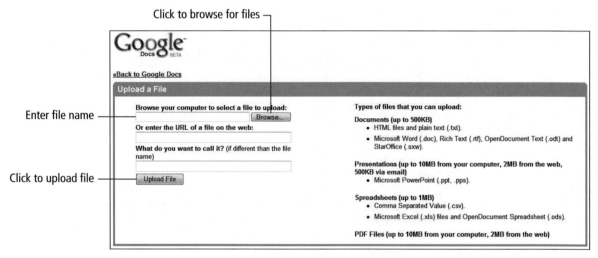

Figure 6.6 Importing a file into Google Spreadsheets.

3. When the Choose file dialog box appears, locate and select the file you want to upload, then click the **Open** button.

4. When the Upload a File page reappears, enter a name for the uploaded file into the **What do you want to call it?** box if necessary.

5. Click the **Upload File** button. The file now opens in Google Spreadsheets for editing.

 File Upload Limits

You can import spreadsheet files in the following formats: Microsoft Excel (.xls), OpenDocument Spreadsheet (.ods), and Comma Separated Value (.csv). Files must be 1MB or less in size. When this book was printed, Google did not support files created with the latest version of Microsoft Excel, Excel 2007 (.xlsx); this feature could be added to a future version of the application.

Activity 6.6

Exporting a Google Spreadsheet to Excel Format

By default, all the spreadsheets you work with in Google Spreadsheets are stored on Google's servers. You can also download files from Google to your computer's hard drive to work with in Excel. In this activity, you learn how to export a Google spreadsheet to Microsoft Excel.

 Note — **Other Ways to Export**

Google also makes it possible for you to export your spreadsheet as a Comma Separated Values (.csv), HTML (.htm or .html), OpenOffice Spreadsheet (.ods), Adobe Acrobat (.pdf), or plain text (.txt) file.

1. From within the current spreadsheet window, click **File** on the menu bar, point to **Export**, then click **.xls**, as shown in Figure 6.7.

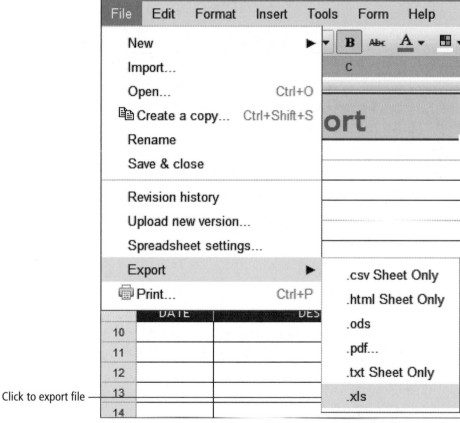

Click to export file —

Figure 6.7 Exporting a file into Microsoft Excel format.

2. When the File Download dialog box appears, click the **Save** button.

3. When the Save As dialog box appears, select a location for the downloaded file, rename it if necessary, then click the **Save** button. The Google Spreadsheets file is now saved in .xls format to your hard disk. You can open it with Microsoft Excel and work on it as you would with any Excel spreadsheet.

Alert! Don't Get Out of Sync

Unlike Google Spreadsheet files, which will automatically synchronize online and offline versions if you've installed the Google Docs Offline application, whatever changes you make to a file in Microsoft Excel affect only the downloaded file, not the copy of the spreadsheet that still resides on the Google Docs site. To reimport the Excel file to Google Spreadsheets, go to the main Google Docs page and use the Upload function. When you reimport a file, Google Docs saves it as a new spreadsheet file rather than saving it over the previous version.

Row Data arranged horizontally in a table or spreadsheet. In a spreadsheet, rows are numbered sequentially.

Column Data arranged vertically in a table or spreadsheet. In a spreadsheet, columns are lettered alphabetically.

Cell The intersection of a row and a column.

Cell address The column letter followed by the row number, used to reference the cell in calculations. The first cell in the spreadsheet is A1.

Objective 3

Enter and Edit Data

As you can see in Figure 6.8, a Google spreadsheet is arranged into rows and columns. *Rows* are horizontal and are numbered. *Columns* are vertical and are lettered alphabetically. A *cell* is the intersection of a row and a column and is where you enter data. The *cell address*, used to reference the cell in calculations, is the column letter followed by the row number. The first cell in the spreadsheet is A1.

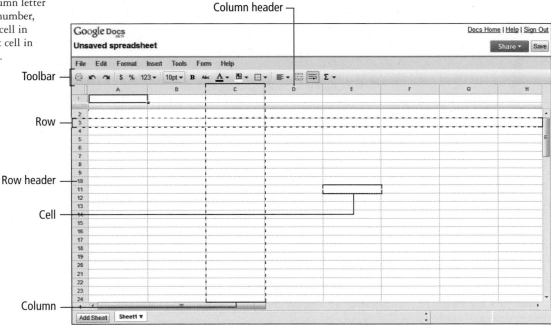

Figure 6.8 Examining the Google Spreadsheets workspace.

Activity 6.7

Entering New Data

You enter data directly into individual cells using your computer keyboard. Google enables you to enter four types of data, as detailed in Table 6.1. In this activity, you learn how to enter data into a spreadsheet cell.

Table 6.1—Types of Google Spreadsheets Data	
Type of Data	**Description**
Numbers	Numbers can be entered in a variety of formats, including currency and percent formats. All numbers can be manipulated mathematically.
Text	Text can contain both alphabetical and numerical characters. Text cannot be manipulated mathematically.
Dates	Dates are numbers formatted to display days, months, years, etc.
Formulas	Formulas tell Google Spreadsheets how to make calculations using data stored in other cells.

The data you enter is formatted based on the type of data entered:

- If you type only numbers, the data will be formatted as a number (with no commas or dollar signs).
- If you type a number with a dollar sign in front of it, the data will be formatted as currency.
- If you type any alphabetical characters, the data will be formatted as text.
- If you type numbers separated by the - or / characters (such as 12-31 or 1/2/06), the data will be formatted as a date.
- If you type numbers separated by the : character (such as 2:13), the data will be formatted as time.

1. Use your mouse or keyboard arrow keys to position the insertion point in the cell where you want to enter data.
2. Use your computer keyboard to type text or numbers into the cell.
3. When you're done entering data into a cell, use the keyboard's arrow keys to move to another cell, press **Tab** to move to the next cell to the right, press **Shift+Tab** to move to the cell to the left, or press **Enter** to move to the cell below the current cell.

 Entering Formulas

Entering a formula is different from entering straight numbers or text. As you'll learn later in this chapter, you have to preface the formula with an equal sign (=).

Activity 6.8

Editing Data

To edit cell data, you must first select the cell, as you'll learn in this activity.

1. Move the insertion point to the desired cell.
2. Press the **F2** key on your keyboard or double-click the cell to open the cell for editing, as shown in Figure 6.9.

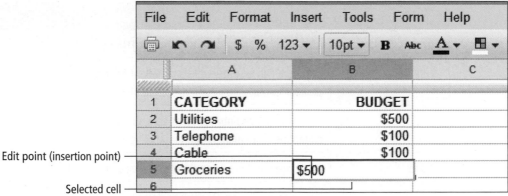

Edit point (insertion point)

Selected cell

Figure 6.9 Editing data within a cell.

3. Move the insertion point to the point within the cell you want to edit, then use the Delete and Backspace keys to delete characters, or use any other key to insert characters.

4. Press **Enter** when you are finished editing to accept your changes to the cell contents.

Activity 6.9

Inserting Rows and Columns

As you work on your new spreadsheet, you may find that you need to insert rows or columns of data into the existing grid. In this activity, you learn to insert rows and columns into your spreadsheet.

1. To insert a new row into the spreadsheet, select any cell in the row above or below the one you want to insert, click **Insert** on the menu bar, then click **Row above** or **Row below**.

2. To insert a new column into the spreadsheet, select any cell in the column to the right or left of the one you want to insert, click **Insert** on the menu bar, then click **Column left** or **Column right**.

Activity 6.10

Deleting Rows and Columns

Google Spreadsheets also makes it possible for you to delete entire rows and columns or clear the contents of individual cells. In this activity, you learn how to perform these operations.

1. To delete a row, select any cell within that row, click **Edit** on the menu bar, then click **Delete row** *number* (where *number* is the row number).

2. To delete a column, select any cell within that column, click **Edit** on the menu bar, then click **Delete column** *letter* (where *letter* is the column letter).

3. To clear the contents of a cell without deleting the cell itself, select the cell, click **Edit** on the menu bar, then click **Clear selection**.

Updating cell references

When you delete a row or column, cell addresses in rows and columns below and to the right of the deletion will change. Any calculations in your spreadsheet will update automatically to reflect the changes in cell addresses.

 Undoing Mistakes

If you accidentally delete data you want to keep, click **Edit** on the menu bar then click **Undo**, or press **Ctrl+Z**.

Activity 6.11

Working with Multiple Sheets

Like Excel, Google Spreadsheets enables you to work with multiple sheets within a single spreadsheet file. Unlike Excel, which always starts with three sheets per file, Google spreadsheets contain a single sheet by default. You can then add additional sheets to this first sheet, as you'll learn in this activity.

1. To add a new sheet to your current spreadsheet, click the **Add Sheet** button at the bottom of the window. A new sheet is added to the right of the current sheet, as shown in Figure 6.10. Each new sheet picks up the continuous numbering of the previous sheet.

2. To switch to a different sheet, click the tab for that sheet.

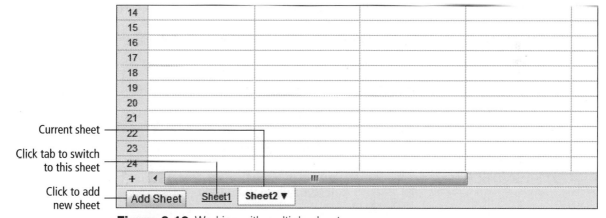

Figure 6.10 Working with multiple sheets.

 Renaming Sheets

By default, Google names its sheets Sheet1, Sheet2, Sheet3, and so forth. If you'd like a more descriptive name for a sheet, select the sheet, then click the down arrow on the tab for that sheet. Click **Rename** on the shortcut menu, enter a new name in the dialog box, then click **OK**.

Objective 4

Format Text and Numbers

A basic Google spreadsheet looks fairly plain—just text and numbers in a grid. You can enhance your spreadsheet by changing the font, font size, and text color and by changing the background color of individual cells.

Activity 6.12

Formatting Font, Size, and Color

Any data you enter into a spreadsheet can be formatted by applying various fonts, font sizes, and color to the data. In this activity, you learn how to format data by specifying font, size, and color.

1. In your open spreadsheet, select the cell or cells that contain the text you wish to format.

2. To change the font, click **Format** on the menu bar, then point to **Font** and click one of the following fonts: Normal (Sans Serif), Normal/serif, Courier New, Georgia, Trebuchet MS, or Verdana.

3. To change the font size, click the **Font size** button, shown in Figure 6.11, then click a size (from 6 to 36 points).

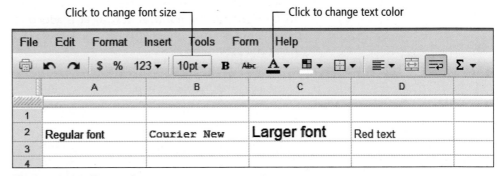

Figure 6.11 Formatting text.

4. To change the color of the selected text, click the **Text color** button, then click the desired color from the gallery.

 Note   **Cell-Wide Formatting Only**

Although you can change text attributes for an entire cell or range of cells, Google Spreadsheets doesn't let you change attributes for selected characters *within* a cell.

Activity 6.13

Formatting Cells

Google Spreadsheets also enables you to format the cells in a spreadsheet. For example, you may want to define a row or column as a **header**, which means that it contains labels for the data in the column or grid. As you'll learn in this activity, you can change the cell background color and add a border.

1. In your open spreadsheet, select the cell or cells that you wish to format.

2. To add a background color to the selected cell(s), as shown in Figure 6.12, click the **Background color** button, then click a color from the gallery.

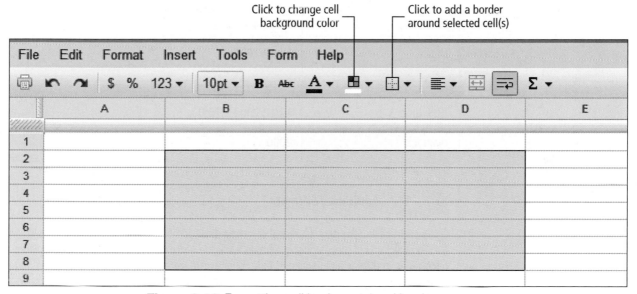

Figure 6.12 Formatting cell background and border.

3. To add a border around the selected cell(s), click the **Borders** button, then click a border type: outside, inside, inside and outside, top only, bottom only, left only, right only, or no borders.

Activity 6.14

Changing Number Formats

Google Spreadsheets also enables you to change the way numbers are formatted within your spreadsheet. Table 6.2 details the different number formats available. You will format numbers in this activity.

Table 6.2—Google Spreadsheets Number Formats	
Format	**Example**
Normal	2000
Rounded	2,000
2 Decimals	2,000.12
Financial rounded	(2,000)

(*Continued*)

Table 6.2 (Continued)	
Format	**Example**
Financial	(2,000.12)
Scientific	2E+03
Currency rounded	$2,000
Currency	$2,000.12
Percent rounded	20%
Percent	20.12%
Date	12/12/2009
Time	2:15:00
Date time	12/12/2009 2:15:00
Plain text	2000

 Additional Formats

Google Spreadsheets offers additional currency, date, and time formats to the ones listed in Table 6.2. To select one of these optional formats, click the **More formats** button, then click **More currencies** to display additional currency options or **More formats** to display additional date and time options.

In this activity, you learn how to apply a number format to the data in a cell.

1. In your open spreadsheet, select the cell or cells that you wish to format, as shown in Figure 6.13.

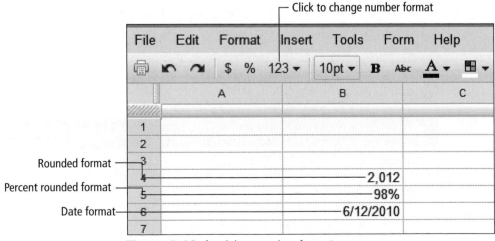

Figure 6.13 Applying number formats.

2. Click the **More formats** button, then click the desired format.

Objective 5

Work with Ranges and Sort Data

Range A group of cells that can be used as a reference in a calculation.

Sort To arrange data in a spreadsheet in a particular order.

A *range* is a group of cells that can be used as a reference in a calculation. *Sorting* is used to arrange your data in a particular order. Both are important skills to be familiar with so that you can analyze and present the spreadsheet data appropriately.

Activity 6.15

Selecting a Range

When you reference data within a spreadsheet, you can reference individual cells or a range of cells. When you reference more than one contiguous cell, that's called a range, like the one in Figure 6.14.

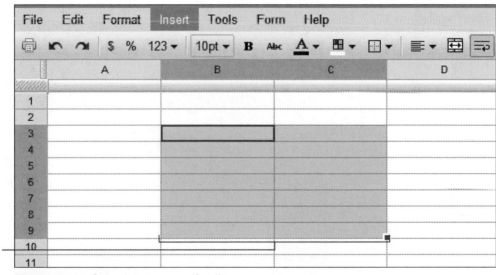

Range (B3:C9)

Figure 6.14 Selecting a range of cells.

 Ranges and Functions

You typically use ranges with specific functions, such as **SUM** (which totals a range of cells) or **AVERAGE** (which calculates the average value of a range of cells).

A range reference is expressed by listing the first and last cells in the range, separated by a colon (:). For example, the range that starts with cell A1 and ends with cell B9 is written like this:

A1:B9

You can select a range with either your mouse or your keyboard, as you'll learn in this activity.

1. To select a range of cells with your mouse, click on the first cell of the range, hold down the mouse button, drag the mouse until all the cells are selected, then release the mouse button.

2. To select a range of cells with your keyboard, position the insertion point in the first cell in the range, press and hold the **Shift** key, then use the arrow keys to expand the range in the appropriate direction(s).

3. You can also use a combination of mouse and keyboard to select a range. Use either the mouse or the keyboard to select the first cell in the range, then hold down the **Shift** key and click the mouse in the last cell in the range. All the cells in between the two cells will automatically be selected.

Activity 6.16

Sorting Data

Changing the sort order of a column of data can help to show trends, such as *ascending* (increasing) or *descending* (decreasing) numerical or alphabetical order. You might want to sort your data by date, for example, or by quantity or dollar value. However, you need to separate any header rows or columns—those rows or columns above or beside your data that define the data—from the data itself.

As you'll learn in this activity, sorting data in Google Spreadsheets is a two-step operation. You first have to freeze the header row(s) of your spreadsheet, then identify the column by which you want to sort. Google will then order all of the nonheader rows of your spreadsheet in whichever order (ascending or descending) you specified.

1. Click **Tools** on the menu bar, point to **Freeze rows**, then click how many rows you want to include as the spreadsheet's header, as shown in Figure 6.15.

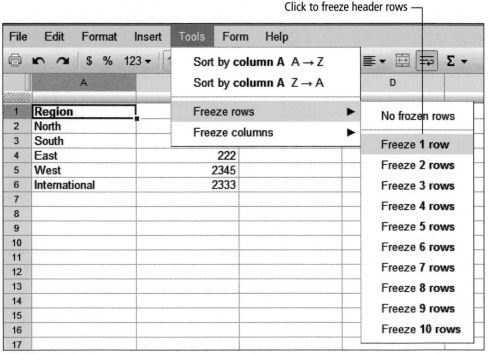

Figure 6.15 Freezing header rows in anticipation of sorting data.

2. Position the pointer over the header of the column you wish to sort by. The header bar now displays a Sort heading, as shown in Figure 6.16.

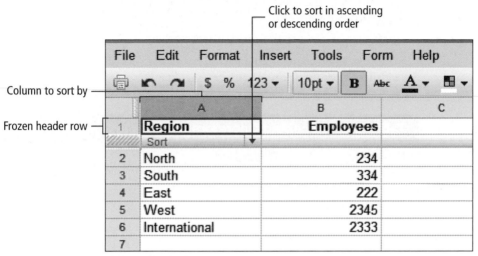

Click to sort in ascending or descending order

Column to sort by

Frozen header row

Figure 6.16 Sorting data in a spreadsheet.

3. Click the **Sort** arrow next to the heading, then click either **A -> Z** (to sort in ascending order) or **Z -> A** (to sort in descending order).

Note **Sorting Text and Numbers**

The A -> Z and Z -> A sorts can also be used to sort by number. An A -> Z sort will arrange numerical data from smallest to largest; a Z -> A sort will arrange numerical data from largest to smallest.

Objective 6

Work with Formulas, Functions, and Gadgets

After you've entered data into your spreadsheet, you can enter a formula to perform calculations with those numbers. You can use these calculations to analyze data with common formulas to calculate your data by addition, subtraction, multiplication, and division. You can also use advanced formulas called *functions*, which are preprogrammed into Google Spreadsheets.

Function An advanced formula, preprogrammed into Google Spreadsheets.

Activity 6.17

Creating a Formula

Formula Calculation instructions, consisting of numbers, mathematical operators, and the contents of a cell or cell range.

A *formula* can consist of numbers, mathematical operators, and the contents of a cell or cell range (referred to by the cell or range reference). A formula includes the following elements:

- An equal sign (=); this = sign is necessary at the start of each formula
- One or more specific numbers and/or one or more cell or range references
- A mathematical operator that tells you what to do with the values of the numbers, cells, or range

For example, to add the contents of cells A1 and A2, you enter the formula

=A1+A2

To multiply the contents of cell A1 by 10, you enter the formula

=A1*10

and so on.

Table 6.3 shows the mathematical operators you can use to create Google Spreadsheets formulas.

Table 6.3—Accepted Operators for Google Spreadsheets Formulas	
Operator	**Description**
+	Addition
-	Subtraction
*	Multiplication
/	Division
^	Exponentiation (to the power of)
=	Equal to
>	Greater than
> =	Greater than or equal to
<	Less than
< =	Less than or equal to
< >	Not equal to
%	Percentage

 Tip **Order of Operations**

Google Spreadsheets lets you create nesting equations by using appropriately placed parentheses. Following mathematical rules, calculations in parentheses and using exponents are done first, then the calculations work from left to right, multiplying and dividing first and then adding and subtracting. So, to divide the sum of cells A3 plus A4 by the sum of cells B5 plus B2, enter **=(A3+A4)/(B5+B2)**.

In this activity, you learn how to enter a formula into a cell.

1. Move the insertion point to the desired cell.

2. Type = to start the formula.

3. Enter the rest of the formula, as shown in Figure 6.17. Remember to refer to specific cells by their cell address, such as A1, B1, etc., or the range reference, such as A1:B3.

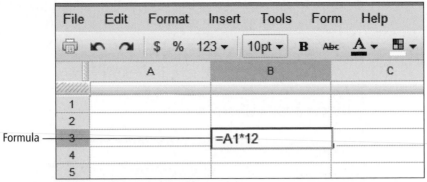

Formula ——

Figure 6.17 Entering a formula.

4. Press **Enter** to accept the formula or **Esc** to clear the formula.

5. When you're finished entering a formula, the results of the formula display and the formula used to create the calculation is not visible. For example, if you entered the formula =1+2, you now see the number 3 in the cell. To view the formula itself, select the cell and then look in the reference area in the lower right corner of the spreadsheet window, or press F2 or double-click the cell to edit the formula in the cell.

> **Tip** ⭐
>
> ### Entering Formulas with Your Mouse
>
> You can use your mouse to enter cell references into your formulas. Start the formula by using your keyboard to enter the = sign and, where appropriate, the operator(s). Instead of typing the cell or range address, use the mouse to select the cell or range of cells to be included. Press **Enter** on the keyboard to finish the formula.

Activity 6.18

Using Functions

You can use Google's built-in functions instead of writing complex formulas in your spreadsheets; you can also include functions as part of your formulas. Google Spreadsheet functions are not case sensitive.

Functions simplify the creation of complex formulas. For example, if you want to total the values of cells B4 through B7, you could enter the following formula:

=B4+B5+B6+B7

Or you could use the **SUM** function, which enables you to total (sum) a column or row of numbers without having to type every cell into the formula. In this instance, the formula to total cells B4 through B7 could be written using the **SUM** function, like this:

=SUM(B4:B7)

Google Spreadsheets uses most of the same functions as those used in Microsoft Excel. All Google functions use the following format:

=function(argument)

Replace **function** with the name of the function and replace **argument** with the appropriate cell or range reference(s). The argument always appears in parentheses.

In this activity, you learn how to enter a function into a spreadsheet.

1. Move the insertion point to the desired cell.

2. Click **Insert** on the menu bar, point to **Formula**, then click **More formulas** to open the Insert a formula dialog box shown in Figure 6.18.

Individual functions—
double-click to select

Click to close
dialog box

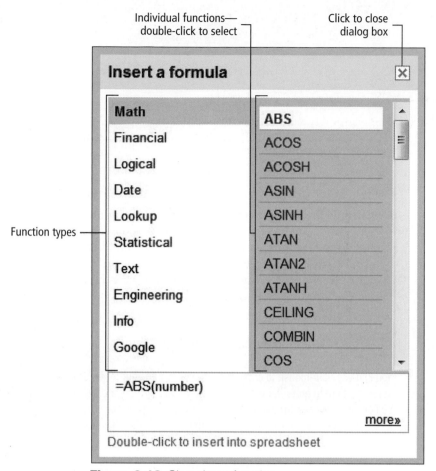

Function types

Figure 6.18 Choosing a function.

3. The functions in this dialog box are organized by type. Select the type of function from the left column, then double-click the function you want to use in the right column.

4. Click the **Close** button on the top right of the Insert a Function dialog box to close the dialog box.

5. The function you selected is now pasted into the selected cell, as shown in Figure 6.19. Move your insertion point into the argument part of the formula (typically between the parentheses) and enter the cell or range references to complete the formula.

6. Press **Enter** to accept the formula.

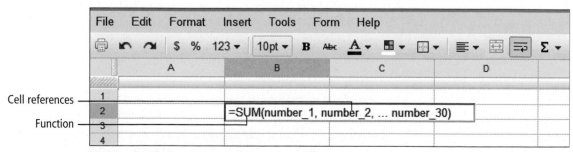

Cell references

Function

Figure 6.19 Function inserted into a cell formula.

Tip

Entering Functions Manually

You can also enter functions into a formula by typing the name of the function.

Activity 6.19

Adding Functionality with Gadgets

Even though Google Spreadsheets is a fairly robust application, it doesn't have all the functionality you find in Microsoft Excel. For example, Google Spreadsheets doesn't include macros or pivot tables, which are features of Microsoft Excel.

You can increase the functionality, however, by adding various gadgets to your spreadsheets. In Google Spreadsheets, a *gadget* adds a feature to a spreadsheet, such as a chart type not included with Google Spreadsheets. Gadgets are created by Google and by other users; you can also create your own gadgets, if you're so inclined. You can find gadgets that create more sophisticated chart types, add pivot table functionality, etc. It's a great way for Google to allow users to add features to their Google Spreadsheet without having to modify the application.

In this activity, you learn how to add a gadget to your spreadsheet.

1. Click **Insert** on the menu bar, then click **Gadget** to open the Add a Gadget dialog box, shown in Figure 6.20.

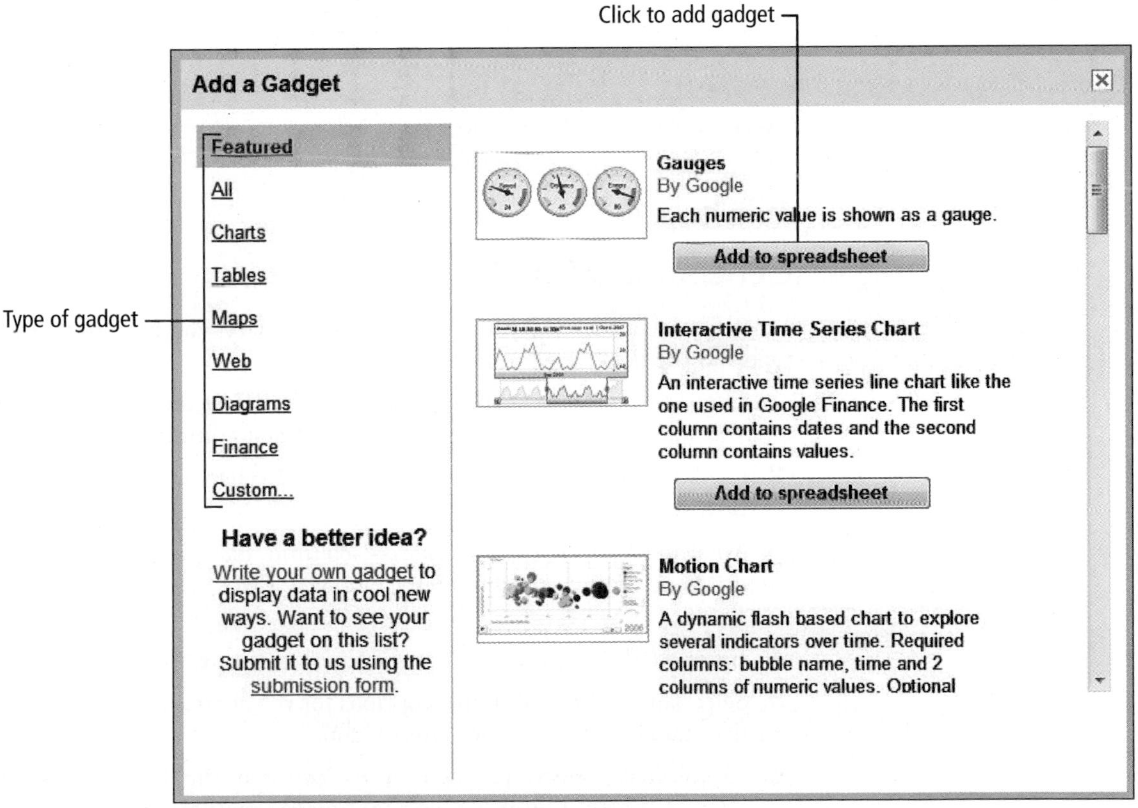

> *Gadget* A small plug-in application used to add a feature to a larger application.

Figure 6.20 Adding a gadget to a spreadsheet.

2. The gadgets in this dialog box are organized by type. Select the type of gadget you want, then click the **Add to spreadsheet** button to add the gadget.

3. What happens next depends on the specific gadget you selected. The gadget effect may be applied directly, or you may need to configure the gadget or select cells or other options.

Objective 7

Chart Your Data

Chart Data presented graphically, such as in a pie chart or bar chart.

Google Spreadsheets makes it possible for you to present your data graphically in a *chart*, such as a pie chart or bar chart. This enables you to view your data visually, as illustrated in Figure 6.21.

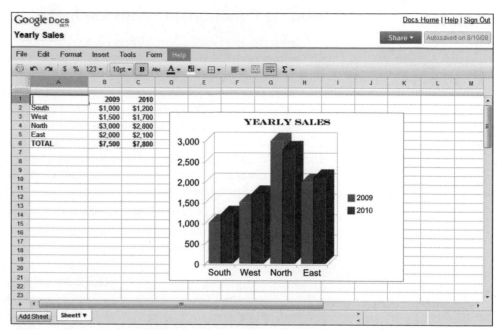

Figure 6.21 A chart added to a Google spreadsheet.

Activity 6.20

Generating a Chart

To create a chart, as you will do in this activity, you have to select both a chart type and the data range to include in the chart.

1. Use your mouse or keyboard arrow keys to select the cells that include the data you want to graph. Do not select any rows or columns that contain totals.

2. Click **Insert** on the menu bar, then click **Chart** to open the Create chart dialog box, shown in Figure 6.22.

3. You can create six types of charts—column, bar, pie, line, area, and scatter—and different subtypes within each chart type. Click the type of chart you want to create.

4. Enter a title for the chart into the Chart title box.

5. Select any additional desired options for the chart, such as a legend, and select a data range if you have not already done so.

6. As you make selections, the Preview section of the dialog box shows what your chart will look like. When you are finished making selections, click the **Save chart** button to add the chart to the current spreadsheet.

Select a position
for the chart legend

Enter chart title

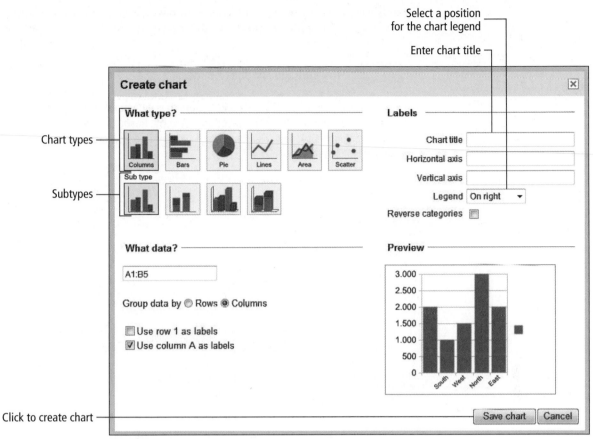

Chart types

Subtypes

Click to create chart

Figure 6.22 Creating a chart.

 Tip **Selecting a Chart Type**

Certain chart types are better for displaying certain types of data. For example, pie charts are best for displaying percentages, while line charts are better for showing trends over time.

Activity 6.21

Modifying a Chart

You can change a chart by selecting a different chart type, adding or removing a legend, or changing the data range, as you will do in this activity.

1. Double-click the chart in your spreadsheet.

2. The Edit chart dialog box opens, which contains the same options as the Create chart dialog box. Make the desired changes to your chart.

3. When you're done changing the formatting, click the **Save chart** button.

Objective 8

Print To create a hard copy printout of your document.

Collaborate To share a document with others online for viewing or editing as a group to create a finished document.

Print, Share, and Collaborate

Printing creates a hard copy printout of your spreadsheets in order to distribute them to others or to review them. You can also share spreadsheets online with anyone who has a Google account. When you share spreadsheets, you can *collaborate* or edit as a group to create a finished spreadsheet. There are two ways to share Google

Spreadsheets files online: you can choose to have others view a spreadsheet without the ability to edit or allow others to collaboratively edit the spreadsheet online.

Portable Document Format (PDF) Adobe Acrobat Reader program files that can be viewed, printed, and shared without having access to the program in which the file was created.

 Note **Printing via Acrobat Reader**

Adobe's *Portable Document Format (PDF)* file format is a common way to distribute noneditable documents electronically. You must have Adobe Acrobat Reader installed on your computer to print a Google spreadsheet. If you don't have Adobe Acrobat Reader installed on your computer, you can download it for free from www.adobe.com.

Activity 6.22

Printing a Spreadsheet

When you're finished creating your spreadsheet, you can print a hard copy. First you must save your spreadsheet into a PDF document; then you can print it, as you'll learn in this activity.

1. From the open spreadsheet, click **File** on the menu bar and then click **Print** to open the Print Settings dialog box, as shown in Figure 6.23.

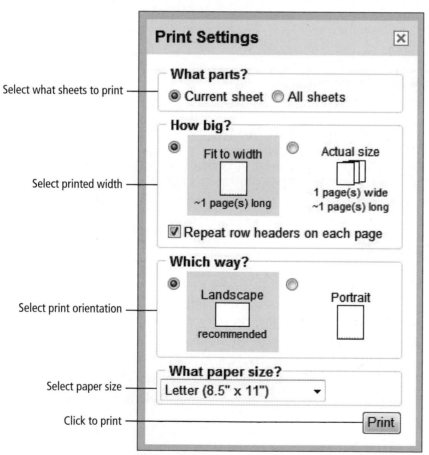

Figure 6.23 Selecting print settings.

2. In the **What parts?** section of the dialog box, select whether to print all sheets in the spreadsheet or just the current sheet.

3. In the **How big?** section of the dialog box, select whether to fit the spreadsheet to the width of the paper or print at actual size.

4. In the **Which way?** section of the dialog box, select either landscape or portrait format.

5. In the **What paper size?** section of the dialog box, select the correct paper size for your printer.

6. Click the **Print** button to export your spreadsheet into PDF format and open the File Download dialog box.

7. Click the **Open** button.

8. This opens your spreadsheet in the Adobe Acrobat Reader program, as shown in Figure 6.24. Click the **Print** button in Acrobat Reader to print the spreadsheet.

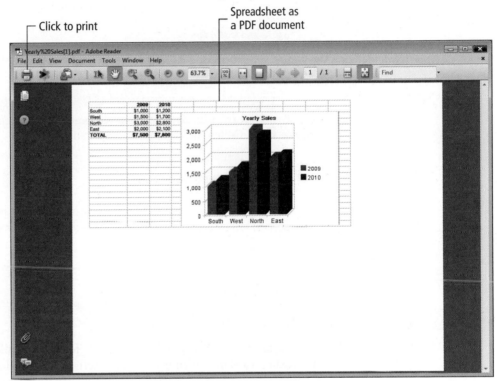

Figure 6.24 Printing from the Acrobat Reader program.

Activity 6.23

Inviting Other Users to View Your Spreadsheet

In this activity, you'll learn how to share a view-only (read-only) spreadsheet.

1. From your open spreadsheet, click the **Share** button and click **Invite people**.

2. When the Share with others dialog box appears, as shown in Figure 6.25, check the **to view** option button.

3. Enter the email addresses of the people with whom you want to share this spreadsheet into the Invite box. Separate multiple addresses with commas.

4. Enter a subject for your invitation into the Subject box.

5. Enter the message to accompany your invitation into the Message box.

6. Click the **Send** button. Your recipients now receive an email invitation that contains a link to the spreadsheet; clicking this link opens the spreadsheet in a new browser window.

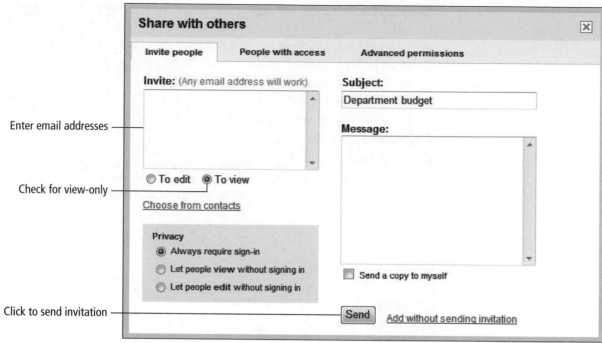

Enter email addresses

Check for view-only

Click to send invitation

Figure 6.25 Getting ready to share a spreadsheet.

 Note **Viewers Can Save**

Anyone invited as a viewer can navigate throughout the entire spreadsheet and also save that spreadsheet to their personal Google Docs online storage area or as a file on their own computer.

Activity 6.24

Inviting Other Users to Collaborate

Google Spreadsheets makes it possible for you to collaborate on spreadsheets with other users in real time over the Internet. Your collaborators need to have Google accounts and be invited by you to share the spreadsheet. In this activity, you learn how to invite others to collaborate on an online spreadsheet.

1. From your open spreadsheet, click the **Share** button and click **Invite people**.

2. When the Share with others dialog box appears, check the **to edit** option button.

3. Enter the email addresses of the people with whom you want to share this spreadsheet into the Invite box. Separate multiple addresses with commas.

4. Enter a subject for your invitation into the Subject box.

5. Enter the message to accompany your invitation into the Message box.

6. Click the **Send** button. Your recipients now receive an email invitation that contains a link to the spreadsheet; clicking this link opens the spreadsheet in a new browser window.

 Note **Collaborators Can Edit**

Anyone invited as a collaborator can edit the spreadsheet in their web browser. Google Spreadsheets enables multiple users to edit the spreadsheet at the same time, so you can have an entire group working together in real time. You can also get alerts when a document you have shared is changed by another user.

Summary

In this chapter, you learned how to create and save new spreadsheets, as well as import and export spreadsheets from and to Microsoft Excel. The chapter included information on how to enter and edit data, insert and delete rows and columns, and work with multiple sheets. You practiced formatting text, cells, and numbers, selecting and referencing ranges, and sorting spreadsheet data. You learned how to work with formulas, functions, and gadgets, as well as how to present your data visually by creating charts. Finally, you learned how to print your spreadsheets and share them with others.

Key Terms

Assessments

Multiple Choice

1. Which of the following Microsoft Excel features can be found in Google Spreadsheets?
    (a) macros
    (b) charts
    (c) pivot tables
    (d) all of the above

2. Google Spreadsheets enables you to export your spreadsheets into which of the following formats?
    (a) Microsoft Excel (.xls)
    (b) HTML (.htm or .html)
    (c) Adobe Acrobat (.pdf)
    (d) all of the above

3. Sheets within a spreadsheet are automatically named as follows: _____.
    (a) Sheet1, Sheet2, Sheet3
    (b) SheetA, SheetB, SheetC
    (c) NewSheet1, NewSheet2, NewSheet3
    (d) FirstSheet, SecondSheet, ThirdSheet

4. To total a column of numbers, use the _____ function.
    (a) TOTAL
    (b) COUNT
    (c) SUM
    (d) EQUALS

5. The formula to multiply the numbers three and five is _____.
    (a) 3×5
    (b) $=3 \times 5$
    (c) =(3 times 5)
    (d) =3*5

6. The number two thousand formatted in currency rounded format looks like this: _____.
    (a) 2,000
    (b) 2000
    (c) $2,000
    (d) $2,000.00

7. Which of the following is *not* a valid range?
    (a) A1:A2
    (b) A1:D1
    (c) A1:D4
    (d) All of the above are valid ranges.

8. Which of the following statements is true?
   (a) Google Spreadsheets lets multiple users collaborate online.
   (b) Google Spreadsheets includes all the functionality of Microsoft Excel.
   (c) Google Spreadsheets lets you format your data with more than 20 different fonts.
   (d) Google Spreadsheets can import and export Microsoft Excel, Lotus 1-2-3, and Quattro Pro spreadsheet files.

9. Which of the following is *not* a supported chart type?
   (a) pie
   (b) bubble
   (c) line
   (d) area

10. To sort a range of data, you must first: _____.
    (a) save the spreadsheet
    (b) freeze the header row(s)
    (c) select the column to sort by
    (d) all of the above

Fill in the Blank

Write the correct word in the space provided.

1. A reference to two or more contiguous cells is called a _____.
2. You use _____ to perform mathematic calculations in Google Spreadsheets.
3. A _____ is a complex formula built into Google Spreadsheets.
4. The intersection of a row and column is called a _____.
5. A range that starts at cell A1 and extends to cell D12 is written as _____.
6. A _____ is a feature that adds more functionality to Google Spreadsheets.
7. To divide the contents of cell B2 by the contents of cell C3, write the following formula: _____.
8. A _____ is someone who has permission to edit your spreadsheet online.
9. Google Spreadsheets lets you add multiple _____ to any single spreadsheet file.
10. When you print a spreadsheet, the spreadsheet is first saved in a _____-format file.

Skills Review

1. Create a new spreadsheet and name it Sales Budget.
2. Create five columns. The first column heading should be blank and the following columns should have headings for North, South, East, and West.
3. In column A, beneath the heading row, create four additional rows with headings for 2006, 2007, 2008, and 2009.
4. Enter data into your spreadsheet as shown in Table 6.4.

Table 6.4—Data for Skills Review Exercise 4

	North	South	East	West
2006	$1,000	$1,000	$500	$2,000
2007	$2,000	$1,500	$750	$2,250
2008	$3,000	$2,000	$1,000	$2,100
2009	$4,000	$3,000	$900	$1,900

5. Create a sixth column, to the right of the West column, with the heading Yearly Total. Manually enter formulas to total the data from each of the four years (2006, 2007, 2008, and 2009).

6. In the row below the 2009 data, create a new row with the heading Region Total. Use the SUM function to total the data in each column.

7. Format with a light blue background the cells that hold the totals. Be sure all data cells are formatted as Currency Rounded.

8. Create a bar chart from your data. Format the chart's legend so that it appears beneath the chart.

9. Save and then print your spreadsheet.

10. Share your spreadsheet with three trusted collaborators.

CHAPTER 7

Using Google Presentations

Objectives

By the end of this chapter you will be able to:

1. Create and Save New Presentations

2. Import and Export PowerPoint Presentations

3. Manage the Slides in Your Presentation

4. Change the Look and Feel of Your Presentation

5. Add and Format Text

6. Add Images, Charts, and Animations

7. Print and Collaborate

8. Deliver a Presentation

Google Presentations is the presentation application in the Google Docs suite. As the name implies, *Google Presentations* is an application similar to Microsoft PowerPoint that enables you to create and give slideshow-like *presentations*. Due to its web-based nature, you can also use Google Presentations to give PowerPoint presentations when you're away from the office. You don't have to take any files with you; all you need is a computer with an Internet connection.

Google Presentations The presentation application within the Google Docs suite.

Presentation Data presented in a slideshow format.

Objective 1

Create and Save New Presentations

To use any Google Docs application, you need a Google account. When you log on to your Google account, you see the main Google Docs page shown in Figure 7.1. This is the homepage for all three Google Docs applications, including Google Presentations. All of your previously created presentations are listed on this page. This is also where you create new presentations.

Presentation file

Click to create a new document

Folders pane

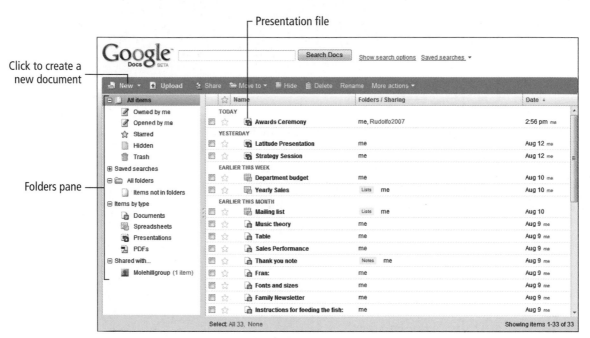

Figure 7.1 The main page for all Google Docs applications.

At the top of the window is a toolbar that contains buttons you can use to manage files or create new ones. The left pane on this page is where you organize your documents. You can see the results of saved searches, store files in folders, view documents by type (word processing documents, spreadsheets, presentations, or PDFs), and display documents shared with specific people.

 New Folders

To create a new folder, click the **New** button, then click **Folder**. Click the words New Folder in the main editing window, then type the name of the new folder. To move a document to a folder, click the checkbox next to the document, click the **Move to** button, click the folder you want to add it to, then click the **Move to folder** button.

The documents stored within the selected folder or filter are displayed in the main part of the window. Presentation files are identified by a presentation icon.

Activity 7.1

Creating a New Presentation

In this activity, you learn how to create a new, blank presentation.

1. Go to the main Google Docs page (docs.google.com). Log into your account if necessary.

2. Click the **New** button, then click **Presentation**. The new presentation opens in its own window on your desktop.

Activity 7.2

Creating a New Presentation from a Template

Alternately, you can create a new presentation based on a predesigned template. A *template* is a combination of text styles, document formatting, and graphics to which you can add your own text and graphics. Templates often contain *placeholder* text, which indicates the type of information you want to include and gives you a sample slide layout. In this activity, you learn how to create a new presentation based on a predesigned template.

1. From the main Google Docs page, click the **New** button, then click **From template**.

2. Google opens a new Templates Gallery window. You can search or browse the gallery for document, spreadsheet, and presentation templates. To view presentation templates, click the Presentations tab, as shown in Figure 7.2.

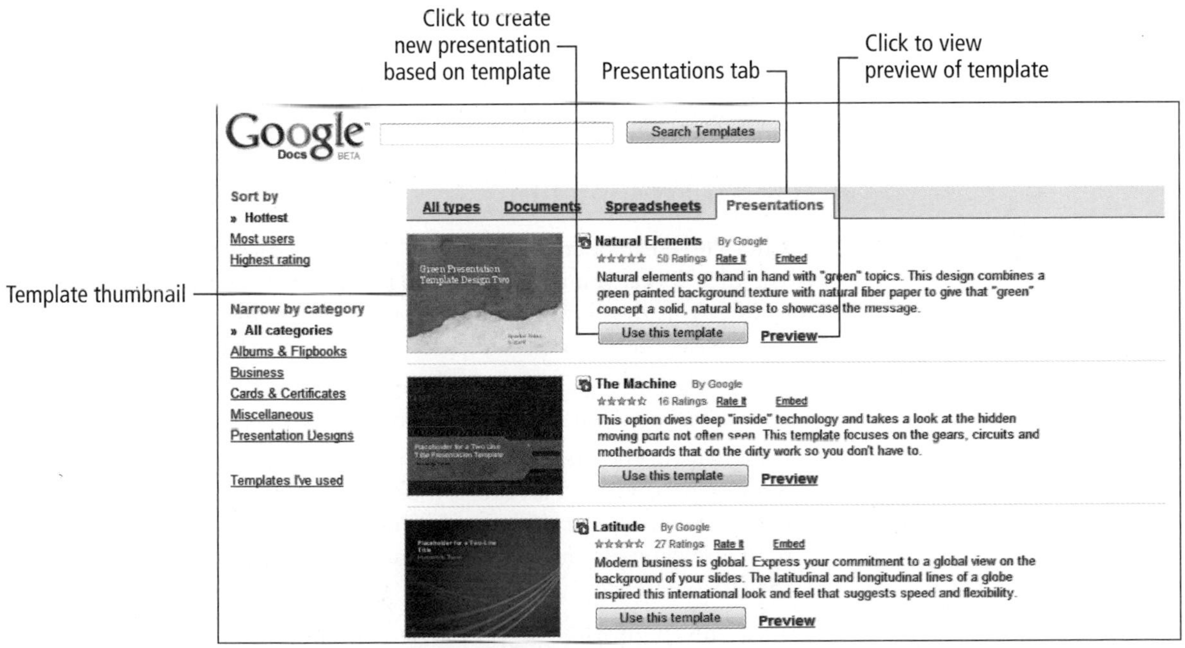

Template A pre-designed selection of text, formatting, and graphics, used to create new document, spreadsheet, or presentation.

Placeholder Text in a template that indicates the type of information to include and a sample page layout.

Figure 7.2 Browsing presentation templates.

3. When you find the template you want to use, click the **Use this template** button to open a new browser window that contains a blank presentation based on the template, as shown in Figure 7.3.

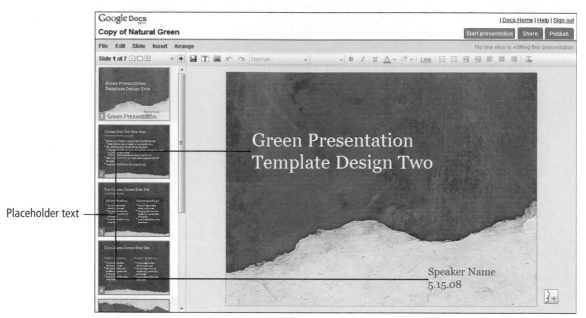

Figure 7.3 Browsing presentation templates.

4. Fill in the necessary blanks in the template or replace any placeholder text with your own text.

Activity 7.3

Saving a Presentation

After you create a new presentation from a predesigned template, you need to save the file. When you first save a file, you must do so manually and give the file a name. After this first save, Google automatically resaves the file every time you make a change to the presentation. In essence, this means that you only have to save the presentation once; Google saves all further changes automatically.

In this activity, you learn how to save a newly created presentation file.

1. From within the presentation window, click **File** on the menu bar, then click **Save** or press **Ctrl+S** on the keyboard. Google now saves the presentation and names it according to the first line of text in the editing window, or using the template name if you used a template. For example, if you had entered the text "Sales Conference," your file would automatically be named **Sales Conference**.

2. To rename a presentation, open it, click **File** on the menu bar, then click **Rename**. When the pop-up window opens, as shown in Figure 7.4, type the new presentation name, then click **OK**.

Figure 7.4 Renaming a Google Presentations file.

 Note **Unblocking Pop-Up windows**

Depending on your security settings, you may not be able to see pop-up windows, If an alert appears at the top of your browser window, click it, then instruct the browser to temporarily accept pop-ups. Before you modify your security settings, you should verify that the site is valid, and if you are in a lab setting, check with your technical support person.

Activity 7.4

Opening an Existing Presentation

Once you've created and saved a presentation, you can reopen it for editing at any time. In this activity, you learn how to open an existing presentation.

1. From the main Google Docs page, click the **Presentations** link in the left pane under Items by type to view all of your presentation files. As you can see in Figure 7.5, presentation documents are identified by a slide icon.

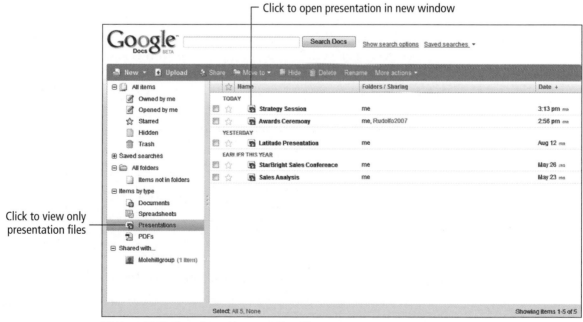

Figure 7.5 Opening a presentation file.

2. Click the presentation's name to open the file in a new browser window.

Tip **Working Offline**

The presentation file you save isn't stored on your computer's hard disk. Instead, the file is stored by default on Google's servers, which means you must be connected to the Internet to access it. However, if you're not connected to the Internet, Google now makes it possible for you to edit your presentations *offline*. To do this, you have to install the Google Docs Offline application. Click the **Offline** link at the top of the Google Docs homepage, and then click the **Get Google Gears Now** button. Follow the simple onscreen instructions to download and install the program. Once Google Gears has been installed, you can open the offline version of Google Docs by entering docs.google.com into your browser or by clicking the **Google Docs** shortcut on your desktop. If you're not connected to the Internet, you'll open the offline version of Google Docs; if you are connected to the Internet, you'll open the normal online version. Whenever you're online, Google Docs automatically synchronizes the files stored on your computer with those stored online so that both locations contain the document version that was most recently edited. You can also work offline when using Google's Chrome web browser, which has Google Gears built in.

Offline When you are not connected to the internet.

Objective 2

Import and Export PowerPoint Presentations

Many organizations use Microsoft PowerPoint to create their presentations. If you or your colleagues use PowerPoint, you can import your PowerPoint presentations into Google Presentations for online editing and collaboration. You can also save your Google Presentations files as Microsoft PowerPoint (.ppt) files on your hard disk.

Activity 7.5

Importing a PowerPoint Presentation

Google enables you to upload your Microsoft PowerPoint presentations so they can be stored on the web and edited online with Google Presentations. In this activity, you learn how to import a PowerPoint file into Google Presentations.

Tip **Presentations on the Road**

Even if you use PowerPoint to create and edit your presentations, you can use Google Presentations to give those presentations when you're away from your desk or even without your computer. By importing your PowerPoint presentation into Google Presentations, you can access that presentation from any computer connected to the Internet. There's no longer any need to take large PowerPoint files (or even your own notebook PC) with you when you travel!

1. From the Google Docs main page, click the **Upload** button.
2. When the Upload a File page appears, as shown in Figure 7.6, click the **Browse** button.

Click to browse for files

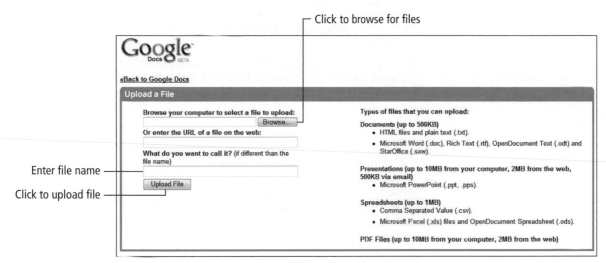

Enter file name

Click to upload file

Figure 7.6 Importing a PowerPoint file into Google Presentations.

3. When the Choose file dialog box appears, navigate to and select the file you want to upload, then click the **Open** button.

4. When the Upload a File dialog box reappears, enter a name for the uploaded file into the **What do you want to call it?** box.

5. Click the **Upload File** button. The file now opens in Google Presentations for editing or presenting.

 File Upload Limits

You can import .ppt- and .pps-format PowerPoint files up to 10MB in size. However, when this book was printed, Google did not support files created with the latest version of Microsoft PowerPoint, PowerPoint 2007 (.pptx).

 Comparing Google Presentations and Microsoft PowerPoint

At present, Google Presentations doesn't offer all the functionality you get from Microsoft PowerPoint. For example, Google Presentations doesn't offer slide transitions and animations or the ability to create charts and tables. Google continues to add functionality over time, so these and other features may be available in the future.

Activity 7.6

Exporting a Google Presentation to PowerPoint Format

By default, all the presentations you work with in Google Presentations are stored on Google's servers. You can, however, download files from Google to your computer's hard drive to work with in PowerPoint. In this activity, you learn how to export a Google presentation to a PowerPoint file.

Other Ways to Export

Google also makes it possible for you to export your presentation as an Adobe Acrobat Portable Document Format file (.pdf) or plain text (.txt) file. Note that not all features of the presentation translate equally well in all formats.

1. From within the current presentation window, click on the menu bar, point to Download presentation as, then click **PPT**, as shown in Figure 7.7.

Click to export file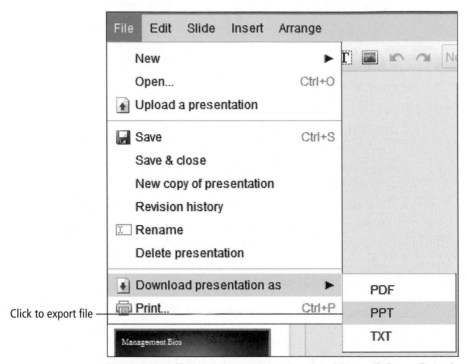

Figure 7.7 Exporting a presentation into Microsoft PowerPoint format.

2. When the File Download dialog box appears, click the **Save** button.

3. When the Save As dialog box appears, select a location for the downloaded file, rename it if you like, and then click the **Save** button. The Google Presentations file is now saved in .ppt format on your hard disk. You can open this saved file with Microsoft PowerPoint and work on it as you would with any PowerPoint presentation.

 Alert ### Don't Get Out of Sync

Unlike Google Docs files, which will automatically synchronize online and offline versions if you've installed the Google Docs Offline application, whatever changes you make to a file from within Microsoft PowerPoint affect only the downloaded file, not the copy of the presentation that still resides on the Google Docs site. To reimport the PowerPoint file to Google Presentations, go to the main Google Docs page and use the Upload function. When you reimport a file, Google Docs saves it as a new file rather than saving it over the previous version.

Objective 3

Manage the Slides in Your Presentation

Slide A slide in a presentation contains text, images, videos, or any combination of the above.

A presentation is composed of a number of different slides. Each *slide* can hold text, images, videos, or any combination of these. A slide can be based on one of five predesigned *layouts* which determine the placement of slide objects:

Layout The placement of objects in a document or on a slide.

- **Title:** the presentation title and subtitle only (ideal for the lead slide in a presentation or to signal new sections in the presentation)

- **Text:** the slide title and a block of text below

- **Two columns:** the slide title and two columns of text

- **Caption:** a blank main area (ideal for inserting graphics or videos) and a text caption at the bottom

- **Blank:** a completely blank slide-you can insert anything on this type of slide

As you can see in Figure 7.8, the slides in a presentation are displayed as thumbnails in the slide sorter pane. The currently selected slide is shown in the main window and can be edited from there. To edit a different slide, just click on it in the slide sorter pane.

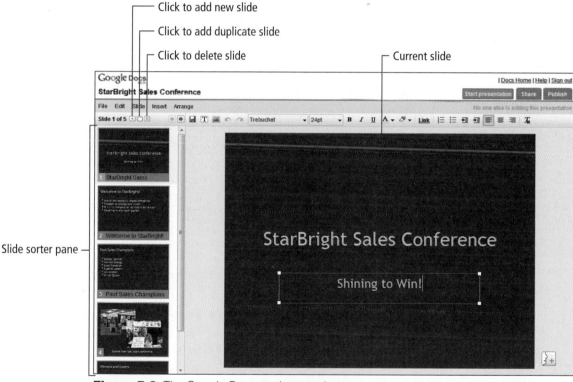

Figure 7.8 The Google Presentations workspace.

Activity 7.7

Adding a New Slide

Slide sorter A pane on the left pane of the Google Presentations window that you can use to select, move, or delete slides.

Every new presentation starts with a single title slide. In this activity, you learn how to add new slides to your presentation. To navigate among multiple slides in a presentation, you can use the *slide sorter*, which is the left pane of the Presentations window and contains a thumbnail of each slide. In the slide sorter, you can select, move, or delete slides.

1. From your open presentation, click the slide in the slide sorter that is the one just prior to where you want the new slide to appear.

2. Click the **Insert a new slide into the presentation** button (the + above the slide sorter).

3. When the Choose slide layout dialog box appears, as shown in Figure 7.9, select the layout for the new slide. The new slide is now added to the slide sorter pane and displayed in the main window.

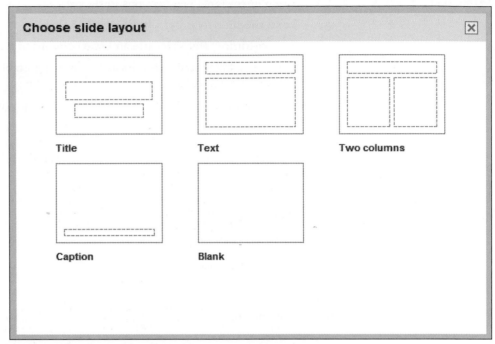

Figure 7.9 Choosing a layout for a new slide.

Activity 7.8

Duplicating an Existing Slide

If you've created a slide with content or formatting that you'd like to repeat elsewhere in your presentation, you can duplicate that slide and then edit the duplicate. In this activity, you learn how to create a duplicate slide.

1. In the slide sorter, select the slide you want to duplicate.

2. Click the **Create a duplicate copy of the current slide** button (just to the right of the + button above the slide sorter). A duplicate of the selected slide is inserted after the selected slide in the slide sorter.

Activity 7.9

Deleting a Slide

In this activity, you learn how to delete a slide from a presentation.

1. In the slide sorter, select the slide you want to delete.

2. Click the **Delete the current slide** button (the X above the slide sorter).

Tip **Deletions Are Permanent**

Before you delete a slide, make sure that you do not need any of the information on it, as you cannot undo a slide deletion.

Activity 7.10

Rearranging Slides

You may need to change the order of slides in a presentation as it develops or customize your presentation for a different audience. In this activity, you learn how to rearrange the order of your slides.

1. In the slide sorter, select the slide you want to move.

2. Use your mouse to click and drag the slide up or down to a new position within the slide sorter.

Tip **Right-Clicking in the Slide Sorter**

To open a shortcut menu that enables you to move slides up and down, delete slides, and make other changes, right-click a slide in the slide sorter, then click a command on the shortcut menu.

Objective 4

Change the Look and Feel of Your Presentation

Your audience will likely not be impressed by a presentation of black text on a plain white background, like the one in Figure 7.10. You gain more attention by using attractive background colors and graphics, as illustrated in Figure 7.11.

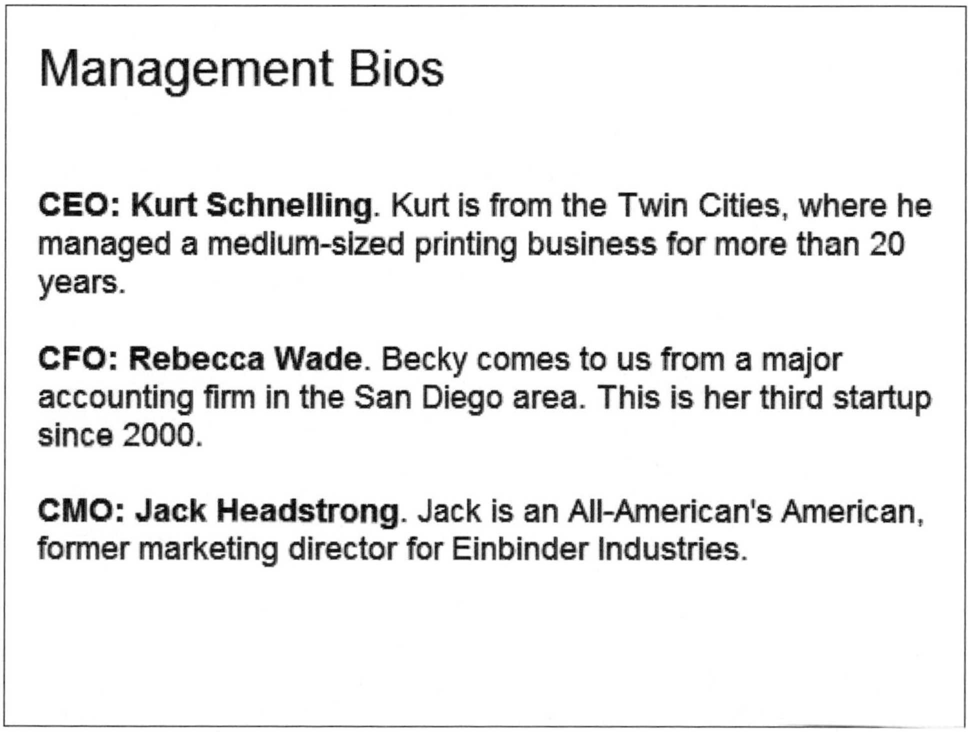

Management Bios

CEO: Kurt Schnelling. Kurt is from the Twin Cities, where he managed a medium-sized printing business for more than 20 years.

CFO: Rebecca Wade. Becky comes to us from a major accounting firm in the San Diego area. This is her third startup since 2000.

CMO: Jack Headstrong. Jack is an All-American's American, former marketing director for Einbinder Industries.

Figure 7.10 A generic-looking slide with black text on a plain white background.

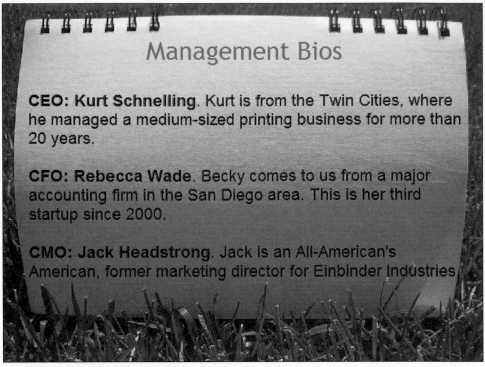

Figure 7.11 A more visually interesting slide created with a predesigned theme.

Google Presentations enables you to choose from several predesigned themes for your presentations. You can also design your own themes by using a custom background color or graphic on your slides.

Activity 7.11

Choosing a New Theme

The easiest way to change the look and feel of your presentation is to choose a new theme. A *theme* is a predesigned collection of background images, fonts, and color schemes applied to each slide in your presentation. In this activity, you learn how to choose a new theme.

Theme A predesigned collection of background images, color scheme, and fonts that are applied to every slide in your presentation.

1. From your open presentation, click **Edit** on the menu bar, then click **Change theme**.

2. When the Choose theme dialog box appears, as shown in Figure 7.12, click the theme you want to use. This theme is now applied to all the slides in your presentation.

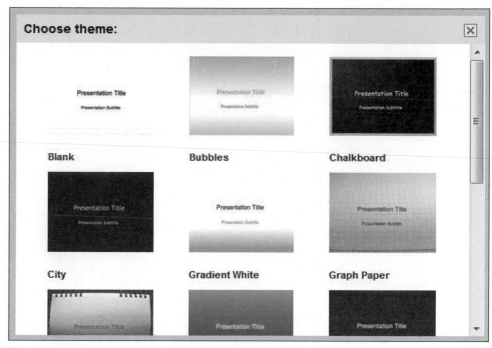

Figure 7.12 Choosing a new theme.

Activity 7.12

Adding Custom Background Colors and Graphics

If you don't like the look of any of the Google Presentations predesigned themes, you can create your own theme by applying a custom background color or graphic to all the slides in your presentation. In this activity, you learn how to create your own themes.

1. Right-click anywhere on the current slide that does not contain a slide object, then click **Change background** from the shortcut menu.

2. When the Change background dialog box appears, as shown in Figure 7.13, click the **Change background** button to select a new background color.

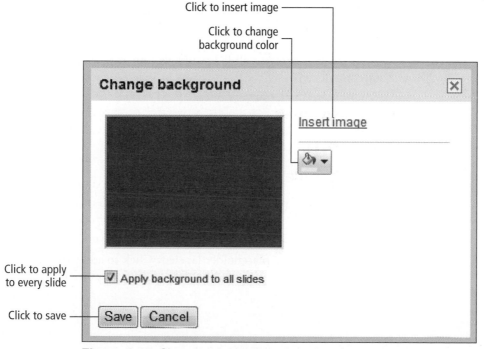

Figure 7.13 Changing the background color of your slides.

3. To insert an image as the background of your slides, click the **Insert image** link in the Change background dialog box to expand the dialog box, as shown in Figure 7.14. Click the **Browse** button to find and select the graphics file you want to use, then click **Open**.

Click to browse for image files

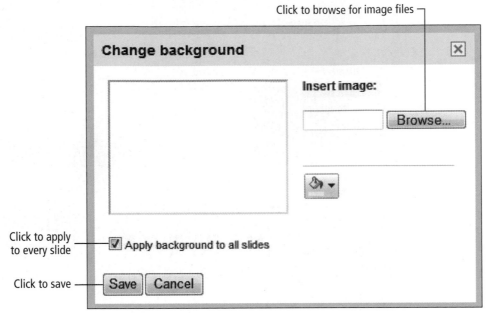

Click to apply to every slide

Click to save

Figure 7.14 Adding a background image to your slides.

4. Click the **Apply background to all slides** option.

5. Click the **Save** button and the new background color or image is applied to all the slides in your presentation.

Objective 5

Add and Format Text

Once you've chosen a slide layout, it's time to start adding content to that slide. Slide content can be in the form of text or images. Each block of text is a separate text object; select an object to add, edit, or format the text within.

Activity 7.13

Entering Slide Title

Most slides in your presentation will have a title that appears at the top of the slide. In this activity, you learn how to add slide titles.

1. Create a new slide with a text or two column layout.

2. The title area is a placeholder labeled "Click to add title," as shown in Figure 7.15. Click this placeholder and type a new title.

Click to enter
your own title

Figure 7.15 Adding title text to a slide.

Activity 7.14

Entering Text in a Text Block

When you need to present a statement or similar detailed information, use a block of text, like the one shown in Figure 7.16. This is like putting a paragraph on a slide, which is what you learn how to do in this activity.

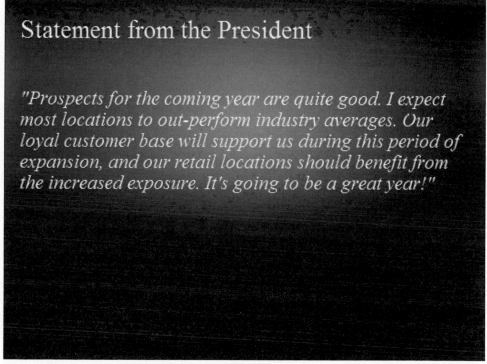

Figure 7.16 A block of text added to a slide.

1. Create a new slide with a text or two-column layout.

2. The text area is a placeholder labeled "Click to add content." Click this place-holder and type your new text.

Activity 7.15

Adding Bulleted or Numbered Lists

A solid block of text isn't the best way to present all information. When you need to emphasize individual points, use a bulleted list like the one shown in Figure 7.17; when you're presenting step-by-step instructions, use a numbered list. In this activity, you learn how to create both types of lists on a slide.

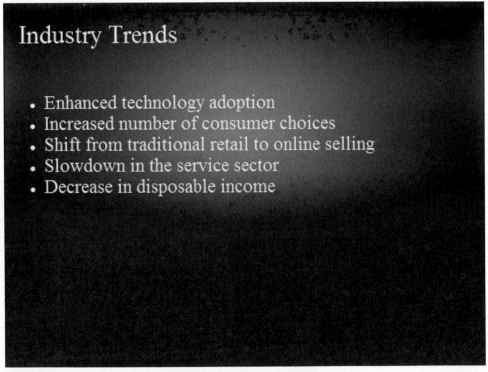

Figure 7.17 A slide with a bulleted list.

1. Create a new slide with a text or two-column layout.

2. The text area is an object labeled "Click to add content"; click this object.

3. Click either the **Bullet list** or **Numbered list** button.

4. Type the first list item.

5. When you're done typing this item, press the **Enter** key on your keyboard. This creates a second bulleted or numbered item. Type the text for this next list item.

6. Repeat step 5 to add additional items to the list.

Activity 7.16

Editing Text

If you make a mistake while entering text on a slide, it's easy to make a correction. In this activity, you learn how to edit a slide's text.

1. Select the text object on the slide that contains the text you want to edit.

2. Position the insertion point at the point where you want to begin the edit.

3. To insert text at the insertion point, begin typing.

4. To delete text to the left of the insertion point, press the **Backspace** key on your keyboard; to delete text to the right of the insertion point, press the **Delete** key.

 Add a Link

To add a web page link to text on a slide, select the text from which you want to link, then click the **Link** button. When the Edit Link dialog box appears, enter the web address (URL) for the web page you are linking to, then click **OK**.

Activity 7.17

Formatting Your Text

Google Presentations also makes it possible for you to format text on a slide the way you'd format text in a word processing document. In this activity, you learn how to use the formatting controls on the application's toolbar, as shown in Figure 7.18.

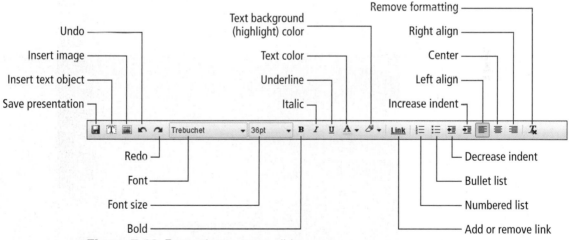

Figure 7.18 Formatting text on a slide.

1. Select the text object on the slide that contains the text you want to edit.

2. Within the text object, select the text you want to format. You can select an entire text block, one or more lines, or individual characters or words.

3. To change the font of the selected text, click the **Font** button, then click a new font from the list.

4. To change the size of the selected text, click the **Font size** button, then click a new size from the list.

5. To change the color of selected text, click the **Text color** button, then click a new color from the gallery.

6. To apply bold to selected text, click the **Bold** button or press **Ctrl+B**.

7. To italicize selected text, click the **Italic** button or press **Ctrl+I**.

8. To underline selected text, click the **Underline** button or press **Ctrl+U**.

9. To change the alignment of the selected text, click the **Left**, **Center**, or **Right** button.

 Tip   **Undo Formatting**

To undo the last change, click the **Undo** button. To remove formatting from a selection, click the **Remove formatting** button.

Objective 6

Add Images, Charts, and Animations

Text isn't the only kind of object you can add to a slide. You can also add pictures and other images, including charts created in Google Spreadsheets. You can also animate a slide by choosing an order for the entrance of each object on a slide when you're making a presentation.

Activity 7.18

Adding an Image

Images can be added to slides for visual interest or to show a graphic to support the slide text, as shown in Figure 7.19. In this activity, you learn how to insert an image file onto a slide.

Figure 7.19 A slide with an image added.

Tip

Best Layout for Images

Images look best on slides with a Blank or Caption layout, although you can insert images onto any type of slide.

1. Select the slide where you want the image to appear.

2. Click the **Insert an Image into the current slide** button.

3. When the Insert Image dialog box appears, as shown in Figure 7.20, click the **Browse** button, then click the image file you want to include.

Click to browse for image file ⌐

Figure 7.20 Inserting an image onto a slide.

4. Click **OK** to insert the image onto your slide as a new object.

5. You can now use your mouse to drag the image object to a new location on the slide or click and drag the image's corner handles to resize the image.

 Tip

Add a Shape

You can also add shapes to a slide, such as boxes, arrows, callouts, and more. Position the insertion point where you want the object to appear, click **Insert** on the menu bar, point to **Shape**, then click the desired shape from the gallery.

Activity 7.19

Adding a Chart

While Google Presentations does not currently include its own chart editor, you can add a chart created in another program to a Google Presentations slide, as shown in Figure 7.21. In this activity, you will create a chart in Google Spreadsheets, then copy it to a Google Presentations slide as an image object.

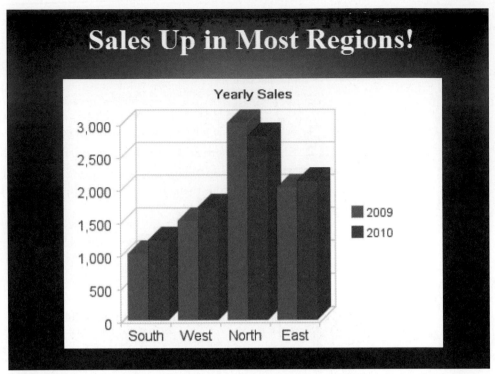

Figure 7.21 A Google Spreadsheets chart inserted into a Google Presentations slide.

 Alert **Not Editable**

Charts imported into Google Presentations are inserted as image objects, and the data in the chart cannot be edited. Charts can only be repositioned and resized.

1. From within Google Spreadsheets, create the chart you want to add or open a spreadsheet that contains a previously created chart.

2. Right-click the chart, then click **Save image**.

3. When the File Download dialog box appears, click the **Save** button.

4. When the Save As dialog box appears, select a filename and location for this file.

5. Switch to Google Presentations and open the slide for the chart.

6. Click the **Insert an image into the current slide** button.

7. When the Insert Image dialog box appears, click the **Browse** button and then navigate to and select the image file for the chart you just created, then click **Open**.

8. Click **OK** to insert the image of the chart onto your slide as a new object.

9. You can now use your mouse to drag the chart to a new location on the slide or click and drag the image's corner handles to resize the chart.

Activity 7.20

Animating Elements on a Slide

Incremental reveal A method of animating the order and method that individual elements (such as text objects, list items, or images) appear on a slide.

While Google Presentations does not currently offer slide-to-slide transitions, you can animate the order and method that individual elements—such as text objects, list items, or images—appear on a slide, using a feature called *incremental reveal*.

When you choose to incrementally reveal an object, it doesn't appear when you first display the slide during a presentation. To reveal an object, you click the **next slide** arrow on the screen, as if you were going to a new slide; this displays the first object chosen to reveal. If more than one object on a slide is formatted for incremental reveal, each successive object is displayed each time you click the **next slide** arrow on the screen.

Incremental reveal is a great way to present a bulleted or numbered list during a presentation. When you apply incremental reveal to an object that contains a list, you can present each list item individually, pause for questions or explanations, then press the **next slide** arrow on the screen to reveal the next list item.

In this activity, you learn how to incrementally reveal the elements on a slide.

1. On the slide where you want to apply incremental reveal, right-click the object you want to appear first, then click **Incremental reveal** from the shortcut menu. A timer icon now appears next to that object on your slide.

2. Select the object you want to appear next, then click **Incremental reveal** from the shortcut menu. A timer button with the number 2 now appears next to that object on your slide, as shown in Figure 7.22.

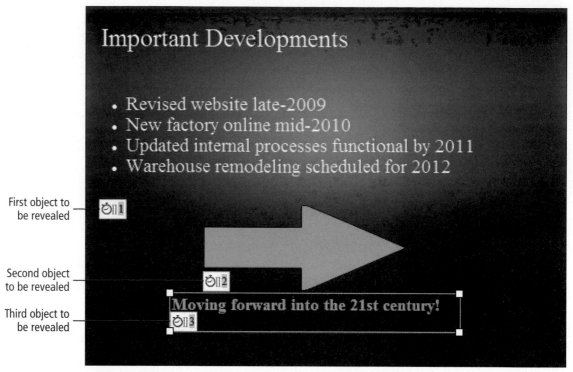

First object to be revealed

Second object to be revealed

Third object to be revealed

Figure 7.22 Objects selected to be incrementally revealed.

3. Repeat step 2 for any other object you want to be revealed on the slide.

4. When you give the presentation, click the **next slide** arrow on the screen to display each selected item in order.

 Tip ⭐ **Change the Order**

To change the order in which objects are revealed, right-click the incremental reveal icon for any object and check a different number.

Objective 7
Print and Collaborate

Google Presentations makes it possible for you to print your entire presentation (one slide per page) to distribute to your audience as handouts or to create speaker notes for you to use when delivering the presentation. You also have the option of letting others collaborate on your presentation over the web.

Activity 7.21
Printing Slide Handouts

Handouts Hard copies of the slides in a presentation, with space for the audience to take notes.

Distributing *handouts*—or hard copies—of the slides in a presentation allows your audience to take notes and to walk away with a copy of the points you make in your presentation. In this activity, you learn how to print slide handouts.

1. From within your presentation, click **File** on the menu bar, then click **Print**.

2. When the Print Preview dialog box appears, as shown in Figure 7.23, click the **Layout** list arrow, then click how many slides you want to print per page—1, 2, 4, 6, 8, 9, or 12.

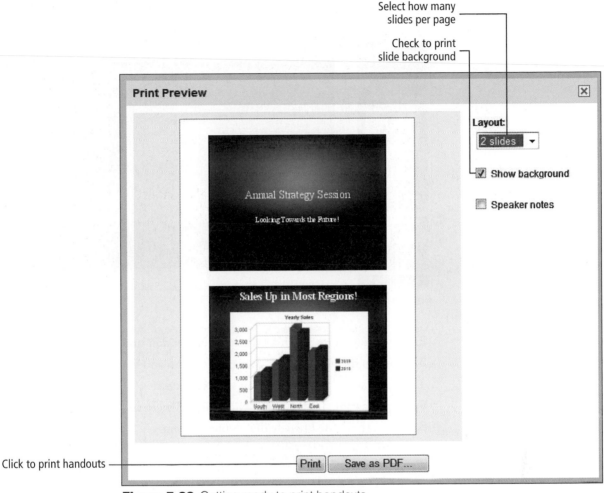

Figure 7.23 Getting ready to print handouts.

3. If you want to display the slide background in your handouts, click the **Show background** checkbox.

4. Click the **Print** button to print your handouts as specified.

Activity 7.22

Creating Speaker Notes

Speaker notes Additional text associated with a slide, used to provide the speaker with information used while presenting.

Many presenters like to prepare speaker notes that they can reference while they're giving a presentation. *Speaker notes* are additional text associated with a slide that does not appear on the slide. In this activity, you learn how to create and print speaker notes for a presentation.

1. From the first slide of your presentation, click the **View Speaker Notes** button at the lower right corner of the workspace. This changes the workspace to open the speaker notes pane, as shown in Figure 7.24.

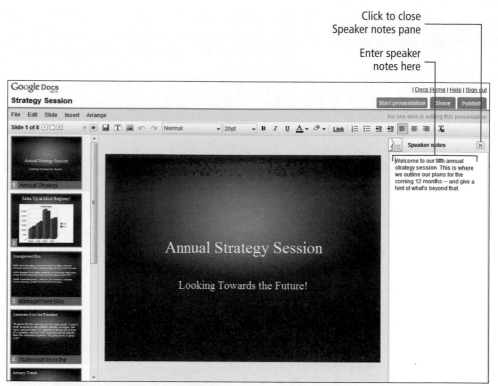

Figure 7.24 Entering speaker notes.

2. Enter your notes for this slide into the Speaker notes pane.

3. Move to the next slide in your presentation and enter speaker notes for that slide.

4. Repeat step 3 for each slide in your presentation.

5. To print your speaker notes, click **File** on the menu bar, then click **Print**.

6. When the Print Preview dialog box appears, click the **Speaker notes** checkbox to print your slides with speaker notes, as shown in Figure 7.25.

7. Click the **Print** button to print your presentation one slide per page, with speaker notes displayed beneath each slide.

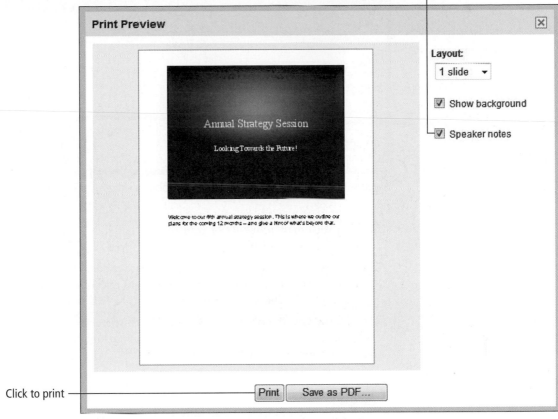

Check to display speaker
notes beneath each slide

Click to print

Figure 7.25 Getting ready to print speaker notes.

Activity 7.23

Inviting Other Users to Collaborate

Using Google Presentations, you can collaborate on a presentation with other users in real time over the Internet. Your collaborators need to have Google accounts and be invited by you to share the presentation. In this activity, you learn how to invite others to collaborate on an online presentation.

Collaborate To share a presentation with others online for viewing or editing as a group to create a finished document.

1. From your open presentation, click the **Share** button at the top right corner of the window then click Share with others.

2. When the Share this presentation page appears, as shown in Figure 7.26, click the **as collaborators** option button.

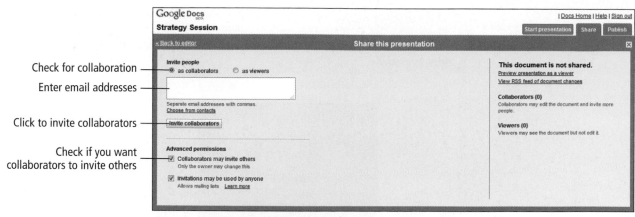

Check for collaboration

Enter email addresses

Click to invite collaborators

Check if you want collaborators to invite others

Figure 7.26 Inviting other users to collaborate on your presentation.

3. Enter the email addresses of your desired collaborators into the Invite people box, Separate multiple addresses with commas.

4. If you want the invitees to be able to invite others to view your presentation, click the **Collaborators may invite others** checkbox. Leave this checkbox unselected to limit the invitees to the ones you have selected.

5. Click the **Invite collaborators** button. Your recipients now receive an email invitation that contains a link to the presentation; clicking this link opens the presentation in a new browser window.

 Collaborators Can Edit

Anyone invited as a collaborator can edit the presentation in their web browsers. Google Presentations lets multiple users edit the presentation at the same time, so you can have an entire group working together in real time. You can also get alerts when a presentation you have shared is changed by another user.

Objective 8

Deliver a Presentation

The main reason to create a presentation is to present it to others. Google Presentations enables you to give in-person presentations or Internet-based presentations that let other users at any location see your presentation in their web browsers.

Activity 7.24

Presenting Your Presentation

After you've completed creating and editing your presentation, you can connect your computer to a projector or large monitor and show it to any size group of people. In fact, you can take your presentation anywhere you travel just by connecting any computer to the Internet, where your presentation is stored.

In this activity, you learn how to use Google Presentations to give a live presentation from any Internet-connected computer.

1. Open the presentation you wish to give, then click the first slide.

2. Click the **Start presentation** button.

3. This opens your live presentation in a new browser window, as shown in Figure 7.27. Press the **F11** key on your keyboard to display the presentation full-screen.

Current slide ⌐

Click to display speaker notes ⌐

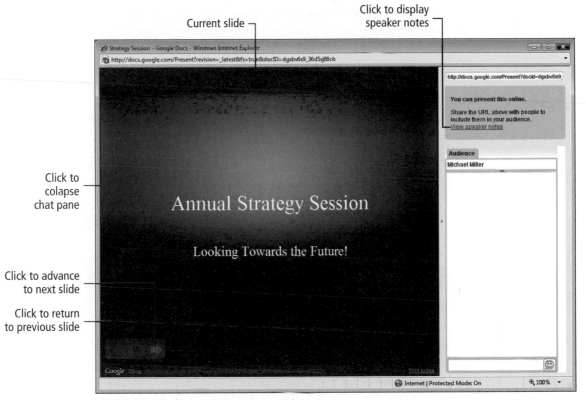

Click to colapse chat pane

Click to advance to next slide

Click to return to previous slide

Figure 7.27 Giving a live presentation.

4. Anyone viewing your presentation online is listed in the chat pane on the right. To hide this pane, click the arrow on the left side of the pane.

5. To view your presentation notes in a separate window, click the **View speaker notes** link.

6. To advance to the next slide in the presentation, click the **Next slide** arrow on the screen or press the **right arrow** key on your keyboard.

 Tip **Incremental Reveal**

If a slide includes objects formatted with incremental reveal, only the slide background and immediate reveal objects will appear when the slide first displays. To reveal the next object on the slide, click the **Next slide** arrow on the screen or press the **right arrow** key on your keyboard.

7. To return to the previous slide, click the **Previous slide** arrow on the screen or press the **left arrow** key on your keyboard.

8. When the presentation is finished you see an End of presentation dialog box. Click the **Restart** button to start the presentation over or click the **Exit** button to close the presentation window.

Activity 7.25

Giving an Online Presentation

With Google Presentations, you can give a presentation in multiple locations over the Internet. Invited attendees view the presentation in their own web browsers as you give it. In this activity, you learn how to invite others to view your presentation and make a presentation to multiple viewers in real time.

1. To invite viewers to your presentation, open the presentation and click the **Share** button at the top right corner of the window, the click Share with others.

2. When the Share this presentation page appears, as shown in Figure 7.28, click the **as viewers** option button.

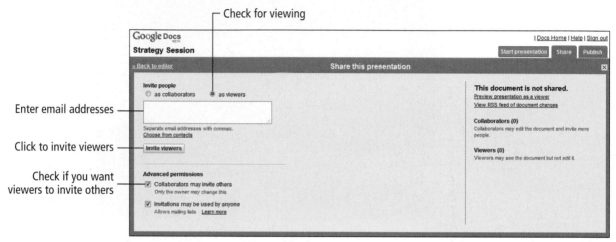

Figure 7.28 Inviting viewers to an online presentation.

3. Enter the email addresses of the people with whom you want to share this presentation into the Invite people box. Separate multiple addresses with commas.

4. If you want the invitees to be able to invite others to view your presentation, click the **Collaborators may invite others** checkbox. Leave this checkbox unselected to limit the invitees to the ones you have selected.

5. Click the **Invite viewers** button. Your recipients now receive an email invitation that contains a link to the presentation; clicking this link opens the presentation in a new browser window.

6. At the appointed time for the presentation, make sure that you and all viewers are logged on and have the presentation open in a browser.

7. From your open presentation, click the **Start presentation** button. Have your viewers do the same. This opens your live presentation in a new browser window, as shown in Figure 7.29.

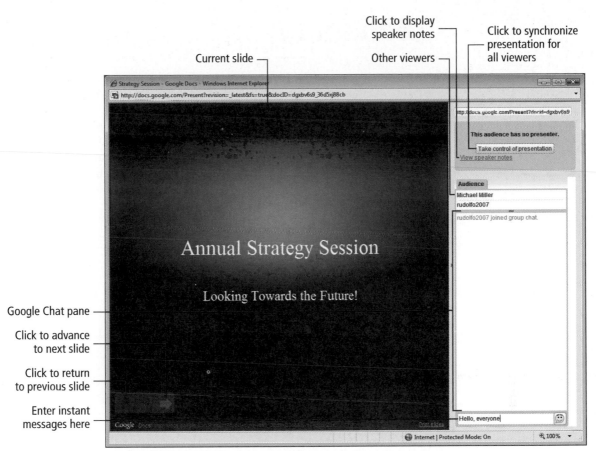

Current slide

Click to display
speaker notes

Other viewers

Click to synchronize
presentation for
all viewers

Google Chat pane

Click to advance
to next slide

Click to return
to previous slide

Enter instant
messages here

Figure 7.29 Giving an online presentation.

8. At the right side of each window is a Google Chat pane which lists each viewer who is currently logged on. You can exchange instant messages with other viewers by entering text into the message box and pressing the **Enter** key on your keyboard.

9. To synchronize the presentation for all viewers, click the **Take control of the presentation** button. Viewers will now see your current slide displayed above the Google Chat pane.

10. Even when you've taken control of the presentation, viewers still have control over the slide displayed in the main portion of their screens. To see the presenter's current slide in the main portion of their screens, each viewer must click the **Follow the presenter** button.

11. To view your presentation notes in a separate window, click the **View speaker notes** link.

12. To advance to the next slide in the presentation, click the **Next slide** arrow on the screen or press the **right arrow** key on your keyboard.

13. To return to the previous slide, click the **previous slide** arrow on the screen or press the **left arrow** key on your keyboard.

14. When the presentation is finished, you see an End of presentation dialog box. Click the **Restart** button to start the presentation over or click the **Exit** button to close the presentation window.

Summary

In this chapter, you learned how to create and save new presentations as well as import and export presentations to and from Microsoft PowerPoint. You practiced adding new slides to your presentation, rearranging and deleting slides, and choosing the right slide layouts. You learned how to change the look of your presentation by choosing a new theme and by adding and formatting text, images, charts, and animations. The chapter included instruction on how to print handouts and speaker notes, share your presentation with other collaborators, and give a live presentation, both in person and over the Internet.

Key Terms

Assessments

Multiple Choice

1. Which of the following statements is *not* true?
   (a) Google Presentations is part of the Google Docs suite.
   (b) Google Presentations is a web-based application.
   (c) Google Presentations has all the functionality of Microsoft PowerPoint.
   (d) Google Presentations lets you give presentations over the Internet.

2. Which is the best slide layout for displaying blocks of text?
   (a) Title
   (b) Text
   (c) Blank
   (d) none of the above

3. To add a chart to your presentation, do the following:
   (a) Click the Insert Chart button.
   (b) Click File on the menu bar, then click Add Chart.
   (c) Import a chart as an image from Google Spreadsheets.
   (d) Add a new slide with the Chart layout.

4. To give an online presentation to others over the Internet, you must first: _____.
   (a) invite others to view the presentation
   (b) email copies of the presentation to viewers
   (c) click File on the menu bar, then click Save for Viewing
   (d) export the file into Microsoft PowerPoint format

5. When you first save a presentation, the file name is created from: _____.
   (a) the name you enter into the Name This File dialog box
   (b) the title slide of your presentation
   (c) your Google account username
   (d) the first few words you enter into the presentation

6. Which of the following features is included in Google Presentations?
   (a) predesigned themes
   (b) chart creation
   (c) slide-to-slide transitions
   (d) table creation

7. To add a title to a slide, do the following: _____.
   (a) click the Insert Title button
   (b) click the "Click to add title" text object
   (c) click File on the menu bar, then click Add Title
   (d) format selected text with the Title font

8. To emphasize individual points that can be in any order, create _____.
   (a) a bulleted list
   (b) a numbered list
   (c) one slide per point
   (d) graphic objects on a blank slide

9. Incremental reveal enables you to: _____.
   (a) hide unimportant objects on a slide
   (b) reveal multiple objects on a slide in successive order
   (c) place one object behind another on a slide
   (d) display the presentation title on each slide in the presentation

10. Which of the following objects can you add to a Google Presentations slide?
    (a) YouTube videos
    (b) picture files
    (c) graphic shapes
    (d) all of the above

Fill in the Blank

Write the correct word in the space provided.

1. Google Presentations enables you to import _____-format presentations from Microsoft PowerPoint.
2. To rearrange the slides in your presentation, click and drag slides within the _____ pane.
3. To add a picture to a slide, click the _____ button.
4. To animate individual objects on the slide, use the _____ feature.
5. To import a chart from Google Spreadsheets, save and then import the chart as a(n) _____.
6. To change the look and feel of each slide in your presentation, select a new _____.
7. When giving a presentation over the web, you can use Google _____ to send instant messages to other viewers.
8. In most instances, you want to use the _____ layout for the first slide in your presentation.
9. To incrementally reveal the next object on a slide, click the _____ arrow.
10. To delete text to the left of the insertion point, press the _____ key.

Skills Review

1. Create a new presentation titled Yearly Goals.
2. Create a title slide for this presentation, with the subtitle Important Tasks for the Coming Year.
3. Format the presentation with the Liquid theme.
4. Create a second slide for the presentation, consisting of a block of text stating your philosophy of life.
5. Create a third slide for the presentation, consisting of a bulleted list of your personal goals for the coming year.
6. Create a fourth slide for the presentation, consisting of an imported picture of yourself.
7. Rearrange the slides in your presentation so that the picture slide is now the second slide.
8. Add speaker notes to each slide in your presentation.
9. Save your presentation and print a handout that includes your speaker notes.
10. Invite two of your friends to a live presentation at the time of your choosing, then give the presentation over the web.

Appendix A

Customizing Google

As frequently as most people use Google during the day, it's good that there are ways to personalize the Google experience. In this appendix, we cover three different ways to customize Google—by personalizing Google search, using the iGoogle personalized homepage, and by using the Google Desktop.

Personalizing Google Search

Most users aren't aware that they can personalize the way in which Google displays search results—and, to a small degree, the way the main search page looks. Well, you can, thanks to Google's Preferences page.

You get to the Preferences page by clicking the Preferences link on Google's homepage. The resulting Preferences page includes a handful of options that can be configured, including the following:

- **Display Google in a difference language.** By default, the Google interface displays with all the text in English. Google can, however, display its main page in dozens of local languages, from Afrikaans to Zulu. To select the interface language, go to the Interface Language section, click the **Display Google tips and messages in** list arrow, then make a selection.

- **Search in a different language.** When you search Google, your query automatically searches for web pages created in any language. You may, however, want to restrict your searches to pages created in a specific language—especially if you only speak that one language. To restrict all your searches to pages created in a specific language, go to the Search Language section, click the **Prefer pages written in these language(s)** option button, then click checkboxes for the language(s) you want your results restricted to.

- **Search safely.** To block unwanted adult content from appearing in your search results, Google offers a content filter that you can apply to your Google searches. Google's SafeSearch filter screens the Google index for sites that contain adult information and then eliminates those pages from your search results. To turn SafeSearch filtering on or off for all future searches, go to the SafeSearch Filtering section and select from one of three options: **Use strict filtering** (blocks both objectionable words and images), **Use moderate filtering** (blocks objectionable images from Google Image Search results only), or **Do not filter my search results** (disables the SafeSearch filter and displays all pages and images, regardless of their content).

- **Display more results per page.** By default, Google displays 10 results per page for each search you make. This allows for a fairly fast display of results. If you want to see more results on your page, go to the Number of Results section, click the **Display** list arrow, then select 20, 30, 50, or 100.

- **Open a new results window.** By default, Google displays your search results in the same browser window you used to initiate your search. If you prefer to have Google open a new browser window containing your search results, go to the Results Window section and click the **Open search results in a new browser window** checkbox. With this option selected, any time you click the Search Google button, a new browser window will open with the search results listed.

- **Suggest queries.** If you want Google to display suggested queries based on partial entries you make in the search box, go to the Query Suggestions section and click the **Provide query suggestions in the search box** option button.

When you're done configuring your preferences, click the Save Preferences button at the top of the page to apply your choices to your current and future Google searches across all Google services.

Personalizing Your Homepage with iGoogle

iGoogle A separate start page that you can use as a portal, not just to Google, but to the entire web.

If you've used Google search at all, you're undoubtedly familiar and comfortable with the spartan Google homepage. But that's not the only way into the Google search engine. Google also offers a separate start page that you can use as a portal not just to Google, but to the entire web. This page is dubbed *iGoogle*, and it's totally customizable.

To view your iGoogle page, go to **www.google.com/ig**. You can also access the page by clicking the iGoogle link on the main Google page. You must have a Google account to create your iGoogle page; you can then log into your account from any computer to see your iGoogle page from any computer connected to the Internet.

The first time you access iGoogle, you are prompted to select options that define your interests (news, humor, sports, etc.), a theme (how your iGoogle page will look), and your location. You can make any selection in this window, then click the **See your page** button to view and make modifications to your personalized page.

To add content to your personalized page, start at the default iGoogle page and click the **Add stuff** link. iGoogle's content is offered in a series of modules called "gadgets"; click a gadget and it appears on your iGoogle page.

To rearrange content on the iGoogle page, use your mouse to drag a gadget to a different location. The layout of the page is "live" all the time; just position the cursor in the gadget's title bar, click and hold the left mouse button, and then drag the gadget to where you want it to appear.

Once you get all your gadgets organized the way you want them, you can then decide how you want iGoogle to look by applying new themes. To apply a theme to your iGoogle page, click the **Select theme** link. This displays the Select a Theme for Your Homepage module; click the theme you want from the list, then click the **Save** button. The theme not only includes a specific color theme, but also graphics for the top of the iGoogle page.

Personalizing Your Desktop with Google Desktop

You use the Google website to search the web, but there's a lot of information you need to find on your own computer as well. You can search for this local information using Google Desktop—a software program that installs on your PC and automatically indexes all your data files, email messages, and more. When you conduct a Google Desktop search, the program searches the index and returns a list of matching files and messages. It's just as easy as using the Google website, and it lets you find all those "lost" documents that are buried somewhere on your hard disk.

As an added bonus, Google Desktop includes a sidebar that sits on your computer desktop and provides access to gadgets that are much like those found on the iGoogle page. Assuming you have the available desktop real estate, the Google Desktop sidebar lets you view your Gmail inbox, the latest news, local weather conditions, your instant messaging contacts, and lots, lots more, all stacked together on the edge of your computer screen.

You can download Google Desktop from www.desktop.google.com. Like all Google applications, Google Desktop is free.

Searching with Google Desktop

Once installed, you can use Google Desktop to search your hard disk (or your entire network) for files and email messages that match a specific query. You do your searching from your web browser, which displays a special Google Desktop page. It works much like a standard Google web search, except that it's not searching the web—it's searching the contents of your computer's hard disk.

There are several ways to search your computer with Google Desktop. You can:

- Click the Google Desktop icon in the Windows taskbar tray, then click **Search Desktop**

- Use the Google search gadget in the Desktop sidebar

- Click the **Start** button on the taskbar, click **All Programs**, click the **Google Desktop** folder, then click **Google Desktop**

- Press the **Ctrl** key on your keyboard twice to display a Quick Search Box on your desktop

Depending on which method you use to start your search, a Quick Search Box may appear in the middle of your computer desktop or Google Desktop may launch its own search page in your web browser. This browser page looks almost identical to the main Google web page. The main differences are that you're not connected to the Internet, the search function is set to Desktop, and there are a few new options at the bottom of the page.

Searching your hard disk is as easy as entering a query into the search box and then pressing Enter or clicking the Search Desktop button. (If you click the Search the Web button instead, Google Desktop connects to the main Google website and initiates a traditional web search.)

Personalizing Google Desktop

Google Desktop is more than just a desktop search tool; it is also a tool that puts more information on your desktop, via the Google Desktop sidebar. This sidebar resides on the far right of your computer desktop and displays a variety of gadgets. You can choose from hundreds of different gadgets to display all sorts of information.

The sidebar is activated by default when you first install the Google Desktop program. You can turn it off by clicking the down arrow at the top of the sidebar to display the menu, and then clicking **Close**. To redisplay the sidebar, right-click the Google Desktop icon in the Windows taskbar tray and click **Sidebar** from the shortcut menu.

To add a new gadget to the sidebar, click the **Add gadgets** button (the + sign at the top of the sidebar) to open the Add gadgets window. In the Add gadgets window, you can view gadgets in a number of different categories. Click the **Add** button underneath a gadget to add it to your sidebar. (To remove any gadget from the sidebar, click the down arrow in that gadget's title bar, then click **Remove**.)

In the sidebar, any gadget can be displayed at any height or collapsed to just its title bar. You can make a gadget taller or shorter by dragging the bottom border up or down with your mouse. To collapse the gadget entirely, click its down arrow, then click **Collapse**. You can also adjust the width of the sidebar by dragging the left edge of the sidebar.

You can rearrange the gadgets in your sidebar in any order. It's a dynamic process; just grab the gadget's title bar with your mouse and drag it to a new position. The other gadgets rearrange themselves to make room for the moved gadget.

 Undocking Desktop Gadgets

Individual gadgets can also be undocked from the sidebar. When you click the down arrow in the gadget title bar and click **Undock from Sidebar**, the gadget is moved from the sidebar to its own window on the desktop. To redock a gadget, click the gadget's down arrow and click **Dock to Sidebar**.

Appendix B

Working with Google Chrome

Google Chrome Google's web browser.

Google Chrome is Google's web browser. But it's more than a traditional browser; it's also a quasi operating system for web-based applications, which makes it ideal for running Google apps. You can download and install your copy of Chrome from google.com/chrome.

Using Chrome as a Web Browser

As a web browser, Chrome is similar to all the other web browsers available today. The Chrome interface resembles that of Internet Explorer and Firefox, complete with tabs for different web pages. Chrome is a bit sleeker than the other browsers, however, with no menu bar, search bar, status bar, or other extraneous bits and pieces. This makes the web page bigger in the window. In essence, it moves the business of the browser out of the way so that you can pay more attention to the web page itself.

To go to a web page, type the URL into what looks like a standard address box at the top of the browser window. This box is more than an address box—Google calls it the Omnibox, and you can also use it to enter search queries. When you start typing in the Omnibox, Google suggests both queries and web pages you are likely to visit. Just select what you want from the list or finish typing your URL or query, then press Enter.

Chrome's tabs let you open different web pages in different tabs, instead of opening one page after another in the same window. To open a new tab, just click the "+" button next to the current tab. You can also open a link in a new tab by right-clicking the link and clicking Open Link in New Tab.

 Minimizing the Chrome

According to Google, the name Chrome derives from the "chrome," or bells and whistles, that accompany a typical user interface. Google sought to minimize the "chrome," which led to the browser's name.

Using Chrome to Run Web-Based Applications

Where Chrome really shines, however, is with running web-based applications, such as Google Calendar and Google Docs. Web-based applications run much faster in Chrome than they do in competing web browsers—more than 50 times faster than with Internet Explorer.

 A Faster Engine

V8 Google Chrome's engine.

Chrome's speed is partly due to its stripped-down interface, but it is more likely a result of the modern JavaScript engine used to run the browser. Chrome's engine, dubbed *V8*, is designed to improve the performance of complex applications—like the web-based applications that Google serves up to its millions of users.

Chrome also lets you make a web-based application function like a desktop application. Start by opening that application in a Chrome tab, click the **Control the current page** button, then click **Create application shortcuts**. When the Google Gears dialog box appears, select what type of shortcut to create: Desktop, Start menu, or Quick Launch bar. When you click OK, not only will a shortcut be created, but the application will open in a new "chromeless" window without the normal browser tabs and menu bars. This window functions like any traditional desktop application window; it can be resized and, when you next open the application, the window opens to the previously saved size.

In the future, you no longer have to navigate to the application's page on the web. You can open the application by clicking the shortcut you just created; the application opens whether you're online or offline, just like a desktop application. In addition, Chrome has Google Gears built in so that you can run your applications whether you're online or offline. This feature alone makes Chrome a worthwhile choice for anyone using Google apps.

Glossary

Anchor text The text that accompanies a link to another web page.

Archive To store old or inactive messages.

Ascending A sort order that displays a column of data in increasing numeric or alphabetical order.

Attachment A file that is sent along with an email message.

Automatic word stemming A feature that enables Google to automatically search for all possible word variations.

Boolean operator Words that are used to refine a search and that come from Boolean logic and mathematics, such as AND, OR, and NOT. Google supports only the Boolean OR operator.

Browsing Locating a website within a directory by clicking through a hierarchical organization of information.

Bulleted list A list of items that can appear in any order.

Cached page A page that is stored on Google's document servers, and may be slightly older than the current version of the page, or outdated.

Cell The intersection of a cell and column.

Cell address The column letter followed by the row number, used to reference the cell in calculations. The first cell in the spreadsheet is A1.

Chart Data presented graphically, such as in a pie chart or bar chart.

Clipboard A Windows storage area for cut or copied text or images that you can paste into a new location.

Collaborate To share a document with others online for viewing or editing as a group to create a finished document.

Column Data arranged vertically in a table or spreadsheet. In a spreadsheet, columns are lettered alphabetically.

Contact A listing of information about a person, including name, email address, and more.

Contact group A collection of Gmail contacts, used to create email mailing lists.

Conversation A group of related email messages.

Copy To store text onto the Clipboard so that it can be inserted into a new location and still remain in the original location.

Cut To remove text from a document and store it on the Clipboard so that it can be moved to a new location.

Descending A sort order that displays a column of data in decreasing numeric or alphabetical order.

Directory A collection of websites assembled by human editors.

Domain A specific type of site on the web, indicated by the domain name after the final "dot" separator. For example, the .edu domain is used to indicate education sites.

Editing To make changes to correct mistakes or to rephrase text, including deleting characters or selections of text, inserting additional text, and moving and copying text.

Event An appointment or other scheduled item in Google Calendar.

Executable program file A computer file that contains a software program.

File extension A 3- or 4-character suffix that indicates the program in which a file was created.

Filetype A particular way of encoding data in a computer file. Most programs store their data in their own filetypes; filetypes are indicated by specific file extensions.

Filter An action that is applied to email messages, such as automatic deletion or starting.

Font A typeface in which letters and characters share similar size, shape, and other characteristics.

Footer A text object that appears at the bottom of every page, including the document's title, page number, or the author's name.

Formula Calculation instructions, consisting of numbers, mathematical operators, and the contents of a cell or cell range.

Function An advanced formula, preprogrammed into Google Spreadsheets.

Gadget A small plug-in application used to add a feature to a larger application.

Gmail Google's web-based email service.

Google The Internet's most popular search engine.

Google Alerts An email that Google sends you when it finds new items of interest.

Google Book Search A method to locate books stored in the Google Books Library Project database.

Google Books Library Project Google's global book repository that allows you to search the full text of any book ever published.

Google Calendar Google's web-based calendar application.

Google Chrome Google's web browser.

Google Directory Google's human-edited directory of websites.

Google Docs Google's suite of online applications; also, the word processing application within the Google Docs suite.

Google Glossary Google's database of word definitions.

Google Image Search A subset of Google's basic web search that lets you search for photos, drawings, logos, and other graphics files on the web.

Google Maps Google's web-based mapping and directions service.

Google News Google's database of current and archived news headlines.

Google Phonebook Google's database of personal names, streets addresses, and phone numbers.

Google Presentations The presentation application within the Google Docs suite.

Google Scholar Google's database of scholarly articles and journals.

Google Spreadsheets The spreadsheet application within the Google Docs suite.

Handouts Hard copies of the slides in a presentation, with space for the audience to take notes.

Header (documents) A text object that appears at the top of every page, including the document's title, page number, or the author's name.

Header (spreadsheets) Specially formatted labels for the data in a table or spreadsheet, used to define a row or column.

Hyperlinking The ability to click on an underlined piece of text to jump to a related web page.

Incremental reveal A method of animating the order and method that individual elements (such as text objects, list items, or images) appear on a slide.

iGoogle A separate start page that you can use as a portal, not just to Google, but to the entire web.

Integrated applications Two or more applications that are designed to work together.

Keyword A term used in a search query.

Label A keyword or tag that describes an email message.

Layout The placement of objects in a document or on a slide.

Line spacing The space between lines of text.

Numbered list A list of items that must appear in a certain order.

Offline When you're not connected to the Internet.

OneBox Specialized search results.

Operator A symbol or word that causes a search engine to do something special with the word directly following the symbol.

Pan To navigate a map in a specific direction.

Paste To transfer text or images from the Clipboard into a new location in a document.

Placeholder Text in a template that indicates the type of information to include and a sample page layout.

Playback To view a recorded video.

Portable Document Format (PDF) Adobe Acrobat Reader program files that can be viewed, printed, and shared without having access to the program in which the file was created.

Presentation Data presented in a slide-show format.

Print Create a hard copy printout of your document.

Query A search for information.

Range A group of cells that can be used as a reference in a calculation.

Row Data arranged horizontally in a table or spreadsheet. In a spreadsheet, rows are numbered sequentially.

SafeSearch A filter used to exclude adult websites and images from your Google search results.

Search index The organization of data to allow for fast and accurate searching.

Signature Personalized text that appears at the bottom of an email message.

Slide A slide in a presentation contains text, images, videos, or any combination of the above.

Slide sorter A pane on the left pane of the Google Presentations window that you can use to select, move, or delete slides.

Snippet A short excerpt from a book or article.

Sort To arrange data in a spreadsheet in a particular order.

Spam Unsolicited commercial email.

Speaker notes Additional text associated with a slide, used to provide the speaker with information used while presenting.

Sponsored link Links on a search results page that are paid for by Google's advertisers.

Spreadsheet A program that organizes data in rows and columns and allows you to perform complex calculations and analysis.

Star A means of identifying selected email messages.

Stop word A small, common word, such as "and," "the," "where," "how," and "what," that Google ignores when performing a query.

Street View Street-level photographs of a location in Google Maps.

Table Information displayed in a grid, organized in rows and columns, to help readers distinguish complex data.

Tag A label or keyword that describes the content of a YouTube video.

Tagging Creates virtual folders, which you can use to search and sort messages by any tag label.

Template A predesigned selection of text, formatting, and graphics, used to create a new document, spreadsheet, or presentation.

Theme A predesigned collection of background images, color scheme, and fonts that are applied to every slide in your presentation.

URL A web address.

V8 Google Chrome's engine.

Viral video A video that gains widespread popularity via Internet sharing.

Wildcard Allows you to search for all words that include the first part of a keyword. For example, search for **book*** to return results for "books," "bookstore," and "bookkeeper." Unlike other search engines, Google does not support wildcard searches.

Word processor An application used to create letters, memos, reports, and other text-based documents.

YouTube Google's video-sharing community.

Index

A

Access fees, 40
Account, creating, 98, 110
Address searching, 55–57
Adobe PDF, 115
Advanced Book Search page, 43–44
Advanced Image Search, 23
Advanced Search page, 17–18
Alerts, 24–27
Allinanchor: operator, 16
Allintext: operator, 15–16
Allintitle: operator, 15
Allinurl: operator, 15
Alphabetical listings, 34
Anchor text, 134
And/or operator, 6–8
Answers.com, 62
Archives, searching, 47–48
Archiving messages, 74, 87
Ascending, 164
Attachments, 81–82
Author searching, 39, 43
Automatic stemming, 84
Automatic word stemming, 10–11

B

Beta status, 25
Book content, viewing, 44–46
Books, searching, 41–46
Boolean operators, 8
Browsing, Google Directory, 32–34
Businesses, searching, 60–61

C

Cached pages, 3
Calculations, 63–67
Calendar. See Google Calendar
Charts, 170–171
Cities, searching, 56
Clipboard defined, 121
Coloration searching, 24
Constants, mathematical/scientific, 65
Contacts, managing, 74, 90–93, 107
Conversions, 66–67
Copy defined, 121
Cosines, 65
Customising Google 211–213
Cut defined, 121

D

Date function, 19
Date range searching, 39
Define: operator, 62–63
Definitions, searching, 61–63
Descending, 164
Directions, searching, 55–61
Directory defined, 32
Documents. See Google Docs

Domain/Web site restriction query, 13–14
Driving directions, generating, 59–60

E

Editing defined, 121
Emailing. See also Gmail
   file attachments, 81–82
   maps, 59
   passwords, 73
   videos, 53
Event defined, 97
Excel spreadsheets, importing/exporting, 154–156
Executable program file defined, 81
Exponents, 64

F

Factorials, 65
File attachments, 81–82
File extensions, 12
File size, searching by, 23
Filetype restriction query, 12–13, 23–24
Filtering email messages, 88–89
Flagging email messages, 85–86
Folders, creating, 150, 180
Footers, 128, 164
Format of alerts, changing, 26–27
Formulas, 165–167
Frequency of alerts, changing, 25–26

G

Gadgets, 169
Gmail
   archiving, 74, 87
   autocomplete, 93
   automatic stemming, 84
   cc/bcc, 79
   composing, 79–80
   contacts, 74, 90–93, 107
   conversations, 76, 83
   deleting, 74, 83
   email, reading, 75–76
   email, sending, 77–81
   event information, adding, 79, 106–108
   file attachments, 81–82
   filtering, 88–89
   flagging (starring), 85–86
   forwarding, 78–79
   Inbox, searching, 74, 84–85
   interface, 73–75
   labeling, 86–87
   message management, 74, 83–90
   passwords, 73
   pop-up blocker, 93, 107
   replying, 77–78

settings, configuring, 74
signature, adding, 80–81
signing in, 74
signing up, 72–73
spam, 74, 89–90
spell checking, 80
Google Alerts, 24–27
Google Book Search, 42–44
Google Books Library Project, 41–46
GoogleBot, 1, 32
Google Calendar
   basic setup, 98
   event information, emailing, 79, 106–108
   events, 103–108
   Gmail contacts, 107
   multiple, setup, 98–99
   multiple, viewing, 103
   overview, 97
   permissions, 109–110
   pop-up blocker, 93, 107
   public, 108–111
   Quick Add, 105–106
   url, personal, 109
   viewing, 99–103
Google Chrome, 214–215
Google Directory, 32–35
Google Docs
   alignment, 125–126
   collaborating, 144–145
   comments, 135–136
   compatible file types, opening, 82
   creating, 114–117
   documents, opening, 117–118
   folders, creating, 115
   headers/footers, 128, 164
   heading styles, 126–127
   images, 131–133
   indentation, 125
   keyboard names, 122
   line spacing, 127–128
   links, 134–135
   lists, 129–131
   offline, 117
   overview, 113
   page breaks, 129
   paragraph formatting, 124–129
   presentations (See Google Presentations)
   printing, 142–143
   saving, 117–118
   spell checking, 141–142
   synchronization, 120
   tables, 136–141
   templates, 115–116
   text, entering/editing, 120–122
   text formatting, 122–124
   upload limits, 119
   Word documents, importing/exporting, 118–120

what's *NEXT?*

Making it easy to teach *what's NEXT!*

Many of today's introductory computing courses are moving beyond covering just the traditional Microsoft® Office applications. Instructors are looking to incorporate newer technologies and software applications into their courses, or in some cases they are offering alternative courses based on emerging technologies.

We developed *The NEXT Series* to provide innovative instructors with a high-quality, academic teaching solution that focuses on the next great technologies. There is more to computing than Microsoft Office, and the books in *The NEXT Series* enable students to learn about some of the newer technologies that are available and becoming part of our everyday lives.

Key Features of *Introduction to Google™ Apps*

▶ Activity-driven instruction so students learn by doing

▶ Full teaching and learning system including end-of-chapter assessments, a Test Bank, and instructional tools such as PowerPoint presentations

Note Note boxes call students' attention to important items

Alert Alert boxes indicate to students where they might get hung up

Tip Tip boxes are used to provide useful tips & tricks

▶ Full color text with lots of figures and screen shots for today's visual learners

ISBN-13: 978-0-13-245747-7
ISBN-10:   0-13-245747-4

Prentice Hall
is an imprint of

www.pearsonhighered.com/nextseries

9 780132 457477

90000